Prima's
Computer Strategy
Games Bible

UNAUTHORIZED

NOW AVAILABLE FROM PRIMA

How to Order:
For information on quantity discounts contact the publisher: Prima Publishing, P.O. Box 1260BK, Rocklin, CA 95677-1260; (916) 632-4400. On your letterhead include information concerning the intended use of the books and the number of books you wish to purchase. For individual orders, turn to the back of the book for more information.

Visit us online at http://www.primapublishing.com

Prima's
Computer
Strategy Games
Bible

UNAUTHORIZED

Michael Rymaszewski
Michael Knight

PRIMA PUBLISHING
Rocklin, California
(916) 632-4400

Project Editor: Lothlórien Baerenwald

ISBN: 0-7615-0846-5
Library of Congress Catalog Card Number: 96-69123
Printed in the United States of America

96 97 98 99 DD 10 9 8 7 6 5 4 3 2 1

Contents

Dedication

To my wife, Leslie

Acknowledgments

It is much nicer to *have written* a book than to actually *write* one. Writing tends to be a long and tiring process, next to impossible without outside help. I would like to thank Lothlórien Baerenwald at Prima for expert editorial work, and Michael Knight for contributing the chapters on *Afterlife* and *WarCraft II*.

Here in Toronto, my thanks go to Norman and Fergus Hogan for their clinking, rustling help, and Winston for continuing to be a source of inspiration.

Finally, special thanks go to my wife, Leslie, who took care of life while this book was being written, and who also cracked the mysteries of *Theme Park* and *Heroes of Might & Magic*.

Introduction

This book is meant to maximize your enjoyment of fourteen strategic games that belong among the best games ever published. Each chapter provides a discussion of a proven winning strategy.

Unlike some game guides, this book is about strategy. It assumes you know the game's manual and interface. With the advice in these pages, you should be able to win at each game's equivalent of the Hard, and possibly the Impossible levels, and you should do very well indeed at the easier ones.

I should say here that I really recommend playing games at the Hard level. At easier levels, many interesting features tend to be absent. It's not unlike hunting a tiger that's had its teeth pulled. *Civilization II,* which will probably turn out to be the most popular game of all time, is a good example of this rule at work. You won't see computer-controlled paratroopers dropping into your nuked city if you're playing at Chief or Warlord. By opting for an easier difficulty level, you forego the pleasure of seeing how smart the AI can be—and you're missing part of the game. Of course, in games that keep scores, you won't do very well there, either.

Winning a game at a high difficulty level—a game at which you've lost a couple of times—can bring great satisfaction. Would you spend a ton of money on a fast car and then never take it out on the highway? Very unlikely. So, to experience each game to the fullest, I urge you once again to play it at Hard . . . or harder.

Finally, there's the question of the selection—the games which were chosen to be discussed here. We (there were more people than just me involved in the decision-making) selected these and not other games on the basis of two factors. The first was to assemble a cross-section of sorts—games that provide a spectrum of what's available and good. Truthfully, *Lords of the Realm* isn't as good a game as, say, *Master of Orion*. However, it appears in this book because it's practically the only good strategic game about the Middle Ages that captures, if only partly, medieval realities. *Theme Park* is not *Civ II,* but in a way, it can be said to be more original. (I hope I won't get stoned for that!) It offers something new, and does so with intelligence and charm. (Have you *ever* thought how challenging it could be to run an amusement park?)

Many people (some of my nearest and dearest included) consider computer games to be trivial. However, the whole business of having pleasure in life is hardly trivial, and I think I can safely say all of the games in this book guarantee a good time. Winning them at a high difficulty level guarantees having a *great* time. Not many things do nowadays. . . .

Michael Rymaszewski,
Author

CHAPTER

1

AFTERLIFE

Publisher:	LucasArts Entertainment Co.
Platform:	PC MS-DOS, Windows95
Release Date:	Spring, 1996
Multiplayer:	No
Rating:	

General Overview

While simulation games in the past have allowed the player to take on several positions of power, whether it be as a mayor, scientist or even a dictator, *Afterlife* provides an even greater role for those power-hungry players: a god. While playing this game, I could not help but reflect back on Dante's *The Divine Comedy,* which I was required to read for a course on Western Civilization. If you have read this classic, you will probably enjoy this game as it brings this story to life. *Afterlife* puts you in the position as the manager of both Heaven and Hell. If this seems sacrilegious at first, put your inhibitions aside. You are not in charge of Earth or even Humans. Your hereafter is for an alien race. Since the game is by LucasArts, we can assume that it takes place "A long time ago, in a galaxy far, far away. . . ." Your job is to provide rewards in Heaven and punishments in Hell for SOULs (Stuff Of Unending Life).

Your hereafter tries to cater to the beliefs of the SOULs. Your job is to provide them with whatever they believed the Afterlife would be like. Heaven and Hell are each independent communities. As the Demiurge, you must plan for your continuously arriving charges by zoning Fates, the housing for the SOULs, and where they will receive their due rewards or punishments. The zones in Heaven represent the seven virtues: namely Contentment, Charity, Temperance, Diligence, Chastity, Peacefulness, and Humility. In Hell, the zones represent the seven sins: Envy, Avarice, Gluttony, Sloth, Lust, Wrath, and Pride. You will also need to hire Angels and Demons to work in these Fates. Your goal is to have an efficiently running Afterlife, and earn more Pennies from Heaven then you spend. While this may seem easy, your Afterlife is not perfect. Remember, you are only a Demiurge. Things can go wrong, and even Heaven and Hell can have Bad Things happen in them.

Golden Rules

 Make sure that the tempo is set to Divine Intervention (pause) whenever your are setting up your Afterlife in the beginning, or when you have to make adjustments to prevent the loss of SOULs. If you do not stop the action, you will continue to lose SOULs while you make your corrections.

 Be careful not to spend too much time in either one of your eternal regions. You may want to monitor them in a zoomed-out view so that you can watch them simultaneously, or go back and forth between the two regularly.

 Use the tools that The Powers That Be gave you on your remote control. The Graphview and Mapview quickly display information on the status of your Afterlife. The SOULview allows you to zoom in on one SOUL and follow its progress. The Micromanager helps you to balance your zones and make them run more efficiently. Finally, your helpers, Jasper and Aria, are available to advise you on how to make your Afterlife run smoothly.

 Monitor the Vibes in each of your realms. In Heaven, you want to have Good Vibes near your Fate zones, while in Hell you will, of course, want Bad Vibes. You can help maintain the appropriate type of Vibes by building different structures such as Topias and Training Centers, and by balancing your zones.

 Provide as much of your own labor force as possible. By building Training Centers, you can train your own Demons and Angels. These are much cheaper than having to hire outside help from other Afterlives. Also, by building Topias, or housing for your labor, you can decrease your costs since you have to pay commuting Angels and Demons extra for their travel expenses.

 Training your own labor force can be a great way to save money. However, you must keep a close eye on them with the Labor Graph. Your imported workers should make up about thirty percent of your labor force. If enough of your local workers become idle, they will stage raids on the opposite realm and destroy structures there. If this gets too out of hand, Ragnarock n' Roll is the result and you are out

AFTERLIFE

of a job. Ports are a quick way to put idle laborers to work. You might also want to drastically decrease the amount of SOULs being trained by your Training Centers.

- Build Ad Infinitum Siphons and connect them to your fate housing by way of roads. These Siphons, which have to be placed adjacent to rocks, empower your buildings allowing them to evolve to their full potential. Unempowered buildings can only evolve to half of their potential. These Siphons give off toxic waste, so keep them away from your Rewards in Heaven, but near your Punishments in Hell.

- Limbo structures can come in handy in case of a disaster on the planet. In such cases, massive amounts of SOULs pour through your gates all at once. Since it will take some time to zone and construct new housing, build a Limbo structure. They act as a holding tank where SOULs can spend a year drinking beer while you make accommodations for them. You can also zone for Generic structures which will take any SOULs. However, these Generic zones are only half as effective as regular Fate zones.

- The Planetview is a nice feature which allows you to influence various factors on the planet. One factor is technology. As technology increases, so does the population and your influx of SOULs. However, once technology has reached the nuclear age, there is a possibility that nuclear war will break out. If this occurs, you will get a lot of SOULs all at once, but the population will be cut severely. You can also influence the level of sins and virtues on the planet. Be careful because changes you make can have dire consequences. For example, increasing Lust will result in larger population. After technology has reached the nuclear stage, you may want to increase Peacefulness on the planet to help prevent a war.

- Be careful of debt. You can build Banks in either of your realms. A total of 20 Banks can be built, each of which can make one loan for a hundred-year period. In Heaven, payments to the Banks are made automatically. The interest increases with the more loans that you

Michael Rymaszewski

have out. In Hell, there is no interest. You just have to repay the lump sum when the hundred years are up. If you do not have enough money, your wages will be garnished and a high interest rate will be included, which also increases with the number of loans that you have out. If you are in debt for 50 years, then the Four Surfers of the Apocalypso will pay you an unpleasant visit.

 Finally, always keep in mind your eternal goal: to provide the SOULs in Heaven with a wonderful experience, and to make the stay for the SOULs in Hell, well . . . Hell. To this end, put all of your zoning close together in Heaven so that the SOULs do not have to walk too far to their rewards. On the other hand, the zones in Hell should be spread out on long and often crooked roads. As a bonus, this game allows you to develop both your divinity as well as your deviousness in perfect balance and harmony—just the traits needed for an up-and-coming Demiurge.

Winning Strategies

IN THE BEGINNING: YOUR FIRST DAY ON THE JOB AS A DEMIURGE

The job of a Demiurge can be a little overwhelming at the start. However, since the game begins with the tempo set at Divine Intervention, you can take your time and set up a good base for your Afterlife.

Lets start at the top—in Heaven. Find a fairly open area with a few rocks nearby. Build a Gate to allow the SOULs to enter this realm. Run a road from the Gate, straight out for about 20 tiles. Next to the Gate, across the road from each other, build a Topia and a Training Center. The Good Vibes put out by these structures will counter the Bad Vibes from the Gate.

Next, you should begin zoning your Fates in 3x3 sections on each side of the road. In Heaven, you get bonuses for building different zones close together. It allows the SOULs to move from one reward to another easily. To help the Fate zones evolve to their maximum potential, they need to be empowered with Ad Infinitum. Adjacent to the nearest rock, build a Siphon. Connect this to rest of your zoning with a road. You are almost ready to open the Gate. All that you lack is a way for those SOULs who believe in reincarnation to get back to the planet.

It is time to build a Karma Station. While your Karma structures really exist in between Heaven and Hell, they are anchored to these realms. You will be building anchors in each plane, but the actual structure will exist in this middle area. Build your station fairly close to a Karma Portal but at least six tiles away from your Fates. Connect your Station to the Portal with Karma Track, and you are ready for business.

In Hell, you also want to find a fairly open area, but you want rocks to be in the middle of your zoning. Since Ad Infinitum Siphons give off toxic waste, you want them near your Fate structures in Hell, but several tiles away in Heaven. Begin with a Gate in the middle of this area, and long stretches of road spreading out in four directions. Each road should have at least one bend in it and a split, so that you get eight end points that are spread out. At the end of each road, zone a 3x3 section for a single sin. You can place a Training Center near the Gate to recruit new Demons, and build a Topia near one of your Fate zones so it can contribute its Bad Vibes to the structures there. Also, if your Fate zones are positioned near rocks, put in a Siphon to charge your structures and spread some toxic waste around the area as well. Build your Karma Station and Track away from your zoning, and your After-life is ready for its first SOULs.

Go up to the Global menu, set the Tempo to Mortal Plodding, and watch the action begin. With the Microview activated, you can check your Fate structures and see how they are doing. You might also want to use the SOULview to follow a single SOUL through his or her Afterlife experience.

THE FATES THAT AWAIT: HOUSING FOR THE MORTALLY CHALLENGED

Each type of Fate zone has several types of structures that can evolve on it. They are listed below, organized by realm and zone.

Heaven

CONTENTMENT—GREEN

Vacation Slides of the Gods	The Good Neighbor
Coffee Shops of the World	Karaoke Korners
Newbody Knows	Seventh Heaven Stretch
The Choir Invincible	Hoofer's Heaven
Final Curtain Theatres	Envy Aid
A Musement Park	Brahmatic Bovine Bliss Ranch

CHARITY—YELLOW

You are Already a Winner	Lost and Found
The Good Space	The Incredibly Lost Episodes
Spinner of Incredibly Good Fortunes	Flea Market
Land of the Lost Toys	The Bazaar
Happy Birthday!	The Final Piece Convention
Casino Royale	Ascetic Mountains

TEMPERANCE—ORANGE

The Perfect Party	Lands of Milk and Honey
Deus Ex Diner	Hog Heaven
Food Court of the Gods	Happy Harvest Farms
Picnicville	Beach Trip
Sickeningly Sweet Sugar Savannas	Eternafest
Bacchanalia	Party Town

DILIGENCE—BROWN

Your Home is Your Castle	The Eternal Afternoon
It's a Cat's Life	Mom and Pop Shops

AFTERLIFE

Library of the Infinite

Paradise University

Cloud Nine Labs

Divine Engines

PanCon

Celestech

Towers-A-Go-Go

The Final Frontier

CHASTITY—PURPLE

Valentine Town

The Perfect Spot Cosmic Backrub

Blueberry Hills

Castaways

Bahbbi-Zho's Drive Ins

The Divine Romantic Comedy

The Only Non-Sleazy Singles Bar in Heaven

Palaces of True Love

Wedding Day Redux

Tunnels of Love

The Perfect Evening

Cherubopolis

PEACEFULNESS—RED

Perfect Playgrounds

Heaven's Complaint Department

Happy Hunting Grounds

Heaven's Embassy

Board Games

Swords Into Plowshares

Fishing Holes

U.S.O.A., Local #777

Peaceful Warrior Pagoda

Splerf Wars

Fight the Power!

The 19th Tee Links

HUMILITY—BLUE

Humble Pie

You Oughta Be In Pictures

The Red Carpet Treatment

Monuments to Humility

Keys to the City

Night of Jillion Awards

Press Conference

Humble-mentary

Roasts

DNA Park

KHVN

Look to the Stars

AFTERLIFE

GENERIC VIRTUES—MULTICOLOR

Happily Ever After	Gardens of Mortal Delight
Newstands of Eternal Wonders	Time Heals All Wounds
"Angel-For-A-Day" Workshops	Personal Freedom Parks
Animal Magnetism	Dreamadise
Fiction Pulp	Lucky Town
Heavenly Hindsight Habitat	Camp Contentment
The Happy Carnival	The Incomparable Band
Radical Malls	Delight Parades
Hope Springs Eternal Spas	SimSimSimSimSim
The Game of Afterlife	Good Heavens Theme Park

Hell

ENVY—GREEN

Deadman's Curve	Out of the Frying Pan
Another Man's Shoes	Survey of the Damned
Very Southgate Mall	Amphitheaters of Anguish
Welcome to Your Flightmare	Hell Octoplex 666
Switchback Mountains	NoBody Burgs
Elevators, Inc.	Escher Pits

AVARICE—YELLOW

Jerky City	The Collective
Bingoslypertukaw!	Booty Island
Trick or Treat	The Wrong Side of the Tracks
You Bet Your Afterlife	Shock Market
Carousels of Greed	Seizure's Palace
Scavenger Hunt	DisCorp

AFTERLIFE

GLUTTONY—ORANGE

Taco Inferno	Sticky's
Pinhead Pizza	Bad Parties
The Pandimensional House of Vermin	Ecoli Shack
Renaissance Paine Faire	No-So-Divine Comedy Clubs
Bahb's All-U-Must Eat	Sleez and Sons Candy
Soylent Yellow	The Bowels of Hell

SLOTH—BROWN

The Itch	Sweat Shops
Bitter Harvest Fields	Faux Heaven
The Secretarial Pool of Fire	Grave Consequences
Convention of the Damned	Slayphus Mountains
The Enchanted Forest of Cable	Beats the Dickens Out of You
Sisyphus Factories	666 Pennants Over the Perdition Theme Parks

LUST—PURPLE

Lust Freezers	Punishing Peep Show Pavilions
The Laundromat	Purple Passion Pulsing Plasma Pods
Bikini Beach Barbecue!	Ghost Town
The Worst Little Whorehouse in Hell	Screaming Subspace Voids
Dates From Hell	Roboto
Ignorance Ain't Bliss	The Big Tease Shower Towers

AFTERLIFE

Michael Rymaszewski

WRATH—RED

Immortal Backalley Battle Warriors
The Post Office Game
Gym Class
Riot!
Illuminatiland
NP-Complete Parking Garages

The Real Underworld
The House of Buggin'
Hellrose Place
Spy Springs
Terroville
War! (What is it Good for?)

PRIDE—BLUE

The Age of Aquarium
SOUL Farm
Hamster Tube
San Quentin Scareantino
The Inquisition
St. Elsecare

Doll House
Simon Says
Unfixable Machines
The Zoo
Complaint Departments
The Loony Bin

GENERIC SINS—MULTICOLOR

Islands of Yip Dogs
Tooth or Dare
Tip of Your Tongue
The Evil Carny
Gross Miscarriages of Justice
Flesh Rending Machines
Telepathy Towers
Cracked Mirror Condos
Riddle Me This
Fear, Unlimited

Flesh Eating Beasts
The Chalkboard
Flesh Eating Plants
Junior High
Camp Mennihackatorso
Like a Goth to Flames
New Age Hells
Deadly Serious Caverns
Infernal Institutes of Irony
A World of Pain

HELL FREEZES OVER: BAD THINGS THAT CAN HAPPEN IN YOUR AFTERLIFE

Birds of Paradise: These Birds fly over Heaven. Wherever their droppings land, that building's efficiency is reduced for up to seventy-five years. The Vista Enhancement Doohicky will keep the Birds away for a radius of eight tiles.

Bats Out of Hell: Similar to the Birds, these Bats fly over Hell. While they reduce the efficiency of most structures, they actually increase it for Punishment structures. The Ugliness Engine will keep the Bats away for a radius of eight tiles.

Heaven Gets the Blues: Thunderclouds float over Heaven, stopping the functioning of everything they cover for 75 years. The Audio Improving Embophone protects your structures for a radius of nine tiles.

Disco Inferno: The Disco Demon dances his way across Hell. While he may look groovy in his polyester leisure suit, his patent leather shoes destroy any structures on which they boogie. The Crinkly Cacophony Contrivance keeps the Demon at a nine-tile distance.

Paradise Pair O' Dice: The Powers That Be play Craps with your Heaven as the table. The dice destroy any structure which they roll over. They will, however, bounce off of the Fluffy Comfort Dispenser at a range of twelve tiles.

Hell Freezes Over: A cold spell hits Hell. Any affected structures will be shut down for 75 years while they thaw. Keep your Hell hotter than an alley cat in heat with a Tactile Gradation Gizmo. This will drive the frost away for a radius of twelve tiles.

Heaven Nose: A giant nose soars over Heaven, sniffing up your zones and depositing the corresponding zones randomly in Hell. The Heaven Scent Atomizer protects Heaven for a raduis of ten tiles, and the Flabbergasating Flatulence Ol-Factory does the same in Hell.

Hell in a Handbasket: Similar to Heaven Nose, this picnic basket gobbles up zones in Hell and drops them off in Heaven. The Creamy Candy Castle and the Wellspring of Unsavoriness ward off this Bad Thing for a radius of eleven tiles in Heaven and Hell respectively.

THE SECRETS OF ETERNITY: SOLUTIONS TO THE SCENARIOS

Dante's Sitcom

While this Afterlife may be pleasing to the eye, it has some major problems. You will need to place several Siphons in each of the realms as well as strategically place all of your special buildings. You may have to zap Fate structures to do this. Make sure that all of your roads connect. You will want to constantly monitor your efficiency as you make these changes.

Dusk of the Demiurges

Your main problem here is that you have too many idle workers. First, turn off your Training Centers. Open up your Labor Graph and leave the window open as you make changes. Build Ports, and zone for new Fate structures to help decrease the unemployment.

2 Evil 2 Live

Are you ready for a challenge? The Powers That Be, unhappy with the way the beings on the planet are developing, decide to wipe them out with several disasters all at once. You will get a huge mass of SOULs arriving at the Gates of your Afterlife in a very short period of time. Build several large Gates, and zone as much as you can. The Tempo will stop the action in your realms, but will not stop the influx of SOULs, so you will have to work quickly.

Splitsville

In this scenario, half of each of your realms is well developed. However, on the other sides of the rivers are nothing but a big Gate letting SOULs enter, but with nowhere to go. Quickly build a road from the Gate to the river, and a Port that connects to a road on the other side. This will buy you some breathing room while you begin to zone for Fate structures on the empty side of the river.

IT'S GOOD TO BE THE DEMIURGE: CHEATS AND OTHER SURPRISES

Get More Pennies from Heaven

Type in the code $@!, and you will immediately receive ten million Pennies, tax and interest free. You don't even have to pay it back. You can do this up to five times. If you use this cheat any more than five times, something Bad is bound to happen.

Bad Bunnies

LucasArts have included their own zany little Bad Thing in the game. If you type in SAMNMAX three times in all capital letters, Max the Bunny will appear and hop around your Afterlife. Save your game before trying this.

The Secret Bonus

This is a little secret put in the game by the designer. In Hell, block off a 7x7 square with a road. Put the Tempo to Divine Intervention. Make sure that the direction arrow is pointing up on the remote control. In the tile at the top point of this square, place a green zone. In the two tiles below it, working diagonally across the square but horizontally across your screen, put in yellow zones. Continue your way down with diagonal lines of the same color. The next colors are orange, brown, purple, red, blue, and then start over again with green. The tile in the bottom point of the square will be red. When you start the game going again, you will see your reward.

CHAPTER 2

CAESAR II

Publisher:	Impressions Software
Platform:	PC MS-DOS, Mac (?)
Release Date:	Summer, 1995
Multiplayer:	No
Rating:	

General Overview

Caesar II is a remake of *Caesar*, a 1993 hit from Impressions. However, in this case, the remake is far better than the original.

The premise of the game is the same: colonize a series of provinces while acting as Roman governor. The colonization process takes place both on the Province Level and the City Level, which inspired comparisons between *Caesar* and *SimCity*. The City Level involves building the provincial capital from scratch, and ensuring that it meets Roman standards. Once you've developed the province and its capital to levels set by the Emperor, you are promoted to a new province. Things get more and more difficult with subsequent provinces—the levels of development demanded by Rome are higher, and the local population is more rebellious. This repetitive aspect of *Caesar II* is the only serious drawback to an otherwise fascinating, entertaining, and beautiful game.

The original *Caesar* put more stress on the City Level. Province development was symbolized by making road connections, building provincial walls, and cohort forts. *Caesar II* takes all these concepts to new heights, and introduces provincial industries. The biggest gripe gamers had about *Caesar* was lack of realistic combat. With the addition of *Cohort*, another Impressions title, *Caesar* gained battlefield screens and gave players a bigger degree of control over their armed forces in the field. In *Caesar II*, this is greatly improved—you control beautiful miniature soldiers in a realistic environment. First developed in a rudimentary form for Impressions' *Lords of the Realm*, the combat system in *Caesar II* offers enough realism and beauty to become a mini-game of its own.

Both *Caesar* and *Caesar II* can be played in the City-only mode. Although the City Level in *Caesar II* is good enough to stand alone as a title, the Provincial Level adds a lot of depth to gameplay.

Golden Rules

 Think before you choose your next province—some are definitely tougher than others.

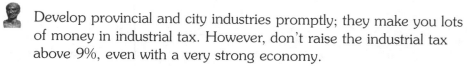

Develop provincial and city industries promptly; they make you lots of money in industrial tax. However, don't raise the industrial tax above 9%, even with a very strong economy.

Keep population tax and conscription rate low. Maximum short-term conscription rate is a little below 20%, but the maximum comfortable and sustainable rate is 8% (less in very difficult provinces). The optimum population tax varies from 3–4%; you can't sustain a rate higher than that in the difficult provinces.

Be wise about your personal savings. If you accumulate too much, you'll be taxed by the Emperor—he gets restless at 3,000 denarii, greedy at 5,000, and positively obnoxious when you accumulate over 8,000. The tax he metes out decreases with the number of provinces you conquer; you don't need more than a couple of thousand to get things going in the early provinces, anyway. Even the most difficult province does not require more than 10,000 in savings, and that's enough to get going really fast.

Don't spend more than necessary on your military. Avoid hiring Auxiliaries except in dire emergencies; use conscription to bolster your legion; draw at least part of your slingers from the plebs working your farms, mines, and quarries.

Work continuously at improving housing values. High housing values make everything much easier. You get more in population tax without raising the tax rate, and everyone's happier.

Keep your people happy! Low population tax and conscription, abundant city amenities, and low unemployment—these are the mottoes of the successful governor.

Time your promotions well—keep the rating necessary to the promotion artificially low until you're ready. Try to avoid ever staying on in a province for an extra term.

Pacify hostile tribes at the very start of your reign. Your cohort will gain morale, and subsequent threats will be easier to deal with.

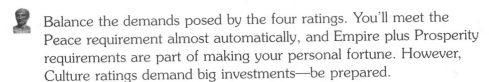

Balance the demands posed by the four ratings. You'll meet the Peace requirement almost automatically, and Empire plus Prosperity requirements are part of making your personal fortune. However, Culture ratings demand big investments—be prepared.

Don't build structures your city doesn't need. You don't need city walls before the Prosperity rating requirement rises to 55%, and you don't need rhetors or circuses if you don't need city walls. Learn the housing value caps provided later in this chapter, and don't expect villas to sprout next to a market.

Winning Strategies

The first thing to keep in mind is that the purpose of the game is to become Caesar, not a rich provincial governor. Many players are tempted to stay on in a well-developed province in order to add to their personal purses. This is self-defeating. With my advice, you'll be able to make sure you're always ready for your next promotion.

To start with, let's look at the world of *Caesar II*.

The Empire

Your career is played out on a board consisting of 43 potential Roman provinces. Each province has a certain difficulty level assigned by the game's designers. In provinces with a higher difficulty level, the local populace is hostile, and you won't be able to tax or conscript it as heavily as in an "easy" province.

Since each promotion requires you reach new heights as governor, careful planning can help you ascend the Imperial throne much faster than choosing provinces at random. The list below groups provinces by their difficulty level:

Level 1—Campania, Cisalpine Gaul

Level 2—Sardinia et Corsica

Level 3—Gallia Narbonensis, Sicilia

Level 4—Illyricum, Pannonia, Thracia, Aquitania, Lycia et Pamphylia

Level 5—Hispania Tarraconensis, Lusitania, Macedonia, Belgica, Cyrenaica, Mauretania, Caria, Syria

Level 6—Germania Superior, Dacia, Gallia Lugudunensis, Bithynia et Pontus, Baetica, Creta, Africa Proconsularis, Mesopotamia

Level 7—Carthage, Achaea, Aegyptus, Britannia, Judaea, Cappadocia, Cyprus, Germania Inferior, Armenia

Level 8—Germania Exterior, Pannonia Exterior

Level 9—Hibernia, Noricum Exterior, Dacia Exterior

Level 10—Caledonia, Asia Exterior, Armenia Exterior

Note that provinces of difficulty Level 8 or higher are only an option if you play the game at higher difficulty levels, from Normal upwards. The most difficult game provinces were never, in fact, part of the Roman Empire—you have the chance to do one better than the Romans ever did. It is not necessary to conquer any of them to become Caesar, except at the Impossible game difficulty level, which I managed to complete in the year 348 A.D.

The difficulty levels assigned to the provinces do not tell the whole story, as a province that's easy to govern could have nasty neighbors. This necessitates a large legion for provincial defense, and large legions are expensive. The details are too numerous to be listed here. If you really want to know them, you'll have to refer to *Caesar II: The Official Strategy Guide* from Prima. What I would suggest is that you save the game right before each promotion. Choose a province, and then survey the land before deciding to put in the tent pegs. If you don't like the looks of it, you can quit and restart at your last save.

There are a couple of general rules to follow when choosing your next province. First, always look for provinces that neighbor other Roman provinces—the less Barbarian neighbors you have, the smaller the external danger. Secondly, when surveying the province, look for maximum variety among local resources. Most African provinces offer wheat and little else, and are subsequently harder to develop.

Thirdly, evaluate the location of the capital. Capitals located close to the border with another Roman province are the ones you want—it's easy to build a road to a border town and establish a trading post. Capitals close to the seashore are also at an advantage. Ports, along with trading posts, are great choices for provincial industries.

Finally, the choice of province depends on what route you want your conquests to take. You may choose to conquer the Near East over Europe, for example.

Remember that Pompous Maximus, *Caesar II*'s other conquering governor, can grab a province from under your nose if you put it off to rule later.

THE PROVINCE

Although you start your reign as governor on the city screen, your first move should be to build your cohort fort. It's only then that you should turn to building the capital city, as outlined in the following section.

You should return to the province screen shortly thereafter to build your provincial industries. I strongly recommend you build trading posts and ports first. They do not require expensive plebeian labor, and provide your city industries with a strong production boost thanks to access to external markets. Note that your city industries can never reach their full production capabilities without an export route (the production is capped at five jars as opposed to seven).

Your next step is to consider the feasibility of building provincial walls. Quite often, a strategically placed stretch of wall can spare you a lot of trouble and expense, allowing a single cohort to perform the work of two. However, you should remember that you can always pause the game and build any necessary walls at the last moment, when the enemy actually makes an appearance. Never surround your capital with walls, except in an emergency, and then quickly demolish the gates on the provincial roads once the emergency is over! Industries in a city cut off by walls from sources of raw materials will produce less, even if the walls have gates.

Connect any towns to which you can afford roads. This facilitates provincial defense while simultaneously boosting your Empire rating. If you've already been promoted a few times, this rating will force you to embark on a second stage of provincial development, often coupled with the building of a second cohort fort. Faraway industries may be easily destroyed by raiders, resulting in big financial losses (you may even lose the game).

THE CITY

This section deals with your provincial capital. Remember you should examine the provincial map first for a while. Note all important features (particularly the location of all provincial industries and tribal settlements), and finally build your cohort fort. Then, and only then, turn to building your city.

You should start building your city with a bang. Don't build a series of shacks, a forum, or a well, and wait for things to improve, because they won't. Plan a small town complete with a market, a grammaticus, a theater, temples, and all the water works. Most city plans feature a river, and most rivers feature a pronounced bend. This is usually the best place to start a town, as you can often supply everyone with water from a single fountain. Also, that location makes your town easy to defend should Barbarians burst onto the city screen (which they never should). Build praefectures to keep the peace, not barracks. The vigiles put out fires *and* quell riots (should they arise), and a praefecture doesn't lower land values as sharply as barracks do.

Given all the basic amenities right at the start, your town should grow very quickly. You should start drafting your citizens into the army as soon as employment dips from 100%. This is also the time to start investing in provincial industries. A few months down the road, when warehouses start filling with commodities, there will also be lots of unemployed citizens—a result of your town's rapid growth—and that's the time to build city industries.

An industrial district invariably has low land values, so you should plan it carefully. You can't exactly isolate it from other housing, as that can mean insufficient labor. City industries actually get a production bonus from housing close by. The low housing values caused by industry presence increase the likelihood of riots, but they also mean that you can build barracks without adverse effect on the quality of your housing.

My favorite solution involves placing two industrial areas to both sides of the original city center. Both have their own forums, baths, markets, and barracks, and later on, also other "culture" objects (schools, theaters, etc). The city layout resembles three rectangles, the biggest one being the original city nucleus. The two industrial zones form two rectangles or squares attached to the first one at its upper corners. In between the two industrial zones—on "top" of the city nucleus—is the area reserved for "culture" structures.

Zoning your industry in this manner also allows you to score a small coup by building two industries of a kind—one in each zone. Their output will still be handicapped because of inherent competition, but less severely so.

After your city has developed to its limits—i.e., housing won't improve without the addition of "culture" structures—I usually add a hospital and a coliseum. These two buildings allow housing to develop to the simple domus stage—the best it can get without city walls. I wait with all other investments until the provincial finances stabilize following these two major expenditures, then continue expanding the city by building whole blocks at a time.

In the later stages of your career, once the required Prosperity rating passes the 50% mark, you'll be forced to build city walls to increase housing values. If you have built all the important housing on one bank of the river, all you have to do is build three walls—the river acts as a fourth. Remember to leave ample space between the walls and the buildings. The proximity of city walls decreases housing values, and you also want to leave some room for growth.

The biggest problem tends to occur when you have to raise housing values in the center of your city, but have no empty sites. I usually do some extensive rezoning at this stage, demolishing factories, moving them to the new suburbs, and building the needed culture structures in their place.

The following sections deal with city planning and structures in detail.

Roads, Plazas, and Gardens

You knew roads were important to Romans, didn't you? They mean a lot in your city. To start with, most buildings require road access. In addition, the citizens you see walking the streets of your city bring important benefits to the areas through which they pass. These are discussed in detail in a later section.

Michael Rymaszewski

All this does not mean you should build roads with wild abandon—they require plebs to maintain, and plebs cost money. Since a building within three squares of a road counts as having road access (though, of course, it won't be able to put "walkers" on their rounds), the most practical city block has six squares per road-enclosed side. Of course, you don't want to limit yourself to blocks like that—you can't fit a Circus Maximus in one, for example—but I found them most practical.

Plazas are basically upgraded roads. They are great at boosting housing values; the earlier you build them, the harder they'll work. However, do not try to build large city squares composed of many plazas. Your city walkers tend to get hopelessly confused and wander around aimlessly.

Gardens are a wonderful way to boost housing values. A strip of gardens behind a row of housing works really well. Note that both gardens and plazas contribute in a small way to your Culture rating, though you have to build quite a lot of them for any effect.

Water Structures

Reservoirs, aqueducts, fountains, baths, and wells all serve to provide your citizens with water for drinking and washing. They are extremely important in achieving healthy population growth and establishing a minimum standard of hygiene. Baths are also a minor contributor to your Culture rating.

You should try and build a city without aqueducts; they are very, very expensive, and complicate city layout. Wells severely limit housing values, and thus are only practical in industrial districts. Reservoirs, fountains, and baths should be strategically placed to ensure maximum area coverage. Remember that baths do not need road access. You can increase their coverage by a square in each direction with each new level of development.

Remember to allocate adequate plebs to water duties, or fountains and baths will dry up periodically, This can cause an alarming drop in housing values which, in turn, can lead to riots. Beware!

Forums, Praefectures, and Barracks

Forums, praefectures, and barracks help you administer your city and keep the peace. Praefectures are perfectly adequate for the latter purpose until you start building large industrial districts.

All three types of buildings produce city 'walkers'—the forum clerk, the vigile, and the soldier—and, therefore, need to be placed next to a road. Forums come in three varieties. The Aventine produces one forum clerk every three months; the Janiculan, one every two months; and the Palatine, one every month. However, for reasons of size and cost, the two smaller forums are much more practical; I hardly build any Palatine forums at all, not even in my biggest cities.

Remember that praefectures and barracks limit housing values. Don't place them in areas that are breeding grounds for villas and palaces.

Markets and City Industries

Markets pose one of the most difficult problems in city design. The walking range of the market trader is very limited, and yet the presence of a market limits housing values to insulas. Quite often, I've had to resort to desperate measures like building a block of three markets around a road extension to provide market access to an upper-class area, allowing the housing to develop into villas and palaces. You can also try to 'buffer' markets with structures such as baths and temples to counter the adverse effect they have on luxury housing. Markets are also essential in industrial areas because market access is critical to the proper development of city industries.

City industries play an extremely important role in *Caesar II*. Without them, you're practically doomed to financial ruin, particularly as the provinces get more difficult. The denarii from industrial tax allow you to keep population taxes low, thus encouraging city growth, preventing riots, and allowing conscription of citizens into the legion. City industries are a top priority after you've built your city nucleus; do not postpone them because of costs associated with the development of *provincial* industries, without which city industries cannot exist!

As a rule, plan each industrial area as a self-contained entity with its own forum, market, baths, and praefectures/barracks.

Shrines, Temples, and Basilicas

All religious buildings perform an important function: they store your gold. The more storage spots you have, the less gold in each, and the smaller the temptation to steal it. Since places of worship boost housing values and improve your culture rating proportionally to their size and cost, you shouldn't skimp on them. Basilicas are never a necessity, but shrines are very handy for improving housing—their single-square size makes them easy to place—while temples offer one of the game's best values in culture structures.

Schools

Caesar II features two types of schools: the grammaticus and the rhetor. You needn't build a single rhetor until the required Prosperity rating forces you to build city walls (the lack of a rhetor imposes smaller limitations on housing values than the absence of walls).

Both the grammaticus and the rhetor provide area coverage without requiring road access, so place them accordingly. Finally, both are important contributors to your Culture rating. The grammaticus also allows your housing to develop into the better insula stage.

Hospitals and Libraries

I've grouped hospitals and libraries together because they have more in common than is apparent. Both are big structures, requiring nine squares or land tiles. Both require road access and forum coverage. However, you'll need the hospital much sooner than the library. I usually build my first hospital following the development of city industries, as soon as unemployment starts creeping up again—the hospital is a big employer. It is also a meaningful contributor to your city's Culture rating, and hospital coverage is an important factor in improving housing. Needless to say, good hospital coverage eliminates the possibility of an epidemic affecting your city (as long as you also have enough fountains and bathhouses).

The library is essential to both high-quality housing and achieving the required Culture rating. It's very expensive, and should not be built until you have a fairly large budgetary surplus.

Remember that hospitals and libraries do not need to be placed close to other city buildings. They just need to be next to the road, and within reach of a forum clerk!

Entertainment Structures

There are three types of entertainment structures, each of which has two classes. Theaters and odeums are variations on the same theme. The more expensive odeum provides a bigger Culture rating boost, and has bigger area coverage. The same rule applies to the arena/coliseum and circus/Circus Maximus combos.

The theater and the arena count as obligatory structures in every capital of any size: Without either, housing grows slowly and doesn't develop to acceptable levels. Start by building a theater, then add an arena. I build mine in the post-hospital era.

Circuses aren't necessary until you reach a relatively high required Prosperity rating. However, they provide the biggest Culture rating boost of all three types of entertainment structures. Coliseums, however, are generally easier to place than a circus, and offer good value in terms of Culture points for the money.

City Walls, Towers, and Gates

City walls are necessary only if the required Prosperity rating is so high that simple domuses don't cut the ice. If you've located your city in a river bend, building city walls is easier than it seems. City walls require pleb maintenance, so it makes sense to build them only when they're really necessary.

You do not need the other types of city fortifications at all; a provincial governor does not let Barbarians enter the city.

The Effect of Structures on Housing Values and Employment

City structures affect housing values, and most of them also provide a number of jobs. The absence of certain structures imposes limits on the development of your housing as set out in the list below.

No Water Supply—housing value limit 2

No Forum Access—housing value limit 6

Next to Business (one tile away)—housing value limit 10

No Market Access—housing value limit 12

Primitive Water Supply—housing value limit 14

Close Proximity to Business (two tiles away)—housing value limit 16

Not Near Baths—housing value limit 18

No Entertainment—housing value limit 20

Near Barracks—housing value limit 24

No Security—housing value limit 24

Proximity to Business (three to four tiles away)—housing value limit 26

Entertainment Level 1—housing value limit 26

Near City Walls—housing value limit 26

Entertainment Level 2—housing value limit 28

Near City Gate—housing value limit 30

Hospital Cover Below 20%—housing value limit 30

Entertainment Level 3—housing value limit 32

No Grammaticus Access—housing value limit 34

Near Praefecture—housing value limit 34

Hospital Cover Below 40%—housing value limit 36

Entertainment Level 4—housing value limit 38

Near Market—housing value limit 40

No City Walls—housing value limit 42

Hospital Cover Below 60%—housing value limit 44

Entertainment Level 5—housing value limit 44

Rhetor—housing value limit 46

Library Cover Below 20%—housing value limit 46

Entertainment Level 6—housing value limit 48

Library Cover Below 40%—housing value limit 50

Hospital Cover Below 80%—housing value limit 52

Library Cover Below 60%—housing value limit 54

CAESAR II

Entertainment Level 7—housing value limit 56

Hospital Cover Below 100%—housing value limit 58

Library Cover Below 80%—housing value limit 58

Entertainment Level 8—housing value limit 60

Library Cover Below 100%—housing value limit 62

The highest housing value possible is 64.

Citizen Happiness and City Growth

You have to keep your citizens reasonably happy. Otherwise, they'll start to riot, and riots can cause incalculable damage. Prevention is the only cure! The principle factors that affect citizen happiness are the province difficulty level, the population tax rate, the conscription rate, the (un)employment rate, and housing values. Of course, the happier your citizens, the faster your city will grow.

The Province difficulty level directly affects the population tax rate. For instance, a 5% tax rate will make the inhabitants of Campania ecstatic, and they'll flock to your city in great numbers. The same 5% tax rate will lead to riots in Egypt, particularly if you're conscripting some of your citizens into the legion.

Limited conscription (2–3%) actually decreases discontent. You can maintain a 6–8% conscription rate with a low population tax rate without any riots in all but very difficult provinces (difficulty level 7 or higher).

Employment comes in two varieties: conscription and jobs provided by city buildings. This does not mean the maintenance plebs!

The following list enumerates jobs created by all of *Caesar II*'s structures:

Aventine Forum—40 jobs

Janiculan Forum—80 jobs

Palatine Forum—120 jobs

Shrine—10 jobs

Temple—20 jobs

Basilica—30 jobs

Baths—20 jobs

Praefecture—25 jobs

Barracks—30 jobs

Grammaticus—30 jobs

Rhetor—80 jobs

Library—60 jobs

Theater—25 jobs

Odeum—30 jobs

Arena—50 jobs

Coliseum—60 jobs

Circus—80 jobs

Circus Maximus—100 jobs

Hospital—80 jobs

Market—20 jobs

Business—60 jobs

Housing values are a very good way to combat unhappiness because raising them also puts more money in the provincial coffers. Do not skimp spending money on necessary city amenities; your housing cannot develop properly without them.

City Walkers

The citizens that walk the streets of your city perform very important functions. Forum clerks ensure tax collection and the operation of hospitals and libraries; market traders ensure market access; industry workers 'find' labor for city industries (inhabitants of houses passed by the worker are potential employees); vigiles put out fires and combat rioters (and Barbarians that make it to the city screen); soldiers fight rioters and Barbarians. It is worthwhile noting that the security bonus passed out by patrolling vigiles and soldiers actually decreases discontent, with soldiers being twice as efficient as the vigiles.

CAESAR II

Every city walker has a 'birth rate' and a certain range—he disappears after walking a certain distance:

Walker	Lifespan/Range	'Birth' Rate
Forum Clerk	6 months/36 tiles	1 every 4 3/2 months
Market Trader	4 months/24 tiles	1 every 4 months
Vigile	6 months/36 tiles	1 every 4 months
Soldier	11 months/66 tiles	1 every 4 months
Worker	12 months/72 tiles	1 every 12 months

To ensure good city development, every block of your housing should be serviced by all types of walkers with the possible exception of soldiers (the soldiers' long range means that once you've built a couple of barracks, you'll see them everywhere, anyway).

PROMOTIONS, RATINGS, AND IMPERIAL FAVOR

You qualify for promotion once you reach the required levels in all five ratings: Empire, Peace, Prosperity, Culture, and Average. This last rating means you have to exceed some of the other ones by a fat margin.

The Empire rating is a sum of two factors: the level to which you've developed the province, and Imperial Favor. Various provincial developments such as road connections or new industries determine 85–90% of your Empire rating; the remainder is decided by Imperial Favor.

Ports and road connections to border towns are the biggest Empire rating boosters. Road connections to provincial towns are the next in importance, followed by trading posts, shipyards, farms and mines, and finally workcamps and warehouses.

Imperial Favor is determined by how well you fulfil the Emperor's requests for gifts of local goods, and how generously you bribe him. A bribe can save your neck if you can't fulfil an Imperial demand and generally improve things in normal circumstances. However, make sure that you don't anger the Emperor by offering him a handful of change. Your bribe should never be smaller than the previous one—and preferably bigger. Don't bribe the Emperor too often, as he can become quite spoiled.

Since Imperial Favor affects your Empire rating, a bribe can help you get the last couple of required points.

The Peace rating is determined by two factors: the passage of time, and events that take place during that time. Every month, your Peace rating automatically grows by 0.2%. Barbarian uprisings, raids, destruction of provincial structures, and finally Barbarians entering the city screen subtract percentage points from the rating. Victories in battle and pacification of tribal settlements boost the rating.

The Prosperity rating depends on . . . money. Specifically, it is affected by your rolling profit (sum total of income and expenditure), the average population tax bill (as shown on the Treasurer's panel), and the size of your city. The size ceases to be a consideration once your city population passes 2,000. From then onwards, your energies should be focused on increasing the average population tax bill. This is increased by either raising the tax rate or improving housing values—or both. In more difficult provinces, improving housing values is the only practical option. Remember that the tax bill is average, and thus, even a couple of palaces won't help much if the rest of your housing is composed of industrial slums.

I found the Culture rating the hardest to satisfy. Towards the climax of your career, you may find yourself building rows of coliseums and basilicas to meet the standards required by the Emperor. Make sure your hospital and library coverage is as good as possible, and prepare to spend considerable sums on all culture structures. The last stages of my career on the Impossible level found me building absurd numbers of circuses, coliseums, etc., as well as turning most of the city map into a big garden!

Remember that Culture rating is affected by your city's population—the more citizens you have, the more cultural amenities you have to provide. Therefore, it sometimes makes sense to abruptly reduce the population by some brutal demolition work, building temples and theaters in place of housing. Although city industries may experience harmful labor shortages, this tactic is very effective in closing gaps of a few percentage points.

Also, bear in mind that your city's population may drop for natural reasons, as when insulas are changing into domuses.

You can make sure you are promoted when you want to be by keeping one of the ratings artificially low. An Empire rating, for example, may be instantly met by connecting a town or two, or you can keep population tax

C
A
E
S
A
R

II

low and jack it up just for a few months. It takes some time before the higher tax will generate riots, and you will be promoted long before then. When the Emperor decides to promote you, he promotes you, even if you've got three Barbarian armies marching on your capital (which let me out of a nasty situation).

You should be aware that all Ratings are population-adjusted, and at the same time, have minimum city population requirements. Your city population has to exceed certain numbers before you can be awarded progressively more Ratings points. You need ten citizens per each Empire and Peace point, and forty citizens per each Culture and Prosperity point. At the same time, Culture is adversely affected by population growth—the more people you have in your city, the more amenities they need. This is what makes satisfying the Culture rating so demanding, particularly if the Prosperity rating is high; the villas and palaces that help with Prosperity house hundreds of people who lower the Culture rating.

SLAVES AND SOLDIERS

Your legion and your slaves, or plebs, are the two pillars of your power. Plebs take care of all city maintenance tasks (without them, there would be no city), work in provincial industries, and supply slingers for your army. Soldiers, of course, keep the Barbarians in check.

Managing Plebs

Here's another province difficulty tidbit: The higher the province difficulty level, the more difficult it is to get plebs. The increase in plebs numbers simulates a natural birth rate, so it's counterproductive to assign big sums to plebs' welfare from the very start. It's best to increase the Roman equivalent of social security by small increments, just big enough to ensure continued growth in plebs numbers.

Do not try to save any money on plebs needed to maintain your city. Any small savings in that area can lead to a catastrophe. Don't build any provincial industries requiring plebeians before you've built up a labor reserve. Make a point of raising a century of slingers as fast as you can, particularly when neighboring Carthaginians, because slingers are the only troop type truly effective against Carthaginian war elephants.

Once you've built a few farms and/or mines, the plebeian laborers are a great reserve force. You can raise an extra century of slingers in an instant.

The Legion

Your legion is composed of four types of soldiers: heavy infantry (professional soldiers), light infantry (conscripted citizens), slingers (conscripted plebeians), and Auxiliaries (mercenary soldiers).

Heavy infantrymen are the best soldiers you can get, with the possible exception of Horsearcher Auxiliaries. They are hired at a rate of one century per five denarii a month. The number of heavy infantrymen in a century decreases with the province difficulty level by five soldiers per level. Thus, in Campania (difficulty level 1) your five denarii a month gets you a hundred professional fighters; in Caledonia (difficulty level 10), you'll get 55.

Heavy infantrymen are your most reliable and hard-hitting troop type. Slow to lose morale when things go badly, they are devastating when attacking in formation (line or column). Heavy infantrymen train at the rate of 20 a month.

Light infantrymen are free of charge, which is very nice, but are noticeably weaker than the professionals in heavy infantry. They are quicker to panic, and are at a slight disadvantage when attacking. However, they move faster than heavy infantry, and thus are better suited for flanking attacks. When in defensive formation (the tortoise), light infantry can generally give a good account of itself. Its soldiers train at the rate of 40 a month.

Slingers are your legion's standard missile troops (in some provinces, you can also hire mercenary bowmen). They are devastatingly effective at short range, but should always be protected by other troops. Relatively easy to panic, slingers should never have to fight hand-to-hand—they tend to get slaughtered. Slingers train at the rate of 50 a month.

Slingers are pretty expensive. When you consider how much a half-dozen extra plebs costs on the monthly welfare bill, they are much more pricey than heavy infantry. Fortunately, you can treat the plebs employed in your farms and mines as your slinger reserve. Just make sure you have full warehouses when you take the slaves off the fields and press them into military service!

Auxiliaries are mercenary troops available for hire—or not, as some provinces don't have any. They are always prohibitively expensive—a mere 50 costs 20 denariis a month, which can get you from 220 to 400 heavy infantry. What's worse, while some are excellent (Armenian Horsearchers), others are rotten (Chatti Spearsmen). Treat them as a last resort . Since you can train unlimited numbers of Auxiliaries in a month, there's no excuse for keeping them on strength on a permanent basis.

Note, however, that if your fifty-strong Auxiliaries suffer any losses, you cease paying for their upkeep. Thus, you can have 49 Auxiliaries in your legion for free at all times.

Winning Battles

In *Caesar II*, battles can be resolved by the computer, or they can be fought by yourself. The computer-led cohort is given a pretty good chance, and unless you know what you're doing, you're better off staying in the governor's palace instead of leading your men on the battlefield. This is particularly true when you fight the infamous Horsearchers (*Caesar II*'s only mounted troops, apart from the Carthaginians), which can be found in many of the Eastern armies. This is because you can easily lose a battle even though your forces are stronger. The outcome of a battle is always decided by the morale of the fighting sides. The side whose morale drops first loses. It's that simple.

Morale is affected by several factors. First of all, there is the cohort's battlefield experience. If your cohort has been repeatedly victorious, its pre-battle morale is excellent, and it can even take on a superior foe. The second consideration is the numbers on the battlefield. If your soldiers are outnumbered, they'll be scared, and vice versa. Finally, morale is greatly influenced by the course of events on the battlefield. A unit's morale drops steadily as it suffers losses, and drops even faster if it's being pelted with missiles. If a century panics and runs, other centuries fighting alongside suffer a drop in morale. Sometimes, this can turn the tide of a battle.

Your soldiers' morale can also be boosted—a century that makes the enemy run becomes very brave. Of course, everything works for both sides.

The moral of the morale story is this: concentrate on making a single group of enemies run, one at a time, and beware of them doing the same to you. I've had battles where my nearly-victorious soldiers suddenly turned and ran just because enemy stragglers managed to get at the stupid slingers. Fortunately, when your soldiers aren't fighting, they regain morale slowly, and by the time they run off the battle screen, they can be often persuaded to re-form and enter the fight again.

My favorite tactic is to line up my legion with heavy infantry in a line in the center, light infantry in tortoise on the flanks, and slingers lined behind the heavy infantry. If I'm using Auxiliaries, I always place them on the wings, and assign them to a decidedly auxiliary role. If everything goes well, I send them into the fray to lose a man or two so that I can have the remaining soldiers for free.

Usually, I wait for the Barbarians to attack. Many armies lose formation when marching, thus becoming easy meat, and you may have similar problems with the less professional of your soldiers. As the Barbarians move closer, I extend the wings slightly forward and target the slingers on the advancing enemy. Finally, when the enemy is just a few steps away, I attack with my heavy infantry from the front and light infantry from the sides.

It's important to remember that Roman troops enjoy a combat bonus when fighting in formation. The bonus applies when your soldiers are attacking in a line or a column, or defending in a tortoise. Soldiers in a tortoise also suffer only half of the missile hits they would have otherwise.

However, ordering your soldiers to break formation and pursue the enemy is often a good move. This is because a soldier under attack from more than one side dies, and three legionnaires attacking from three sides work better than a single one attacking in formation.

SPREADING PAX ROMANA

As mentioned, your first action in every province is the building of the cohort fort. Usually, it's best to place it at the corner of your capital city square (on the provincial map, of course).

Hire a century of heavy infantry at a time (they won't train faster just because you pay more) and keep a trickle of slingers coming. When unemployment rears its head, introduce conscription. You should have a century of light infantry by the time your second century of heavies is ready.

Hire some Auxiliaries if you want to play the fifty minus one maneuver, and set about pacifying the province. Do not go after faraway settlements with your single cohort and leave the capital unprotected for a long period of time! If you must do that anyway, do it as quickly as possible. There is a period of grace at the beginning of your rule in a new province; Barbarians won't get troublesome until sometime later.

Pacification of tribes lets your Prima Cohorts score a couple of easy victories and improve its morale to Excellent. Be aware that various settlements are defended by armies of various sizes. The army defending the tribe is always composed exclusively of light infantry, with 150 infantrymen for every level of tribal power. Thus, a weak tribe will field 150 infantry, a local tribe— 300, strong—450, and powerful—600.

Having pacified whatever you could without risking your neck, let the Prima Cohors grow in strength. Most provinces call for your cohort to have at least 800 men if you're going to be there for some time, and by mid-career that's the rule—you gotta serve your years before you can move on. You should only build a second cohort fort if Barbarian pressure is too strong for one cohort, or when there is no other way to protect some of your new provincial industries (sometimes, you'll be forced to build an industry in the middle of Barbarian territory because of an Emperor's fancy). Unfortunately, some provinces will also call for a third, even a fourth cohort. However, third and fourth cohorts are usually around 300 strong; the big raids and invasions are dealt with by the Prima Cohors and maybe the Rabbits, while additional cohorts just fill in the resultant holes in defense and possibly take on smaller Barbarian incursions

I cannot imagine a province which would require you to build half a dozen forts, let alone the maximum eight permitted.

The most dangerous Barbarians you can encounter are mostly massed on the fringes of the Roman empire. Picts, Britons, Saxons, and Frisians are to be watched in Western Europe. The Parthians and all the Horsearcher army types make lethal adversaries in the East. Visigoths and Vandals raid as far as Dacia, while Galatians, Parthians, and the Huns dominate the southeastern corner of the Empire. Greek regulars and Mediterranean type armies constitute worthy opponents. Numidian pirates, which strike European shores, are very tough (although never numerous), and Arabs tend to bring huge armies with plenty of bowmen. Also, you should beware of charging axemen which are a feature of many Germanic armies. If the charge is successful, it can result in a catastrophic drop in morale among your soldiers. Break it up by attacking from the flank.

Easy opponents include African armies, Slavic armies (Dalmatians, Macedonians), and, surprisingly, the Gauls.

CHAPTER 3

CIVILIZATION II

Publisher:	Microprose Software
Platform:	PC MS-DOS
Release Date:	Spring, 1996
Multiplayer:	No
Rating:	

Plot Summary and General Overview

Civilization, first published in 1992, is quite possibly the greatest computer game ever created. The original version sold nearly a million copies and turned hundreds of thousands of computer owners into gaming enthusiasts. Versions for Windows, the Macintosh, and finally a mutliplayer *Civ* called *Civnet* appeared over the next few years. I was one of the early *Civ* addicts—I lost a good New Year's Eve party because I started to play *Civ* for the first time on the last afternoon of the year.

Civilization II lives up to big expectàtions created by its predecessor. The SVGA graphics and isometric view offer a great visual improvement over the original. The combat model is much better. There's more of everything— more Advances waiting to be discovered, more Wonders of the World, more military (and non-military) units. It's as addictive as the original was, which probably means that several thousand people will lose their jobs, and a few hundred will get divorced. The great gameplay, for which the original *Civ* is famous, is still there; add the new features and the chrome, and you have what could be called a supergame.

The premise of the game is very traditional: Starting with a unit or two of settlers, you must conquer the known world—or the unknown world—by sending a spaceship with colonists to the nearest star system, Alpha Centauri. This is not easy, even at the lower difficulty level; at higher difficulty—King or above—it's quite hard. The satisfaction you'll feel when your spaceship finally blasts off, or when your paratroopers capture the last foreign city, will be as great as if you had just graduated or gotten the dream job you'd always wanted. After playing *Civilization II,* you may well feel that any other game is just a game, and that's all.

Unfortunately, there are a few small negatives (I feel very hesitant writing about those. It's as if I was spitting at a Deity . . .). The winds of political correctness that have been blowing at Microprose for some time have left their mark. For example, the creators of *Civilization II* chose Empress Maria Theresa of Austria to represent the Germans. Oddly enough, Henry VIII, the one with six consecutive wives, often replaces Elizabeth I as the English leader. Perhaps someone at Microprose heard old Henry liked women.

My advice: Get the game, because if you like games, you'll love it. But please remember what Microprose, perhaps overwhelmed by the responsibility of working on such a big title, forgot: It's only a game.

Finally, a word about the winning strategies discussed below. They have been developed while playing *Civ II* at the Deity level. I've tried them out at the Emperor and King level, and they work even better there. Easier levels may offer you more choices because the game will be more forgiving. Your score won't be anywhere as high, though, nor your satisfaction from winning anywhere as big. *Civ II* is winnable even at the hardest level, so why not give it a try?

The advice on these pages has been written specifically for *Civilization II,* version 1.11. However, a lot applies to the original *Civilization* and *Civnet*—these two earlier versions of the game are almost identical. I've pointed out the differences where appropriate.

Golden Rules

⚔ Position your cities well. Switch the grid on and contemplate things for a while; imagine subsequent cities and how they will fit in later. Aim for a good balance of food and resources, and make sure you place a fair number of cities on the coast. Be on the lookout for resource-less grasslands/river squares; they are the perfect sites (in *Civ II,* a city produces a single shield regardless of location, so the square in question gains a resource).

⚔ In a way, the game should be called *Expansion II.* Keep expanding, starting new cities, and immediately looking for space to start some more. If you bump into another civilization early on and find there's no space to grow, immediately erase the new neighbors. You'll gain several ready-made cities as a bonus, and sometimes even a Wonder or two.

⚔ Garrison each city with three units—two defensive, one offensive, or three good at both—and keep a small, highly mobile standing army to deal with sudden threats.

- Connect all your cities by road, and later build a railroad network. This is essential for effective defense. Connected cities also experience slightly less corruption.

- Build a good navy. Naval power is a major factor in most *Civ* games. A troop transport with eight units sunk en route means you have eight less land units to deal with later.

- Use money as a tool, don't hoard it. Speeding up the production of a granary in your first city can mean five more cities 5,000 years down the line. Paying for quicker completion of profitable marketplaces and banks is particularly worthwhile. Later on, quick completion of mass transit systems and recycling centers can eliminate the threat of pollution to the degree where you can wage nuclear war without global consequences. However, do keep a reserve that lets you buy a couple of big improvements or expensive military units at a moment's notice.

- Make sure you know what you're telling your scientists to work on. A later section details what I found to be the best research route. Feel free to devise your own, but have a plan first and don't get side-tracked.

- Protect your Reputation. Don't start wars. Provoke others into launching sneak attacks by keeping a constant, nagging presence in their territory. Make full use of diplomacy to foment the computer players. At the same time, pick one civilization to be your ally. I've found that the best allies are civilizations a class below mine. They have good enough cities to trade with, but at the same time, don't count in the final rush for the brass ring.

- If you must be brutal, go all the way and become a Fundamentalist. No one's going to expect much of you after this, so diplomatic penalties are lessened. However, make sure you've advanced far enough to discover a host of good "military" advances, and use spies to keep advancing in knowledge. Fundamentalism, as we all know, is bad for knowledge.

⚔ Make establishing trade routes a high priority. If you don't establish the maximum three trade routes per city, you'll be in trouble—that's all there is to it. Remember that foreign trade pays much better, but domestic trade isn't to be sneezed at. A single caravan gives a permanent trade bonus to both the home and destination cities.

⚔ Set your sights on specific Wonders early on, and accumulate caravans prior to beginning construction. In this way, your Wonder will be ready in record time. If you're sure no one's going to beat you to it, use food caravans to speed up construction (you still want the Wonder's benefits ASAP and your building city to go back to churning out other improvements and units). If you think someone might beat you to it, accumulate goods caravans and build the Wonder within a single turn. If someone else does it, you still have the goods caravans with which you can start trade routes.

⚔ Be aggressive and don't let anyone push you around. However, that doesn't mean being stupid—you can kowtow to someone to buy time. Plan aggression carefully. You shouldn't make a move unless you are sure you can capture at least one city within a couple of turns. That means assembling a carefully balanced army in the right spot before any shots or arrows are fired.

⚔ Treat the spaceship win as an option, and go for the world conquest. If you succeed, your end score will be much, much higher. Building an industry to meet the needs of your war machine automatically means having an industry capable of turning out spaceship parts quickly. Of course, no war machine is complete without modern military units. Space technology is just a short step sideways from weapons technologies, so changing directions is not a problem.

Winning Strategies

Civilization II is a complex game. There is a multitude of Advances to discover, many city improvements and Wonders to build, and practically dozens of military units to choose from. All those factors may prevent you from fully appreciating the fact that the success of your tribe rests on the smooth and uninterrupted running of three engines: Food, Resources, and Trade.

THE ECONOMICS OF CIVILIZATION

Your civilization has to strike the right balance in the production of food (wheat stalks on the city display), resources (shields), and trade (arrows). Striking the right balance (and adjusting it in accordance with your civilization's changing needs) is absolutely necessary if you want to win.

Food and resources can only be obtained from the land, so to speak. They are produced by the citizens of your cities working the land within the city area. Trade may be obtained both from the land (and water—ocean squares are particularly good), and through trade routes that you create with caravan and freight units.

It follows that correct positioning of your cities is of great importance— it's dealt with later on in detail. Here, we'll just examine the implications each of those three factors have for you and your tribe.

Food

Food, naturally, is what lets your civilization exist in the first place. Here's rule number one: Not a single city of yours should be without a surplus of food. The bigger the surplus, the better. Some players (initially, I was one of them) try to avoid civil disturbances caused by the large size of their cities by limiting food production. It's a very short-sighted policy that gives a few minor short-term benefits (you don't have to worry about the problem, basically) in exchange for a major long-term headache that can result in losing the game.

You must make sure each of your cities has a food surplus at all times. Check the city display often to make sure this is the case. Some game events may seriously cut into your city's food supply in a way that could escape your attention:

> **Building a new settlers unit.** New settlers mean that the population of their mother city has just decreased by one. The computer automatically re-allocates the city's work force so that it

produces as much food as possible. Nevertheless, settlers demand food for support, and under certain circumstances, that may result in a food shortage for the city. The most common mistake is building too many settlers units. A city that has a surplus of three food or less should never support more than one settler unit. You may let it support two if the surplus is five or more—the more, the better. If you're ruling a Republic or Democracy, settlers demand two food per turn.

Presence of foreign units. Unless you've signed an alliance with another civilization, any foreign units occupying a square automatically close it to your city workers. In the original *Civilization*, the computer liked to land units all around your cities until you had no choice left but starvation or war. In *Civ II*, you can ask them to leave. Whenever there are foreign units lurking near one of your cities, check the city display to make sure production isn't being affected.

Pollution. From the moment you discover Industrialization, pollution is an increasingly acrid problem, so to speak. Pollution cuts food from a square in half. Since pollution is partly the result of a large city population in the first place, the consequences are often dire—you'll find the food box contents diminishing instead of growing.

Revolution. The period of anarchy between governments grows in length with time. By the 1800s, a revolution is likely to last several turns. Throughout that time, food production is the same as under despotism, with penalties for any square producing more than two stalks. Of course, by that time, most of your food-producing squares yield three or four food per turn, so the penalties mean a severe shortfall. If you didn't build the Pyramids or granaries in each city, you may be in trouble. Any city which has accumulated just a row or two of stalks in its food box may easily lose a population point (or single citizen from the city display).

Note that the list above includes just the not-so-obvious factors. There are plenty of obvious ones, too, from global warming to inadvertently building a mine in an oasis. Simply check food production *every* time you open a city's display, and you should be able to avoid any unpleasant surprises.

CIVILIZATION II

There are many ways in which you can increase the food production of a city—irrigation, re-assigning worked squares, terrain transformation, or redrawing the borders of neighboring cities to transfer a good food-producing square from one to the other. One of the big changes in *Civ II* is that you can also build food caravans. They institute supply routes—one food per turn for every route. The problem with these is that once they're set up, they cannot be canceled. You can, of course, always build another food caravan sending the food back to the original supplier, but that takes time and shields.

The only instance in which I would consider forming a food caravan is when I really need to place a city in an inhospitable spot for strategic reasons—say, a border town in a mountainous region. Military matters often demand solutions that defy common sense, so in a way, it's logical.

Finally, a word about your electronic opponents. Below King level, they're handicapped by having their city food storage boxes wider than yours (taking more stalks per row to fill the box). At King, you're even. At Emperor, the computer player's food box is 10 percent smaller, and at Deity, 20 percent.

Resources

Food is all very nice, but your tribe won't progress far without resources, or shields. Maintaining high production levels is essential to winning the game at the higher difficulty levels, where the computer player enjoys clear-cut advantages. As with food, things are the same at King level, with a 10 percent boost for the computer for each additional difficulty level.

Resources are generally harder to find than food, which is entirely appropriate. However, since their availability determines how quickly you can get things done, they are just as important as food is in your winning game plan.

In my experience, a good formula to follow is that a city's total production (total number of shields—not just those available after subtracting support) should equal the number of its population points plus two. This does not apply to brand-new cities. Quite often, starting a city in a location where its initial production is low guarantees optimum production after it's reached a certain size. This is because ordinary land squares that provide more than a single shield do not, as a rule, yield more than one food. Squares with special resources, such as a pheasant or a whale, may be good at both, and that's what makes them so precious.

Michael Rymaszewski

The food-or-resources rule means that a city working mines or forests must make up for the food shortfall by working fertile food-producing squares. It's good to remember that it is impossible to achieve a decent level of production without guaranteeing a good food supply to start with.

Boosting shields in your city is somewhat more difficult than increasing food supply. However, there are some fixes and solutions:

- **Re-assigning the city's work force to resource-rich land squares.** This is a fix, not a solution, and is best applied when you want to complete building something in a hurry (such as a Wonder or a military unit in a city under attack). However, if you examine city displays on a regular basis at some point in the city's development, you'll be able to boost production by a shield or two without sacrificing too much food, if any. This is most often possible in aqueduct-sized cities (8+ population points, 360,000+ citizens).

- **Building mines and railroads.** These solutions are the only ones that are truly effective, but they are time consuming. It's good to have two settlers/engineers working the same square—one building a mine, the other the railroad.

- **Changing/transforming terrain.** Changing terrain takes less time than transforming it, and there's one change in particular which is very fast. This is turning plains/grassland into forest, which, given a railroad, will yield you three extra shields per square. Since the few shields problem is most common in cities which are surrounded by plains/grasslands, this does not usually cut into a city's growth ability or influence its maximum size too badly. Tip: Build the railroad (or even a road if you haven't discovered Railroad yet) before you change the terrain. Building roads/railroads takes much less time on a plain than it does in a forest.

- **Factories and manufacturing plants.** These dramatically increase a city's shields, up to double the original amount. The downside is the accompanying pollution, which often results in food shortages (and cuts production back, too).

✖ **Nuclear or hydro power plants, or the Hoover Dam Wonder.**
Don't ever build coal-fired power plants—the pollution problem
tends to become unmanageable! Do not even consider the Hoover
Dam if it won't benefit at least five factories (some of which may be
still in the planning stage). Nuclear plants are cheaper than hydro
plants, and only carry a risk of disaster if the city with the plant goes
into disorder. Both types of plants boost the city's shields nicely, but
don't ever make the mistake of building them in cities without
factories or manufacturing plants!

✖ **Disbanding units.** Civ II features this nice change from its
predecessor. Disbanded units contribute half of the shields they cost
to the construction of whatever's being built in the city in which you
disband them. It goes without saying that you should never disband
units in the field, except when *not* doing it threatens to bring down
your Democratic government. Of course, you should only disband
obsolescent units; I find that a *very* effective way of speeding up unit
transitions, such as when changing over from musketeers to
riflemen. Obviously, this is a fix, not a solution.

The Demographics screen, accessed from the World menu, provides valuable
intelligence as to where your civilization stands in terms of production. "Manufactured Goods" simply means total number of shields. Ignore the million
tagged onto the number—it's there for purely decorative purposes. You
should always strive to be the first in Manufactured Goods, because that means
your cities have more shields than anyone else's, and that, in turn, means you
get things done at least as quickly as other leading civilizations (at Emperor and
Deity, you cannot say for sure you're fastest, because the computer players
have smaller production boxes). It's very, very difficult to win a game of *Civilization* or *Civilization II* if you aren't number one in production.

Trade

Booming trade is a prerequisite of winning at *Civilization II* at any but the
very easiest level. However, since trade is not essential to the growth of cities
or the production of units, its extremely important role is often under-appreci-
ated or even ignored.

I am linking trade to income in this chapter for a reason. This is because trade is the only way to increase income and you must have income to maintain anything you build in your cities. Thus, income takes precedence over science and luxuries—which is not to say science is not important.

You must give trade the same priority you give to resources (sometimes, that means switching your city to maximum resource production so that it builds caravans faster). Fortunately, increasing trade isn't all that hard:

- ⚔ Make sure every grasslands and plains square worked by a city has a road. The computer always selects the squares with the biggest food production when placing new workers, so check your city display each time the population has grown by a point. The same thing goes for every new settler/engineer unit. Check the city display, because the computer may have assigned a citizen to working a land square without a road.

- ⚔ Anticipate things a little, and build a couple of roads in the right squares (optimally, grasslands with resources) before using the settler to start the city. Maximum possible trade from the very first turn of its existence gives your city a good start. It can grow a little larger before it produces its first settler unit without losing any potential trade.

- ⚔ Water means extra trade. Give priority to river squares within the city's area—a forest with a river yields one trade, a forest without a river doesn't. Build an adequate number of coastal cities that can take advantage of the ocean's trade bonus (each square yields two trade), and look for ways to include inland lakes in the city limits (lakes also net two trade, as does any expanse of water).

- ⚔ Discover trade early on. The first caravans you build will probably be destined for a Wonder–building city to assist with the construction. However, you should institute at least one trade route per city for any city that reaches five population points (150,000 people), even if you haven't made contact with any other civilizations. Each "internal" caravan brings you trade in two cities—the starting point and the destination—and that yields two trade. Detailed information on caravans is furnished later on.

CIVILIZATION II

✖ By the 1500s, ensure that every city of five or more population points has at least two trade routes. You should make contact with at least one other civilization by then, and the new trade routes should be much more rewarding.

✖ Make establishing trade routes with other civilizations an important priority throughout the game. When you make contact, it's worth your while to throw all your effort into establishing the maximum three trade routes per city. There are rare exceptions to this rule: You may not want to start trade routes with someone whom you intend to conquer in short order, or with a powerful civilization that you are directly competing with. Remember, the caravans/freights you send out result in trade in the destination city as well, so you may be boosting your immediate rival's trade as well as your own (of course, all foreign trade involves giving a boost to a foreign economy).

✖ Finally, try manipulating the city workforce after all three trade routes have been established. Quite often, putting a single citizen to work an ocean square instead of a forest or mine results in an increase of trade from trade routes. The trade route bonus is calculated on the basis of local trade in the two cities involved; increasing local trade may thus bring very happy results. It's not uncommon to gain three extra trade in an instant!

Once you've got decent trade going on in your cities, everything becomes much easier. Your scientists make discoveries more quickly, money flows into the treasury, and everyone's happy.

Trade Details

The profit you make from each caravan is twofold. Most importantly, a caravan or a freight establishes a trade route that brings in extra trade to its home city for every turn thereafter until the end of the game. It's quite possible for a big city to have three trade routes netting between 20 and 30 trade, each and every turn. The extra trade a caravan brings is calculated on the basis of the local trade arrows in host and destination cities (foreign trade does not count). The more arrows in both cities, the better the trade between them.

The other thing to remember is that domestic trade is always worth much less than foreign trade. An example illustrates this as well as any mathematical formula: Two big cities forging a domestic trade route under a Republic or Democracy can expect to pull in 4 extra trade per turn, per city, which isn't bad. However, should the same two cities belong to two different Republican or Democratic civilizations, the trade bonus becomes enormous (often reaching double digits).

Caravans and freights also bring a secondary profit. Although I call it secondary, it may sometimes be huge, and it takes the form of an immediate cash-and-light bulb bonus the moment your caravan/freight arrives in the destination city (it does not matter whether you're actually establishing a new trade route, or not). This immediate cash/light bulb bonus is calculated in a similar way as the permanent trade bonus—number of local trade arrows in both cities, nationality. However, distance also plays a role, as does the fact of whether the two cities are on the same land mass, or are separated by water. Finally, a big part of the bonus is determined by the contents of the caravan. If they are in demand in the destination city, the bonus is much higher (this is where all that dye-silk-coal-wine business comes in). Remember that the contents of a caravan do not affect the permanent trade bonus. However, if you deliver whatever's currently in demand, you can get several hundred coins and an equivalent number of light bulbs by delivering a caravan from one Republican city to another foreign one, halfway across the world.

Since the sums—and research bonuses—that are involved can be very considerable, do not hesitate to replace old, low-paying domestic routes with foreign ones once you make the contact with other civilizations. You may find that although your Science Advisor calculates the discovery rate at every eight turns, you're actually making one every third turn (there is a cap on the maximum boost research can get from caravans, but it's a loose-fitting cap). Just watch the retort signifying research progress change color when a really profitable caravan comes in!

Consider using occasional caravans as a means of improving cash flow, and research speed when you have several cities that don't really have anything to build. This does happen! The relatively small size of the city may not warrant building second or third-level research/monetary improvements, and its shield numbers may not allow it to support more units than it already does. The only thing that makes sense is then to make diplomats/spies or caravans/freights, even when the city already has three good trade routes. You may hoard the caravans for a future Wonder if you don't need the monetary/light bulb boost, and spread diplomats/spies among your cities (a must in the endgame at the Deity level. Your James Bonds can prevent an enemy act of subversion or sabotage).

First Steps

The sections above discussed the three fundamental concepts in the game. What follows roughly retraces the course of events during a game, with separate sections devoted to issues that arise as you play.

LOCATING CITIES

The first decision to confront you as you begin playing is where to put your first city. The answer is obvious: Place it so that it has the maximum of everything—food, resources, trade.

At the start of the game, your world is shrouded in blackness, with an area the size of a city area visible around your first settler (or settlers at the Deity level, you're routinely given two). If you build the city right then and there, trusting in the wisdom of the computer, you'll get your civilization off to a flying start. On the other hand, a better site may become obvious once you've moved your settler just once . . . okay, one more move . . . now, let's just see what's there—and your potential initial advantage is lost, while it turns out the starting site was best, after all.

Things don't always go this way. About 50 percent of the time, I manage to find a better site for my first city within the first two turns (again, this applies to the Deity level. Moving two units twice uncovers quite a lot of extra ground). However, there is a definite trade-off here. My conclusion is this: If you don't like the site the computer has chosen, allow yourself up to two turns—three in absolutely exceptional circumstances—to explore the surroundings. A fortunate placing of your city may speed up its growth, thus making up for the couple of turns at the outset. More importantly, at the Deity level, it helps to have a better idea of the surrounding terrain right at the start—you get that little bit of extra warning.

I also make it a point to build a road before I start the first city (at the Deity level, you may do both simultaneously because you've got two settlers). The extra light bulb does wonders for early research. For instance, you can acquire much-needed Bronze Working twice as fast.

Positioning subsequent cities isn't as much of a nail-biter because by then, you have an idea what the lay of the land is. As a rule, you should spread them out so there is minimum overlap, yet every land square is covered by city areas. It's very helpful to turn the grid on before ordering your settler to start building; you'll see exactly where to place him.

If you're faced with one of those hard choices—overlap or unused squares—go for the overlap. It's better to have two cities than one, even if both are just a tad smaller. Just don't let the overlaps grow too large. A city may have up to four squares shared with other cities without any truly serious consequences.

One final note. When placing your first and subsequent cities, be on the lookout for rivers, and place your city on a river/grasslands or river/plains square if you can. The trade isn't as important as the 50 percent defensive bonus.

EXPANSION—THE EARLY YEARS

During the first 50 or 100 turns of the game, it's likely your civilization will be on its own. The only other presence is that of the barbarians, but they don't appear very often unless you chose the 'Raging Hordes' setting.

If, as I recommend, you're playing at one of the higher difficulty levels, your first concern is not only city defense, but also the happiness of its citizens. Fortunately, under Despotism (the system you start with), the two birds here can be killed with one stone: Military units keep peace as well as protect your incipient settlement from external threats.

Start by building at least two military units. It's preferable that you build phalanxes, and you may want to consider setting your first city's production to settlers right away. If you've taken care to maximize trade in your city (both squares that are worked produce at least trade each), your wise men

CIVILIZATION II

will discover Bronze Working before the first settler is ready. You can then switch production to a phalanx at no penalty (penalties apply only when you switch production between these categories—Wonders, improvements, and units).

Keep one unit inside the city while you explore the surroundings with the other. Your city should be building its first settler unit (it may be building a third military unit if you've started the game with two settlers). Your wandering soldier should locate a good site for a second city before the settlers are ready. At the Deity level, use the waiting time well, and instruct your second settler to build roads wherever they make sense, while other units explore the land.

Keep early expansion flowing smoothly and quickly. Every city should be supporting a settler at all times. Start production of new settlers the moment the former ones found a new city. Every other unit should be military. It's better to be safe than sorry, and it's easy to be sorry at the higher difficulty levels. Remember that under Despotism, all the military units are upkeep-free (unless the number of units supported by a city exceeds its population points), and that you have an allowance of three maintenance-free units per city under Monarchy and Communism.

SCIENCE AND WONDERS

Almost as soon as you start your first city, you'll meet your Science Advisor, who will humbly ask which civilization advance you want to research next. *Civ II* features very many advances—many more than the original *Civilization*—and the most effective research path is radically different.

In the original *Civilization,* the emphasis was on acquiring Advances that resulted in immediate benefits—new units, city improvements, Wonders, and so on. Most of the "soft" Advances such as Philosophy, Medicine, etc. could wait until the middle stage of the game, when it was often possible to acquire them through an exchange with another civilization, through war, or by stealing Advances with the help of diplomats. Not so in *Civilization II;* the emphasis now is mostly on developing better political systems and schools of thought. This somewhat nebulous term can be stretched to cover political systems, Philosophy, Monotheism, and the like.

First Advances

Your first priority upon beginning the game is to provide some sort of defense for your cities. I found that researching Bronze Working and the Warrior Code are enough to keep my cities relatively safe throughout the opening hundred turns or so. Later on, things change, depending on whether you have made contact with another civilization and the state of the resulting foreign relations.

Following these two advances, I concentrate on acquiring Monarchy as soon as possible. In the original *Civ,* it was possible to maintain Despotism until it was time to switch to the Republic. This is no longer the case. Monarchy has been made much more attractive through the elimination of upkeep costs for the first three military units, and by reducing the food requirement of a settlers unit from two food to one. You should convert to Monarchy as soon as you can. If you do it early on, in the BC era, the transition will be quick and painless. If you switch governments before 1500 BC, you may even experience no anarchy—the change of government becomes effective immediately. To acquire Monarchy, you have to research Alphabet, Code of Laws, and Ceremonial Burial. This last discovery will come in particularly useful, since at the higher difficulty levels, unrest is a constant concern. It's good to acquire the capability to build temples early. At Deity, it is practically the first improvement you have to build in a new city.

Setting Your Sights on Wonders

Following Monarchy, you should set your sights on Literacy. This is because you want to build the Great Library Wonder. Not worth much in the old *Civilization* (it expired quickly), the Great Library is now of immense help in winning the game. The new *Civ* features so many advances, most players will find it impossible to research all of them. You'll have to rely on other means to some extent. Those other means consist of exchanges of knowledge with other civilizations, and obtaining new advances through cunning or through war (espionage, capture of cities). However, the Great Library provides you with advances as soon as two other civilizations discover them. If your game involves just one or three opponents, the Great Library does not have such value; but it is indispensable in any game involving a number of civilizations, especially when playing at the higher difficulty levels.

CIVILIZATION II

On the way to Literacy, you should consider acquiring Currency and Trade. Although building marketplaces is a waste of time early on, when tax income is minimal, you'll find caravans most useful in completing Wonders quickly. If you know that another civilization is building a Wonder you are interested in, you should consider building caravans instead of the Wonder, and completing the Wonder in a single turn. You'll be warned by the game when the other civilization is a turn away from completing the construction; and at the very worst, you'll still have a bunch of very useful units which you can immediately use to initiate new trade routes. Since it is rarely possible to pick the advance you want most every time research comes up for review, you may be able to acquire Currency and Trade by default on your way to Literacy.

Having acquired Literacy, set your sights on Philosophy. This important Advance opens the gates to a host of others. What's more, you'll be given a free Advance if yours is the first civilization to discover Philosophy. You should apply it towards your next goal—Monotheism. Monotheism allows you to build Michelangelo's Chapel, which is also one of the best Wonders in the game (in the original *Civ,* it's next to worthless). Michelangelo's Chapel saves you a lot of time and shields that you'd otherwise spend building cathedrals or coliseums to contain unrest. As mentioned, unrest is always a serious, pressing problem at the higher game difficulty levels.

The road to Monotheism is studded with Advances that have excellent practical applications. Mysticism doubles the effectiveness of your temples. Polytheism provides you with war elephants, a good mounted offensive unit. Upon discovering Monotheism, you'll not only be rewarded with the possibility of building Michelangelo's Chapel, you'll also get the ability to build crusaders—the strongest offensive unit for quite a time, although not as useful as knights because of poor defense.

At this point, I recommend you go one step further and acquire Theology. Feudalism is a prerequisite, but again, it provides you with a very useful unit—pikemen, which replace the phalanx. Pikemen enjoy doubled defense against mounted troops, thus rendering them largely null and void if not backed by heavy medieval artillery in the form of catapults, or legions. Theology, on the other hand, immediately increases the contentedness of your people by one per city, at least until you discover Communism. It also gives you the opportunity to build Michaelangelo's Chapel, but consider the geography of your empire before building it. Bach's Cathedral turns two unhappy citizens per city into content ones—as long as the city is on the same continent or land mass as the Wonder. If your empire consists of several separate land masses, this isn't a high-priority Wonder.

Having acquired Theology, it's time to put your scientists' minds to practical pursuits. The Great Library will have provided you with a wealth of knowledge. You'll get messages about the acquisition of a new Advance almost every other turn, particularly when playing a seven-civilization game at a high difficulty level. Your goal now is to acquire nautical knowledge (unless your world consists of just one huge continent, which is highly unlikely). Get to Navigation as fast as you can. If your empire spans two or more land masses, build the Magellan's Expedition if possible. Naval combat plays a very important role in the game, and Magellan's Expedition provides you with an unbeatable edge in the shape of two extra moves per ship, per turn. Basically, this means you'll be able to run away from the enemy most of the time, and sink troop-laden enemy transports much more effectively. Submarines benefit most—the Expedition almost doubles their movement speed. In addition to military considerations, building this Wonder also lets you establish trade routes with distant civilizations with relative ease, and these are the trade routes that pay (more on this later).

Setting a New Course

Once you've acquired Navigation, consider adding Physics and Magnetism. Magnetism provides you with your first "real" fighting ships—the frigate is a tough and fast unit, especially given Magellan's Expedition. Your next step should be to acquire Invention, Gunpowder, Steam Engine, and Railroad. These Advances mark the transformation of your civilization into a relatively modern one. They may also force you to do a lot of back-tracking in your research if you haven't got the Great Library (there's a long line of Advances needed for Invention, so really do try hard to build this great Wonder!).

The switch to Gunpowder marks a dramatic increase in expenditures. The new barracks cost twice as much in maintenance; therefore, I would recommend you set your sights on Economics and Adam Smith's Trading Company

CIVILIZATION II

next. On the way, you'll need such useful Advances as the Republic (you'll probably have gotten it from the Great Library) and Banking.

At this point, it's time to turn your mind to war. You have to start fighting at some point in the game. Otherwise, you have little chance of winning, unless you're playing at a very easy level. This does not necessarily mean you are committing yourself to victory through world conquest. If you do not start a rumble with the other major players in time, they'll get to the Space Age before you, and then you'll have to start a war to prevent them from winning by colonizing Alpha Centauri. The computer opponents react to war by increasing their tax rates (the harder you hit them, the more money they try to raise), and thus slow research down. If you're playing at Emperor or Deity, it's more than likely you'll be somewhat behind in research in the final stages of the game (after the Great Library expires), and thus, you'll be in worse shape for a war than earlier on.

Note that I don't recommend building Leonardo's Workshop. Leonardo is a favorite with many players because it replaces old units with new ones the moment you gain the appropriate Advance. However, you have to gain that Advance first, and even then, the new unit is a rookie, while your old unit may well have been a veteran. This sometimes can paradoxically result in getting weaker units! A veteran knight, for instance, has six attack and three defense, but the rookie dragoon that replaces it has five attack and two defense, thanks to Leonardo.

Because of the warlike turn in my policy at this stage of the game, I recommend researching Advances with military applications. Your goal should be to acquire Conscription, Tactics, and Metallurgy as quickly as possible (usually the Great Library supplies you with Metallurgy well before then). You already have improved naval technology in the shape of the Steam Engine and the ironclad; now, boost your naval power by adding Electricity (destroyers) and Steel (cruisers). Then acquire Tactics for a radical update of your whole military; you get alpine troops, which are the best choice as a defensive unit, and cavalry. My veteran cavalry easily squashes tanks and marines, particularly when it catches them on open ground, which is not so difficult to arrange.

The above Advances will have permitted you to acquire Machine Tools and thus, artillery units. I make Flight my next priority. Veteran fighters are great against defenders protected by city walls. You may lose a few, but with the support of ground troops, fighters can make capturing walled-in cities rather easy.

In Search of *Wunderwaffe*

After that, it's usually Advanced Flight for me, and Amphibious Warfare. This last choice should be considered earlier if your game world consists of many land masses. Marines are great at assaulting cities directly from the transport they're on. Usually, a couple of salvos from your escorting warships can make the marines' job even easier.

Acquisition of subsequent Advances varies game to game. Basically, a lot rides on which political system you want to adopt at this stage. If you're inclined peacefully and want to slide into Republic or Democracy, you should make Space Flight and SDI defense two concurrent priorities. The computer players will go after you with a vengeance once you get going on your rocket, and the SDI will come in very handy, believe me.

The final advances that really matter to me in my chosen strategy are almost all geared towards waging war with maximum effectiveness. I try to obtain Robotics for the howitzers. (Finally, there's a unit that can move forward and attack while ignoring the protective effect of the city walls!) Rocketry is extremely important. It yields both the cruise missile and the nuclear missile. The former is great for destroying defenses behind city walls, the latter is great for destroying everything within a radius. All that remains is to move in with the paratroopers (Combined Arms is another important advance in the endgame).

Personally, I prefer to pursue the wars I started to their bloody conclusion, and only build a space ship as a last-resort sort of choice. This is because the score you can get upon conquering the world is better than anything you can hope to achieve with space travel. In addition to the victory bonus, you get loads of points for all the conquered cities and captured Wonders.

MOVING AWAY FROM MONARCHY

To this end, I make Communism a high priority. In addition to providing an excellent political platform for waging war (every military unit in a city keeps *two* citizens content), Communism (paradoxically) increases the productivity of your civilization by eliminating a lot of corruption. At this stage of the game, your big monarchy is probably experiencing severe corruption in its far-flung cities that even courthouses cannot resolve. You'll see a sharp change in your finances—often, a slight deficit is replaced by a healthy surplus—and sometimes also in your discoveries rate, which may improve by a turn.

If things look difficult, I also get Fundamentalism—the perfect political system for waging an all-out, desperate war. I haven't had to change to it often. Usually, my Communist regime runs things with very uncommunist-like efficiency. Retaining Communism also allows my scientists to continue research work unhindered (Fundamentalism carries terrible research penalties).

Once you've got everything researched, however, Fundamentalism becomes a terrible weapon. You suddenly have stacks of money. All the happiness-affecting improvements and Wonders produce cash, one coin per former content face. Setting high luxury rates may cause your Fundamentalist cities to celebrate the "We Love the High Priest" Day, which makes them operate as under a Democracy—no corruption and an extra trade arrow. You can buy half a dozen units every turn and still have cash to spend! Cheap fanatics and no unit maintenance costs for the first ten units mean that Fundamentalism can be exactly what you need to achieve world domination, especially since your diplomatic penalties for treacherous acts are reduced.

Getting James Bond on Your Side

The greatest advance for waging war well is somewhat unmilitary in character. This is Espionage—a particularly effective weapon in Communist hands, as all spies produced under Communism are automatically veterans. Veteran spies are absolutely great in every respect. They can repeatedly infiltrate cities to investigate them, conduct sabotage, and commit other nefarious deeds (I confess my morality has so far stopped me from using a spy to plant a nuclear device). Spies can even sabotage enemy units in the field. They destroy 50 percent of a unit's hit points, turning the health bar yellow. Veteran spies can accomplish all these tasks and return to the nearest friendly city unharmed time and again. Secret warfare—I suppose that's my secret reason for going Communist instead of Fundamentalist.

OPTING FOR PEACEFUL COEXISTENCE

If you decide to go the peaceful route despite my fork-tailed entreaties (it's all in the interests of bettering your score through glorious VICTORY), then there isn't any doubt you should acquire Democracy as quickly as possible. Build the United Nations (Communism) before the others do (it's a favorite with the computer players). At the same time, make sure you maintain a strong army.

Democracy, or Fortified Peace

In Democracy, fortresses built by your settlers become very important. A unit in a fortress three squares or less from a friendly city does not cause any unhappiness by being away from the home city. Use this feature to erect strongly-defended borders. You may want peace, but if your Democracy is successful and powers your civilization to the lead, the computer players will set about you in earnest. They like to capture a town and immediately sue for peace, which your Democratic senate is eager to accept. Erecting fortresses, and the whole business of making and placing units inside them, is troublesome but effective. It creates a closely guarded boundary. Space fortresses two squares apart so that their zones of control (this notion is explained in the manual) prevent enemy units from breaching your borders.

It's possible to wage war while a Democracy (in old *Civ*, it was quite easy—you could always refuse to talk to enemy envoys). However, this involves going to a great deal of trouble. In addition to the United Nations, you'll need Wonders such as Women's Suffrage and Cure for Cancer. Also, you may have to build expensive police stations in particularly powerful troop-producing cities. You can re-assign them to another, small city that does not produce any units, but small cities don't tolerate absent units well. There are only so many population points, or citizens on the city display, that you can manipulate.

Opportunity Knocks, or Republican Rule

The Republican government allows you to pursue a somewhat opportunistic course, alternating between peace and war. You'll have to be quite the provocateur, but on the whole, getting your way while ruling a Republic isn't impossible.

CIVILIZATION II

A Republic allows an experienced player to wage war with almost the same abandon as Monarchy. Early discovery of Industrialization and the granting of Women's Suffrage lets you move military units as you please. The only drawback is that as soon as you start winning, there may be a period of brief, enforced peace.

The Republic makes you independent in another way, too. Because of the trade bonus, domestic trade routes are quite attractive. You don't have to placate a rich neighbor so that your caravans and freights can forge trade routes unhindered.

MANIPULATING FOREIGN POLICY

One of the greatest challenges of *Civ II* lies in the need to maintain a Respectable Reputation while basically trying to knock your opponents into dust. Also, going the Republican or Democratic way means there's a Senate constantly blowing raspberries at your ambitious plans, and scuttling them brutally.

The best way to maintain a Spotless Reputation while having your own way is, of course, through political manipulation. Be very nice to everyone to start with, and never break your word. When you feel it's time for war, two tactics can help:

- Constant provocation. Blockading ports with naval units, continuously encroaching on your victim's territory with your troops (even though you are forced to withdraw each time), sending over swarms of spies and diplomats that make unit movement (and life in general) difficult for the computer player. All these moves may arouse ire sufficiently for your victim to start a war with a sneak attack. If you help things along by simultaneously becoming a pain to deal with (making repeated requests for tribute, etc.), you are almost guaranteed a hostile reaction, as long as the other party isn't in absolute awe of your power (unlikely at the higher difficulty levels).

- Sometimes, all the provocations in the world won't work. Go the diplomatic route. Since you're very friendly with everyone, you should have no trouble in talking another civilization into declaring war on your victim. Send emissaries repeatedly to the guys that declared the war for you, or even ally with them right away, and they'll ask you to join the party on their side. Being seemingly talked into a war by someone still brings penalties, but they're much smaller.

The question of Reputation is a strong reason in favor of playing *Civilization II* at one of the higher difficulty levels. At the easier levels, the other guys tend to be nauseatingly friendly, and no amount of boorishness can provoke them into war. Note, however, that provoking someone into war through hostile diplomatic dialogue, not unit movements, may cause your government to collapse.

If you've committed many international *faux pas* in the early and middle game, you should try very hard to build the Eiffel Tower. However, don't even think about it if you've grown really strong. Nobody's going to like you anyway, so who cares what your Reputation is?

THE *CIV* GENERAL

A large part of your success in *Civilization II* depends on your prowess as the leader of your armed forces. You can be great at developing great cities, but they won't stay yours for long if you also aren't a good general and admiral (later, also air marshal).

Defending What's Yours

Your first duty is to ensure the security of your cities. This is fairly easy to achieve. Since soldiers keep unhappy citizens content, you kill two birds with one stone.

Out of all the military units in a city, only the first three have an effect on the mood of the populace, and only the first three units supported by a city are maintenance-free. It's no surprise that the optimal city garrison consists of three units. My favorite combination consists of two defensive units and one offensive. This allows me to kick barbarian and other posteriors before they even get to attack. If your young city can afford only two units, I strongly suggest you build one defensive, one offensive—at least until you discover Gunpowder, or better yet, Conscription.

To make things clearer, here's a brief rundown on how my city garrisons change with time. The first unit is invariably a phalanx, and the second, an archer. Archers are good both on the defense and offense, but they are a little expensive in the very early stages of a civilization. So, while the bigger of my cities might have a phalanx and two archers, others may have one archer and two phalanxes.

I replace phalanxes with pikemen as soon as they become available, and archers with knights or catapults. A particularly precious city usually has a garrison of three knights, or two knights and a catapult. It bears remembering that knights perform well both on the offense and defense. Their movement of two also allows them to be transferred rapidly to reinforce other garrisons should the need arise.

However, if a city is under strong threat, or if its surrounded by terrain that offers a defensive bonus, I make a point of including a veteran catapult among the defenders. A veteran catapult can successfully deal with musketeers, and even riflemen on occasion, so it's a good investment that performs reasonably well long after the first cannon appears. The same goes for knights, which gradually take the role of a strong reconnaissance unit.

Getting back to the city and its garrison, as soon as I've got Gunpowder, I replace pikemen with musketeers. Military units tend to get expensive with Gunpowder, so my replacement of knights with dragoons often isn't complete for a long time. From Gunpowder onwards, I tend to replace troops in city garrisons as the situation dictates—according to threat, value of the city, and affordability.

City defenses now consist of other improvements in addition to the venerable city walls. City walls double (not triple, as in the old *Civ*) the defense of garrison units against land attacks, coastal fortresses double it against naval attacks; and SAM batteries double it against air attacks. SDI, of course, protects from nuclear strikes (although your city may still be nuked with a device brought in by a spy).

The Internal Interventionary Force

In addition to the city garrisons, I keep a small, highly mobile army on hand for dealing with emergencies. This usually takes the form of several mounted units, as they can get quickly anywhere. Of course, all of my cities are connected by a road network that not only links cities, but also provides additional connections in potential trouble spots. There's nothing worse than having your relief force stymied by an enemy perched on a hill or a mountain while your city is being pummeled to bits!

My interventionary force usually consists of knights—at least three units, but not more than five, with the other two units often being of a different kind. I may include antiquated horsemen or a chariot. I dissolve this army the moment I have developed railroads to the extent where I can quickly reinforce any city, anywhere, from any other city's garrison.

Do not ever treat roads and railroads as a purely economic measure! They perform an extremely important strategic function, as well. You should make a point of building an inter-city rail network in the later stages of the game. It allows you to transfer any unit anywhere within a land mass, any time.

In the final stages of the game, I garrison cities with riflemen (when relatively safe) or alpine troops (when under threat)—of course, I often mix the two. I still prefer to add pure-bred offensive units to garrisons of more important cities; other cities often simply have three riflemen.

In the final stages of the game, I build SDI defenses in every city over the size of 8, and SAM batteries as needed. I update some garrisons with mechanized infantry and tanks. Usually the two or three most important cities I have contain an armored fist of several mechanized infantry and tank units. I also place cannon, and later, artillery, in cities that are under a potential or actual threat.

The Navy

Naval units also play an extremely important role in the game. Many of the game worlds feature a multitude of islands and continents, and until you start building airports, the only transport available is by ship.

You should start building triremes very early on, and send them on exploratory journeys—first along the coast of your land, then outwards. I risk losing the occasional trireme to find out what lies further on, because I found it pays dividends in the end (and the SFX are rather cool, too, when the trireme sinks). At the trireme stage, however, there are too many other priorities to build a navy composed of very weak ships. My coastal defense, therefore, consists of a couple of triremes that have nothing else to do, and which double as transports as the need arises.

Things don't change with the arrival of the caravel. Naval units are still relatively poor value for the money, and I do not actively maintain a coastal defense per se. However, I usually do form a task group of two or three caravels that explore the perimeters of my empire in times of peace, and lay in wait for enemy ships in times of war. If you attack another caravel with two caravels in a row, you're guaranteed success, and it makes sense to lose a ship in exchange for at least a ship and another unit (the caravel can carry three).

The frigate is the first worthwhile fighting ship. A veteran frigate can successfully take on a transport, and two can sink an ironclad almost any time. I usually discover the Steam Engine very soon after Magnetism, though, and so never have more than a handful of frigates. However, the ones I do have perform very well as extended reconnaissance units, fast troop and settler transports, and corsairs on enemy sea routes. Here's a good tip: When starting a new city on a new continent or island, you can use the frigate to augment the city's garrison in its weak, uncertain beginnings. A frigate packs quite a punch!

In the old *Civ,* ironclads used to mark a radical transformation of the war at sea. In *Civ II,* they still do, but the change isn't as great because *Civ II* frigates are much more powerful than in the original game. Moreover, the introduction of destroyers with Electricity means the ironclads rule the seas for a relatively short time. Destroyers have the same combat values as ironclads, but much better movement, so they usually get to pick when to fight. Their movement also makes them the best troop transport interceptors, and corsairs for prowling enemy transport routes.

Steel comes right after Electricity, and gives you cruisers. The cruiser is the first naval unit capable of bombarding strong city defenders into submission, although I still would not recommend going against a city with a coastal fortress. You should build at least one cruiser the moment you can, and give it an escort of destroyers. When you see how your flotilla can perform in action, you'll doubtless build more.

The final naval units you get to build are the battleship, the AEGIS cruiser (which *replaces* the old, Steel-borne cruiser in newer versions of *Civ II*), the submarine, and the carrier.

Important Note: Use ships, and indeed all military units, in groups. Even the most powerful unit cannot achieve much on its own.

The battleship is predictably good at both naval battles and shore bombardments. You'll want to use your battleships carefully—they're very expensive! Treat them the way the real-life Navy treats them—as the commanding ship of a flotilla, the linchpin of a task force. They're far too valuable and a little slow to be used as corsairs. If you want to create a serious naval diversion that includes bombarding some of the enemy's port, give your battleship a full escort.

The AEGIS cruiser is a newer, better cruiser that boasts doubled anti-aircraft defenses. As time goes on, air power becomes very important, and the AEGIS cruiser provides better defense to all the ships stacked with it (in the very first versions of *Civ II,* the AI often fails to select it as the defender against air attack, making its worth questionable).

The submarine is pretty much useless unless: a) you have discovered Rocketry, because a sub can carry Cruise missiles, or b) you have Magellan's Expedition. Its three-square movement rate simply isn't enough to attack and escape far enough to avoid detection during the enemy's turn. The only possible application for a sub that's Cruise-less and Magellan-less is to let it lurk near an enemy port or favorite enemy landing spot (the computer has these).

The carrier is very useful at assaulting islands/continents too far away for your land-bound air force. You may try smuggling a settler in to build an airfield, but that can be dicey. Better include a carrier in every invasion fleet, and don't forget to include fighters as well as bombers in its complement of aircraft. Carriers can also carry nuclear missiles. If you have to capture an enemy capital halfway across the world to prevent their space ship from ending the game, make sure you have a carrier with nukes along (and a transport loaded with settlers for cleaning up the resulting pollution). It's possible to capture a whole string of enemy cities in one turn by nuking them, sailing a transport right into port, and activating the units on it from the city display. Tanks and mechanized infantry have three moves per turn, and given the extensive road and rail network of most civilizations, it's always possible to conduct an impressive blitzkrieg.

Air Power

Air power changes the character of every war you fight. The moment you discover Flight, you should make plenty of fighters (unless you're a Republic or Democracy). Let them gain veteran status while fighting easy targets (non-military units or weaker military units on terrain with no defensive bonus). Then unleash them in numbers, say six at a time, against a city wprotected by city walls. with support from your ground forces. You'll quickly capture your target.

Advanced flight brings bombers, which are predictably devastating against any unit, but are best employed bombing defenders inside city walls or power-ful naval units. At the very end of the research tree lies Stealth Technology, which lets you build a new generation of fighters and bombers. They are much more effective, but usually arrive too late to be of decisive consequence.

In the meantime, well before Stealth, comes Rocketry. This allows you to make cruise missiles, which are excellent at reducing a city's defenses to rub-ble (figuratively speaking) with minimal risk and without the pollution penal-ties of a nuke attack. A series of cruise missiles fired into a city is all the preparation you need for your troops to march right in. You lose a missile in every attack, true, but it still costs less than all those lost bombers and battle-ships. If you're playing at the Deity level, take note, and build SAM batteries if you can't guarantee the safety of your cities.

The Deity Memorandum

When playing at Deity, you'll see the computer players behave in ways they don't at lower difficulty levels.

A favorite tactic is to bribe your cities (all it takes is one diplomat, remem-ber?)—computer players pretty nearly always have a lot of money. This is where a Democracy can come in pretty handy; Democratic cities and units are immune to bribery.

Another tactic is to nuke you without any warning, and if the nuked city is within range, follow that strike with paratroopers. These are lethal tactics, and it's best to do what's only possible to prevent from ever taking place.

The best way to do so is by keeping the computer players on the run. Do not be afraid to fight many wars at once, although, of course, it's best to fight just one at a time. Powerful computer players are fairly easy to provoke into a sneak attack. Once you've got your war without putting a stain on your Reputation, all you have to do is keep your enemies busy on their grounds (that's the best way to prevent them from attacking you on your ground). Capture a city or two, hold onto them, and advance as much as possible, but with an emphasis on defense. The computer player goes into a paroxysm of fury and dispatches a stream of troops at the city it lost, and with skillful generalship, city walls, and barracks, you can achieve a ten-to-one kill ratio. If you can't hold onto your conquest, remember to gut the city you're about to give up. Sell off all its improvements, leaving the city walls for the very last.

Never concentrate on just one aspect of an ongoing war. Don't get hypnotized by the waves of enemy troops smashing against the walls of your bridgehead. Look elsewhere. Build partisans, and embark on a massive campaign of economic warfare, pillaging mines as a first priority. It slows down military production, and a veteran partisan on a hill isn't that easy to kill. Use spies in numbers—veteran spies can sabotage a city's production time after time and return unharmed. Conduct diversionary attacks. A brisk naval bombardment of a city on the other shore, followed by a landing of a bunch of pillaging partisans, distracts the computer player quite well. Capturing a city at the other end of its empire works even better, but involves having considerable military muscle.

Do not forget diplomatic war. Provided you've kept your Reputation clean, you can almost always talk someone into declaring war on your enemy, although it may cost you a little. Although your new ally is likely to make peace promptly, it's an excellent distraction for the AI.

When you get really strong, no one's going to like you. The computer players form pacts against you, but they often don't go beyond exchange of knowledge. I've found some pact signatories to be very eager to make

CIVILIZATION II

peace with me once we've actually met, but then I usually enjoy a Spotless Reputation.

Remember to be cunning. Don't advertise your moves. Don't launch an offensive with two or three units at a time. Get a proper army in position, and support it with the air force and the navy. When you try to capture cities by sending in a stream of ground units alone, it will frequently take you a very long time and heavy losses to achieve anything. With proper air and naval support, and later a preliminary cruise missile bombardment, the whole business of capturing cities is laughably easy. It's actually more difficult to hold them against the invariably furious counter-attack.

FINAL NOTES

Expansion is the name of the game. Don't get caught up in forever improving your existing cities. Go and build new ones, or capture them from somebody else.

Money is a means to an end, not the end in itself. While you should keep a reserve big enough to build an expensive improvement or a couple of units at a moment's notice, don't hoard your money. Use it to speed up construction of improvements—income-boosting improvements are the first candidates. Later on in the game, it's useful to finance quick construction of mass transit systems and recycling plants. Things tend to get pretty sticky with many factories!

Be bold. The AI may have this and that, but it doesn't have one thing you do: your imagination!

CHAPTER

4

COMMAND & CONQUER

Publisher:	Westwood Studios
Platform:	PC MS-DOS
Release Date:	Summer, 1995
Multiplayer:	Yes
Rating:	

General Overview

Commanding an increasingly sophisticated army, you fight your way through a series of progressively tough missions. You can choose to lead the forces of the good Global Defense Initiative (GDI) or those of the bad Brotherhood of Nod. Each side features units with distinctly different capabilities, and the missions are arranged in a learning curve—a structure common to many games, notably *Warcraft.*

Although *Command & Conquer* is far from an original concept (even the game engine was borrowed from Westwoods earlier hit, *Dune II*), the game is extremely well put together. *C&Cs* hit status was confirmed by the Spring, 1996 release of *The Covert Operations*—an add-on CD containing fifteen new stand-alone *C&C* missions, and many new mutliplayer battlefields.

C&C is not for the faint of heart. The games slick graphics and sharp sound effects include people being burned alive. If you want to beat this game, you better be a killer at heart—and no, you don't have to tell anyone.

Golden Rules

Build your base in a location that is hard to find, easy to defend, and close to tiberium fields. (Usually, the corner of the battlefield is a good location.)

Build all important structures away from likely points of entry. In the absence of natural barriers, build your own. Guard base entrances with defensive structures (such as turrets or guard towers), and make sure the base is laid out so as to minimize traffic problems. Ease of movement is important for troops defending your base from a raid or assault.

Build your structures at the right time. You should be able to produce both infantry units and vehicles as quickly as possible, especially in multiplayer games. In general, put your highest priorities on building a communication center. In multiplayer games, you should also focus on building an airstrip/weapons factory and base defenses.

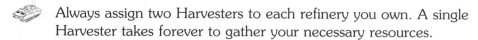

Always assign two Harvesters to each refinery you own. A single Harvester takes forever to gather your necessary resources.

Spend your credits well. Begin by building a base defense force and a recon force. Then, depending on the situation, produce only the units you need.

Don't venture out too far before you are strong enough to repel a minor base assault. In multiplayer games, start exploring right away. The sooner you locate your opponents base, the better the chance of victory.

Play it smart. Some missions can only be won through attrition, but the majority of your victories come through striking at the enemy's weakest point. Choose force over finesse only if there's no way of winning through an engineer raid. Even then, it is advisable to support the base assault with a diversionary attack or unexpected raid taking place in another spot, especially in multiplayer games.

Don't be afraid to retreat when faced by overwhelming opposition—he who fights and runs away lives to fight another day. Set up ambushes, and draw pursuing enemy forces into them. Although this is much more difficult in *The Covert Operations,* in *C&C* the computer player gets taken in every time.

When planning the base assault, try to knock out enemy power plants/construction yards before you mount the main attack. If you cant, try an engineer raid that detaches from the main assault force.

Avoid friendly fire casualties—self-inflicted casualties can easily constitute a quarter of your losses, especially if you're leading the Nods with their flamethrowers.

Always fight with your units in formation. Every unit should always be placed exactly where you want it, or in the process of moving to that spot.

Keep the pressure up throughout the mission. Relentless pressure exhausts both computer and human opponents.

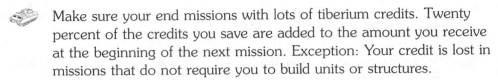

Make sure your end missions with lots of tiberium credits. Twenty percent of the credits you save are added to the amount you receive at the beginning of the next mission. Exception: Your credit is lost in missions that do not require you to build units or structures.

Build sandbags or place units on the sites of destroyed enemy buildings in single-player mode. The computer can't rebuild destroyed structures if something is already there.

Winning Strategies

To execute a winning strategy (let alone to plan one), you must always remember that a handful of well-led infantry units can easily destroy a much larger, but poorly commanded force. This is true regardless of the opponents armor and vehicles. Understanding each units unique features and advantages is crucial to victory over the computer AI as well as human opponents.

Traditionally, strategy games place a lot of emphasis on resource management and planning. In *C&C*, resource management is limited to gathering and utilizing tiberium. The cost for each unit/structure is listed in the game manual. While the games economic structure is unlikely to give you any difficulties, deciding where to spend the credits will. Its very easy to squander your tiberium wealth foolishly.

C&C is a real-time strategy game. This means that your unit management has to be both good and timely. Beyond a certain level, you'll frequently notice everything seems to be happening simultaneously—you're being attacked in two different spots, your Harvesters gone crazy, and there's no way you can gimmick your way out of this situation. You have to do everything personally.

GDI UNITS

With the exception of the self-repairing Mammoth tank, GDI units are more traditional than Nod units.

Infantry

GDI infantry consists of grenadiers, bazookamen, and minigunners. Grenadiers are the toughest and fastest; bazookamen are both slow and vulnerable, and minigunners fall somewhere in between (closer to grenadiers than bazookamen).

In my opinion, GDI grenadiers are the best infantry in the game. They are very good at fighting all Nod infantry, including the dreaded flamethrowers. They also do well against vehicles and structures. Bazookamen, on the other hand, work well against structures and vehicles, but do very poorly against other infantry. Note that bazookamen, being slow and vulnerable, always need to be protected by other units.

Minigunners constitute your basic cannon fodder—they're cheap and efficient at fighting Nod minigunners and bazookamen, as well as light vehicles. A strong squad of minigunners can also destroy a power plant or a Hand of Nod quite quickly, but won't perform as well against larger structures (such as airstrips, construction yards, and so on).

Multiplayer games and some missions feature commando infantry also. The commando is an awesome, incredibly fast unit. His sniper rifle outranges all other infantry weapons and never misses—and he can fire at pursuing enemy troops, move away while reloading, then fire again; and he can blow up enemy buildings. But be warned: there often are minigunners emerging from the rubble. To avoid damage to your unit, place the cursor over the explosion and click as soon as it changes into a gunsight (meaning there's an enemy soldier hiding in the smoke).

Engineers

The engineer is, arguably, the most important single unit in the game. His ability to capture enemy buildings means money and great tactical flexibility. Many missions are won when an engineer captures the enemy construction yard.

The engineer raid, staged with the help of Armored Personnel Carriers or transport choppers, is the single most lethal tactical maneuver in the whole game. However, the engineer is a slow-moving unit, and very vulnerable. Note that in single-player mode, GDI is particularly well-equipped to stage

COMMAND & CONQUER

engineer raids, whereas the Nod vehicle lineup does not feature the APC. (It *does* in multiplayer games, though, so be warned!)

Light Vehicles

GDI vehicles start with the hummer, your reconnaissance vehicle of choice. Its cheap and fast. In addition to recon tasks, hummers perform very well when grouped in anti-infantry squads of two or three—three hummers working together can defeat an equivalent number of bazookamen. However, the hummer is pretty vulnerable, so make sure you use its speed to its best advantage.

The APC is probably the single most precious vehicle in the GDI lineup. Better armed and armored than the hummer, it can also carry five infantrymen and/or engineers. Its superior sighting range makes the APC a great recon vehicle. Both the hummer and the APC are armed with machine guns that can destroy a Nod light tank, but make sure you have several light vehicles fighting a single tank.

Armor

The Abrams tank constitutes the backbone of any GDI mobile force. It is well armored and has a powerful cannon that outranges the one mounted on Nod tanks. The Mammoth—the second tank in the GDI lineup—is tremendously expensive, and you need to have a repair bay before you can build it. Its double cannon and double missile launcher make it the most heavily armed vehicle in the game, and it has armor to match. It also has the ability to self-heal up to fifty percent; however, it is agonizingly slow. This makes its usefulness debatable in situations where you need to move fast. In general, Mammoths are much more useful in single-player games.

Both the Abrams and the Mammoth require some sort of protection from infantry; a squad of hummers works well, and so do rocket launchers.

Rocket Launchers and Orcas

The rocket launcher becomes available after you build the advanced communications center. It is one of GDIs most effective weapons. It fries Nod infantry units and excels at demolishing enemy structures. It is also the only effective mobile defense against the lethal Nod attack choppers. The rocket launcher isn't too good against armor, and its easily damaged; make sure you protect it with tanks.

Judging by what I've heard, the Orca helicopter is GDIs most-loved vehicle. It is very good against Nod buildings and vehicles, but rotten against infantry. However, the Orcas ability to help on a distant battlefield at a moments notice makes it important in single-player games, and absolutely essential in multiplayer games. Remember to use Orcas in groups, particularly when attacking anti-aircraft fire.

Harvesters

Harvesters are essential to your war effort. Without them, you won't have any guns to carry out your plans. It's good practice to have two Harvesters servicing each tiberium refinery. In addition to more credits, you'll enjoy more security— Harvesters often fall prey to the enemy, especially in multiplayer games. Its not really worth getting a Harvester by building and selling a refinery. The AI that guides the Harvester between the refinery and the tiberium fields can get very confused when the original refinery is missing. This may cause a lot of problems on a busy battlefield, and I strongly suggest taking the time and trouble to order a Harvester from your friendly airstrip/weapons factory.

Note that in *The Covert Operations,* Harvesters demonstrate superior intelligence. They find their way around much better, and will crush Nod motorbikes along with infantry.

Warthogs, Gunboats, and Technicians

Warthogs are aircraft that carry out GDIs air strikes. They drop napalm with predictably horrifying results on infantry, soft-skinned vehicles, and buildings; they don't do much harm to armor.

Computer-controlled Warthogs can be easily fooled. Since they always target your northernmost unit/structure, you can avoid damage by posting a single decoy minigunner well north of all your other units/structures. If you have the patience and skill with the mouse, you can also make Warthogs drop napalm on their own side. This requires that you dash your northernmost unit into the midst of your enemies when the air strike comes. The results are very gratifying.

COMMAND & CONQUER

Gunboats are somewhat beyond your control because they sail a pre-determined course. However, you can instruct them to fire at specific targets if those targets are within range. Simply click on the gunboat, then place the cursor over the target. If it changes into a gunsight, its a go.

Civilians fall into three categories: the technicians you get when selling a building, friendly inhabitants of settlements that dot numerous game battle-fields, and *unfriendly* inhabitants. In spite of a propensity to run around with their hands up, all civilian types pack a ten-shot pistol, and occasionally even manage to destroy a badly mauled unit.

Note that although your technicians are just as fast as the commandos, they are useless for reconnaissance purposes, because they don't have a sighting range.

NOD UNITS

Generally speaking, Nod units have less firepower than their GDI counter-parts, but there is a much wider variety of units available. If you know how to choose and use them, Nod forces emerge as much better-equipped than their opponents.

Infantry

The Nod infantry lineup is similar to GDIs—it features three infantry types, engineers, and commandos. Multiplayer games and one or two of *The Covert Operations* also feature Nod chemical troopers.

Minigunners are more important to the Nod forces than to the GDI forces. They are the easiest to use of all Nod infantry types (the bazookamen are slow and vulnerable, while Nod flamethrowers have a disconcerting knack for frying their comrades-in-arms). Also, in *C&C* (but not in *The Covert Operations*) Nod turrets cost 250 credits to build and yield two minigunners, plus 125 credits when sold. Finally, their low price makes Nod minigunners the decoy of choice for GDI air strikes.

Flamethrowers are the Nod answer to GDI grenadiers. Used expertly, they can be lethal to the enemy; used inexpertly, they are lethal, period. To avoid self-inflicted casualties and to maximize damage to the enemy, place solitary flamers at the head of your troops. Flamethrowers wouldn't be worth all that trouble if it weren't for the fact that they can quickly destroy buildings, soft-skinned vehicles, and entire infantry units.

Nod bazookamen are slightly more important than GDIs. They provide good protection against Orcas at a low cost, and since Nod armor is weak, anti-tank weapons are an important asset.

The Nod commando is identical to the GDIs in all respects, but has an easier job—he does not have to blow up SAM sites bristling with minigunners. Finally, in multiplayer games (and one of *The Covert Operations*) you get to play with chemical troopers. At 300 credits a pop, they are hardly a bargain, and nothing about their battlefield performance justifies that price tag.

Light Vehicles

The Nod army features a couple of vehicles that are the psychopathic beach bums dream: the machine-gun toting dune buggy and a rocket-armed motorbike.

The dune buggy has one enormous advantage: it's cheap. At 300 credits, its exactly the price of a bazookaman. Buggies are very fast and maneuverable, and make good recon vehicles. Used in packs of three or four, they make great infantry hunters.

The Nod motorbike is the fastest ground vehicle in the game, which makes hit-and-run attacks an effective tactic. Since it fires rockets, the Nod bike can be used in groups of two or three to destroy buildings. Because of its speed, it also makes a great anti-aircraft weapon, and is generally well worth the rather stiff price of 500 credits. The only drawback is that its very easily damaged, leading to a corresponding drop in performance.

Armor

The Bradley light tank is the only conventional tank on the Nod side. It has inferior firepower and armor to the GDIs Abrams, and has to be used in squads of at least three to be truly effective. Fortunately, at 600 credits, its relatively cheap.

The Nod flame tank is an excellent anti-infantry weapon, and does respectable damage to GDI tanks when given the chance. However, its twin flamethrowers have a fairly short range, its armor isn't very thick, and when pitted against GDI armor, the flame tank does pretty poorly. Its devastating against soft-skinned vehicles, however.

The third tank in the Nod lineup is the Stealth. As the name indicates, its by far the best recon vehicle in the game. Armed with double rocket launchers, Stealths are good at destroying enemy structures and offer the ultimate form of anti-aircraft defense. You won't even see the tank until its begun firing, and the computer likes to deploy Stealths in defense of its Harvesters. Be careful!

Solitary Stealths are great at running over unsuspecting enemy soldiers in *C&C;* in *The Covert Operations,* the computer-controlled infantry seems more alert.

Artillery and SSM Launcher

Nod artillery and SSM launchers share one characteristic: they are great at hitting enemy infantry/structures at long range, and extremely vulnerable to enemy fire.

The Nod self-propelled artillery unit is very cheap at 450 credits. Extremely slow, fragile, and inaccurate at long range, it nevertheless offers a lot of firepower for the price and is an excellent unit to have along in assaults on enemy bases. However, its dreadful slowness makes any kind of withdrawal impractical.

The SSM launcher is featured in multiplayer games as well as in many of *The Covert Operations.* The awesome range of its twin missiles makes it particularly well-suited to base bombardment. Note that the missiles cannot be used against aircraft, and that the SSM launcher is particularly vulnerable to Orca attacks. The missiles enjoy some success against infantry, but aren't too effective against vehicles—particularly armor.

Attack Chopper and Transport Helicopter

With the exception of multiplayer games, the Nod attack chopper is a rare bird. It appears in just a handful of missions in *C&C* and *The Covert Operations.* You can also acquire the ability to make Nod choppers if the GDI opponent has Orca helicopters *and* you capture the GDI construction yard.

Armed with a chaingun, the Nod chopper is great against infantry, and pretty damaging against vehicles and structures. Also, its presence forces a human opponent to build advanced guard towers, hampering offensive efforts; and until the enemy deploys mobile rocket launchers, your Nod chopper will practically rule the skies above the battlefield. A pack of three Nod choppers can even deal with an Abrams tank.

The transport helicopter appears in select missions in both *C&C* and *The Covert Operations,* as well as in multiplayer games, where it contributes to the vicious character of multiplayer tussles. This is because the availability of a transport chopper immediately enables you to conduct the ultimate *C&C* maneuver: the airborne engineer raid/assault.

STRUCTURES

Basically, *C&Cs* structures serve one of two purposes: they are either used to wage war on the enemy (guard towers, turrets, and so on) or to provide you with the means to do so by producing units. The only structure that cannot be neatly fitted into either category is the communications center, which principally provides you with an overhead map of the battlefield that also shows all visible units.

The buildings and structures in *C&C* are interdependent. First of all, they must all be connected to one *another when they are being built.* This distinction is very important, for it leads to *C&Cs* ultimate, conquer-all tactic—the traveling sandbag (see below).

Secondly, you cannot build certain structures without having built certain others first. You need a construction yard before you can build anything else, a power plant to build barracks and refinery, a refinery to build an airstrip/ weapons factory, and so on. Keeping this in mind is important to good base design. It enables you to visualize the building sequence and its implications.

All the structures you build can be sold. They fetch half their construction price, and yield some personnel in the form of minigunners, technicians, and the occasional engineer (principally during the sale of a construction yard— but I have also received an engineer from the sale of an airstrip/weapons factory). Its important to remember that some structures come with a vehicle, and that their selling price will reflect that. For example, a 2,000-credit refinery holding no tiberium will sell for only 300 credits, because 1,400 credits of its cost remain yours in the shape of the Harvester. Similarly, a 1,500-credit helicopter pad sells for 150 credits—you keep the 1,200-credit helicopter.

Basic Buildings

The construction yard is the most precious building you have. Protect it not only from attacks, but also from prying eyes. This is especially true in multi-player games, which often feature diabolical engineer raids.

The yard is not easy to destroy, and I recommend you use a combination of weapons to get the job done quickly. A good example is a kamikaze tank attack followed by a nuclear/ion cannon strike before the initial damage can be repaired. Since destroying/capturing the enemy's last construction yard means certain victory, make it a priority whenever its feasible at all. Remember to apply the reverse thinking, and protect your yard at all times!

Power plants are your second Achilles heel. A power shortage means no radar map, no advanced base defense, and reduced effectiveness of all your producing structures such as barracks or Hand of Nod.

Power plants come in two varieties: advanced and simple. The advanced ones are more costly because they supply twice the power of simple plants. Since all power plants can be easily destroyed, it is advisable to build several simple plants instead of the advanced version—you will suffer less severe power shortage and smaller financial losses in case of an attack. Also, when building a base, don't mass your power plants in a single block that can be easily taken out.

The tiberium refinery is what powers your war machine. Locate it as close to tiberium fields as possible, bearing in mind that it is a building you have to protect at all times.

Unit-Producing Buildings

The infantry and the vehicles in the game are produced in buildings that differ, dependent on whether you chose GDI or Nod. However, their functions are identical.

The Hand of Nod or GDI barracks produce infantry and engineers. Its worth noting that GDI needs barracks to make APCs in its weapons factories; in multiplayer games, both sides need a barracks/Hand of Nod to produce commandos (upon completion of Temple of Nod/advanced communications center). It makes sense to locate your barracks/Hand of Nod close to the construction yard, so that you can always pop out a couple of minigunners in an emergency.

Note that if you build more than one barracks/Hand, you will be able to produce new infantrymen at an increased speed. You select in which building you want the unit to be produced by double-clicking on it. However, I found out that this often does not work as it should.

Remember that you still have to build other structures in addition to the Nod airstrip supply vehicles/GDI weapons factory in order to produce some weapons—the Mammoth needs a repair bay, the Stealth tank a communications center, and so on. Capturing or destroying these buildings is always a major blow to your opponent, especially in multiplayer games.

While infantry is important in many single-player missions, the role it plays shrinks drastically in multiplayer games where the emphasis shifts to building vehicles, helipads, and airstrip/weapons factories—and even the mighty commando is little more than machine-gun fodder. You'll still use infantry in engineer raids, of course, and the Nod bazookamen continue to play an important role in anti-aircraft defense. In short, do not spend many credits producing infantry. In multiplayer battles, one tank is worth a dozen infantrymen.

Multiplayer games also stress the importance of a third type of unit-producing structure: the helipad. Absent from most single-player missions, the helipad confers the ability to make helicopters. While the transport chopper is always an incredibly useful unit, the attack chopper is often relatively unimportant in single-player games. This is because you mostly get to use the chopper when playing GDI. and the computer-controlled Nod army always has plenty of SAM sites and Obelisks. Knocking out the SAM sites to let your choppers operate freely means providing a bigger surplus of power for the Obelisks, which in turn means they'll be virtually impossible to knock out by targeting power plants.

Defensive Structures

Defensive structures include barriers (sandbags, fencing, concrete wall) as well as buildings that actively fight enemy forces (simple and advanced guard towers, turrets, SAM sites, Obelisks). The term defensive is rather misleading, as all of the structures listed above can be used offensively. In fact, I found the sandbag to be the single most effective structure in single-player games!

COMMAND & CONQUER

Enemy troops confronted by sandbags stop and stand still until you send some guns along to put them out of their misery.

Sandbags can be used to extend your base and erect structures far from its site. To do this in a cost-effective manner, you should sell sandbag #1 as soon as you have built sandbag #2, and so on. This results in a single sandbag traveling to wherever you want it. Once you've reached the desired site for a new building, erect it next to the sandbag. The same technique can be used to erect defensive/offensive structures in the middle of enemy bases, with the added bonus that you can block off the base entrance as you sandbag your way in.

Use sandbag barriers extensively against the computer opponent. You may want to build fencing or concrete walls in potential trouble spots—a sandbag can be blown away with a single shot, whereas a concrete wall can take some pounding.

Not surprisingly, the traveling sandbag and defensive barriers don't work as well against human opponents, who recognize them for what they are. Keep that in mind, and don't feel your base is safe just because you build a wall around it. Humans know walls can fall.

The three types of barriers are shared by both GDI and Nod. Other defensive structures are more specific for each side. The GDI lineup features simple and advanced guard towers. Simple guard towers, which use up just a little power, are fairly good at dealing with infantry, and average at dealing with vehicles—most Nod vehicles have poor armor. They are very good at protecting your base from engineer raids. A simple guard tower next to your construction yard offers a lot of security for relatively little money. However, simple guard towers aren't meant to hold off a purposeful enemy assault, and require assistance.

Advanced guard towers eat up quite a lot of power—if you build any, make sure your power plants are protected! A power shortage may disable your guard towers just when they are needed. Since advanced guard towers are also frightfully overpriced, you may want to avoid building any at all. When playing GDI in multiplayer games, I found that the rockets fired by the advanced guard tower work against aircraft. They are also great against both infantry and vehicles, but their short range is a big problem, as is their inability to hit a unit standing right next to the tower.

Both advanced and simple guard towers are relatively fragile. They can be easily taken out without being given the opportunity to fire back, so always provide some support—preferably armor.

Nod structures are much better. In *C&C,* the turret is a steal at 250 credits. In *The Covert Operations,* however, turrets cost 600 credits each. Nevertheless, given the turrets range (longer than that of GDIs guard towers), it usually makes good sense to build a couple in every mission, if you get the chance. Turrets are also my offensive structure of choice, although they are pretty hopeless against infantry.

The SAM site is a Nod specialty that combats only aircraft. It is very expensive at 750 credits, and eats up a lot of power—build them only when they are really necessary (as in the Level 5 Nod campaign or in multiplayer games, where aircraft are abundant). Avoid the temptation to build SAM sites as defense against GDI air strikes—it's far better to use a decoy. You should also consider selling a badly damaged structure, and building it from scratch in another spot. No matter how badly damaged a structure, it always fetches fifty percent of its construction cost, and repairs can be expensive.

The Obelisk of Light is the best defensive weapon in the game. It has the staggering capacity to destroy any infantry units with a single shot, and most vehicles with just two. However, it consumes a lot of power, and operates better if you have a huge power surplus. The moment you build an Obelisk, your power plants become a weak spot. You must protect them well.

Always combine defensive structures when actually building base defenses and not using them offensively. An advanced guard tower paired with a simple guard towers works better than two advanced guard towers, and the combination of an Obelisk with a turret and a SAM site is a tough nut to crack. You'll notice that the computer-led Nod tends to protect its Obelisks in that manner, and you'd be wise to emulate this tactic in multiplayer games.

Remember that defensive structures also serve as whistle-blowers. In multiplayer games, it is absolutely vital to keep the location of your construction yard secret for as long as possible, and denying access into your base becomes a top priority. Make sure you build barriers and place guard towers or turrets at your base entrance. If you're fighting against Nods equipped with Stealth tanks, there shouldn't be more than two map squares between the guard towers/turrets (i.e., you can place two vehicles side by side between the towers).

UNIT FORMATIONS

Unit formations are key to winning in *C&C*. Troops fighting in formation have a much better chance of defeating the enemy, and can give a good account of themselves, even without your intervention in the course of battle. Given the fact that the AI likes to attack in two spots simultaneously, unit formations are a great help to every *C&C* commander. Sadly, I found out that most *C&C* players do not use them, relying instead on their ability to fight on two fronts at the same time. From my experience, unit formations are outright indispensable in many of the more difficult missions, such as the ones in *The Covert Operations.*

Unit formations are broadly divided into defensive, offensive, and universal—this last label applying to formations best suited for unit movement, yet allowing for rapid deployment into either defensive or offensive positions.

Broadly speaking, defensive formations involve placing your troops individually to achieve a high concentration of firepower in a given area—the area where you expect the enemy incursion to take place. The defensive formation sees infantry deployed in front of vehicles. It is good if you can create opportunities for enfilade fire, i.e. firing on the enemy from the flank.

If your defensive lineup features infantry only (no vehicles), the rule is to put infantry with the shorter firing range in the front so that everyone can open fire at the same time. Nod flamethrowers, however, should always be placed in front of other troops, with plenty of space between the individual flamethrowers. Otherwise they'll burn your guys as well as each other along with enemy soldiers.

If your lineup features vehicles only, the defensive formation sees armor in front and soft-skinned vehicles behind and on the wings—they should be ready to strike any enemy bazookamen threatening the armor with their machine guns/rockets.

Offensive formations see vehicles placed in front of the infantry, with armor leading. If you have just infantry, the offensive formation differs between GDI and Nod. Nod infantry, as usual, features flamethrowers in front, only this time I group them in pairs. Chances are they'll be flaming something in front of them, not to the side—in which case, they won't automatically fry each other. The flamers are followed by minigunners, then bazookamen. The GDI offensive infantry lineup features squads of grenadiers leading minigunners, which, in this case, are simply a protective screen for the bazookamen bringing up the rear.

The vehicle-only offensive lineup features light vehicles on point, and armor following with other soft-skinned vehicles (like rocket launchers) close behind.

Bear in mind that flexibility is important. At Level 14 in the GDI campaign, for example, you'll conduct a search-and-destroy mission in which you should use an offensive formation in defense. The formation, as such, exists to create overlapping fields of fire. If you find that a particular battlefield lets you develop site-specific formations, then go for it.

Universal formations—the ones used for moving units in a way that allows going on the offensive or defensive at a moments notice—follow a few basic rules. The fastest units are in front, since they can retreat quickly to join the rest of your force. Infantry follows vehicles very closely, and moves to front when changing to defense. Of course, if the opponent consists of five flame tanks, you want to hide the men and move armor forward. Remember to be flexible.

Firing Ranges

Firing ranges are a very important aspect of the game. If your unit has a longer firing range than the enemy, it can destroy the enemy without being fired back.

Firing ranges are consistent throughout *C&C,* but not in *The Covert Operations.* For instance, in Hostile Takeover, Nod artillery easily destroys GDIs guard towers, both simple and advanced, without being threatened. If you try the same tactic in Deceit, you'll lose unit after unit. (Any irregularities are noted in the mission summaries.)

Minigunners have the shortest firing range (about two map squares). They are followed by grenadiers, flamethrowers, and the Nod flame tank(just over three map squares each), and the bazookamen, the Nod Bradley tank, and machine-guns mounted on hummers, dune buggies, and APCs (four map squares). Note that the bazookamans range applies to bazooka-type rockets also used by Nod motorbikes, Stealth tanks, and Orca helicopters. Note also that firing ranges of GDIs guard towers (simple and advanced) are supposed to extend four map squares. However, you'll find that if you position a four-square weapon (e.g. bazooka or machine gun) carefully, it can fire at a simple guard tower without getting damaged.

The Abrams tank cannon has a range of well over four map squares, and is roughly identical to the Mammoths cannon. Mammoth rockets have a range of five squares, as do Nod turrets. Nod artillery, GDI rocket launcher, and the Obelisk of Light all have the same range in practical terms. Finally, the Nod SSM launcher has the biggest range of all—almost fifty percent more than the GDI rocket launcher.

Mission Summaries

What follows is a brief summary of each missions most important points. For detailed walkthroughs and maps, see Prima's *Command & Conquer Secrets and Solutions—The Unauthorized Edition.*

COMMAND & CONQUER

The mission trees in *C&C* provide several choices at many levels. I've included my own recommendations for every level in both Nod and GDI campaigns. Note that missions that appear as choices have a suffix following the level number (e.g., Mission 5a). This suffix corresponds to the one awarded to the mission by the games designers—you'll find a corresponding a, b, c, or d in the lower right-hand corner of the Options panel when you select Game Options while playing a mission.

GDI Missions

Mission 1: This is basically a tutorial in setting up a base. The gunboats take out the Nod turrets, and the Nod opposition is very weak. Setting up a good defensive perimeter is enough to win this mission. Pardon me—you have to hunt down a couple of enemy soldiers frozen with fright in the trees.

Mission 2: This is a base assault tutorial. You are given three engineers to capture selected Nod buildings in the Nod base to the north of yours. Fend off the enemy assault the mission starts with, repair your buildings, set up a base defense, then go on the offensive. Its a small battlefield, and the opposition isn't strong. Preserve your vehicles as long as you can, and remember to group your minigunners into squads rather than moving them singly or in one large group. Protect the engineers—they're fragile.

Mission 3: This is slightly tougher. Set up base near your starting point. Destroy the SAM sites in the right sequence—first the one to the west of your base, then the two near the cliff edge to the north. Your grenadiers can destroy these from below the cliff if you position them right. Finally, push north through the pass in the middle of the battlefield. The last SAM site is to the northwest, and its destruction will bring you air strike support as well as an opportunity to lay an ambush for Nods running to assist their comrades. Coordinate the air strike with the beginning of your base assault, and everything will go well. I suggest you make as many grenadiers as possible, and use this mission to familiarize yourself with the capabilities of this excellent infantryman.

Mission 4a: This is the second most difficult choice of Level 4 missions: it teaches you how to use the APC. After the brief fire fight at the very start, load all your infantry aboard those vehicles and go north, right to the edge of the battlefield, then turn west. You'll come to a cliff overhanging the Nod base. Use your grenadiers to dispose most of the Nod troops guarding the crate you're to steal back—start by destroying the Hand of Nod. Then retrace your steps, and cross the bridge just north of your starting point, heading west. Follow the road, then proceed north after it ends, to find the entrance to the Nod base. If you lose all your units, you are given another APC and some grenadiers.

Mission 4b: This is the easiest of Level 4 missions—again, you get to use the APC. The trick here is to coordinate vehicle and infantry movement—i.e., to fight in formation. Once you've achieved that, dealing with the scattered opposition is fairly easy.

Go south from the starting point, then turn east and cross the river with some caution—there may be a Nod ambush on its other side. Turn south, cross another bridge and possibly win a major fire fight, then go west. The town of Bialystok is located in the southwestern corner of the battlefield. After you've cleared it of any Nod presence, garrison it with a small force and hunt down the remaining Nods.

Mission 4c: This is the most difficult of Level 4 missions. It's very similar to Mission 4a—you have to rush the APCs carrying your infantry past some determined opposition. Lead with the hummer and don't stop to fight—just squash as many enemy soldiers as you can with the APCs.

Go northwest from your starting point until your reach the edge of the battlefield. You should see the road that runs south along the battlefields eastern edge. It features some twists, and its guarded by bazookamen hiding in the trees. Just tell the drivers to step on it. A Bradley tank at the southern end of the road has to be destroyed—use the grenadiers with APC support. After that, go west along the shoreline till you hit the Nod base. Engage the Nods in front of the Hand with part of your force, and send something fast south and west through the Nod base to get at the crate. If you lose all you have, another APC with grenadiers becomes available.

Missions 5a, 5c, and 5d: These are identical. You get to use the Abrams tank and make light vehicles in all Level 5 missions. They are a big step up in complexity from the previous ones.

Go east from the starting point—of course, arrange everyone in formation before you set off. The GDI base is in the southeastern corner of the battlefield. Establish a defensive perimeter (don't forget to defend from the north!), repair the base, and clean the Nods out of the area south of the river that runs across the battlefield.

After establishing control over the bridge, push one force along the river to the east—it can destroy the Nod construction yard from below the cliff. Coordinate that attack with the main assault, which should hit the Nod base from the east and north of the cliff featuring a SAM site.

Mission 5b: This is much more difficult than other Level 5 missions. Although the objectives are identical, the map is not.

After forming up, go south at top speed across the bridge, turn east, and there's your base. Rush to the bases eastern entrance to fend off Nod attacks there, then repair your base and build up your forces. Go on defensive in the west, and offensive in the east; the eastern part of the battlefield features tiberium fields you need to control. Use the river fork to your tactical advantage—a river is hard to cross—then mount a big pincer movement. The Nod base is north by east of your base. One (the weaker) force should approach it from the west, and the other, from the southeast. Preserve your Abrams tanks so that they can take part in the final battle—they make a big difference.

Missions 6a and 6b: These are identical, and constitute the most difficult level in the whole GDI campaign. You'll find it very hard to accomplish this mission without repeated saves, as your commando is likely to suffer damage each time he blows up a SAM site.

Proceed north from your starting point—the commando can shoot everyone from a safe distance. Watch out for bazookamen hidden in the trees, and for the minigunners that emerge from the smoking ruins of each freshly destroyed SAM site. After you destroy the two sites just north of your starting point, you'll be given a transport chopper.

Use the chopper to ferry your commando east of the spot marked by a smoke grenade. Proceed north along the western edge of the battlefield, killing solitary Nod infantrymen with your commando and following him with the chopper. After destroying the SAM site near the northwestern corner of the battlefield, clear the map as much as you can by walking the commando along the cliff, then ferry him in the chopper to the cliff that shows east. You have to time this very carefully, and may have to touch down with the chopper at the base of the cliff before you can find a landing spot on top. Once you've hopped upstairs, unload your commando immediately, shoot any infantry, and destroy the SAM site on the cliff—its just east of your landing spot, which is why you should land right on the edge of the cliff. Land farther in, and the SAM battery will fire at your chopper.

After destroying this fourth SAM site, repeat the chopper-hopping maneuver to transfer your commando on top of yet another cliff. This ones to the north, and the entrance is right beside the cliff your commando is on. Move him into the base, shooting any Nod infantry of sight (beware of flamethrowers!), then go north and east. You're supposed to blow up the airstrip in the northeastern corner of the Nod base. Blow up anything else, and instead of advancing to Level 8, you'll have to do Level 7.

Mission 7: This is a moderately difficult mission. Set up your base near the starting point, and block off two approaches—from the east, along the shore, and from the north. Push north until you reach the top edge of the battlefield, then go west until you come to a turret over the Nod base. Destroy it.

In the meantime, you should have assembled a base assault force. Strike east along the shore, turning north at the first opportunity. Your column should join up with your northern force near a round cliff roughly in the center of the map, which features a turret and a SAM site. Destroy the turret promptly, then hit the western entrance to the Nod base with everything you've got.

Mission 8a: This is the easier of Level 8 missions. The opposition isn't strong in spite of a bleak beginning.

Start by repairing your base, organizing your force into squads, and establishing a defensive perimeter. Remember to protect your base from the north. Assemble a small striking force, and push east until you come to a village containing some moderately weak Nods. After you've killed them off, root around along the western edge of the battlefield—there's a money crate in the trees just south of the river.

Build a base assault force while clearing the field of Nods, then mount your assault. You can destroy the Nod construction yard from below the cliff to the south of the Nod base—its near the maps eastern edge. Once you've made sure the Nods can't rebuild, attack through the base entrance.

Mission 8b: This is decidedly the more difficult of Level 8 missions. Go southwest from your starting point, then west until you find Doctor Moebius and his hospital. Place your base north of the village, on the other side of the river. There will be Nod airborne assaults coming in two spots: on the small plain east of the village, and next to the blossom tree near the southwestern corner of the battlefield—these are practically next door to the hospital, and are particularly dangerous. Make sure you guard both spots. You may also sandbag them off if you have the money and the patience.

The sandbag can be used to quickly win this mission with minimum casualties. Just build north through the bridge over the river, and right into the Nod base in the northwestern corner of the map. Take this base first, then attack the second Nod base—in the northeastern corner—from the south and from the northwest.

Mission 9: This is a relatively easy, but also relatively complicated mission. Start by building your base and a strike force. In the meantime, use the infantry (which a transport chopper delivers for you) in the south to destroy the Nod turrets. Attack with grenadiers first, and everything will be fine. Destroying all turrets south of the river enables you to retrieve a money crate in the southwestern corner of the map.

Do not destroy the northern turrets till the endgame. Instead, strike out west—you'll see a river. Cross it, turn south, and presto, you've found a practically unguarded entrance to the Nod base. An engineer raid through that entrance coupled with an assault will accomplish this mission in record time. You may consider destroying the northern riverbank turrets so that the gunboats arrive when your assault starts. They are not good for much apart from drawing the Obelisks fire, but in doing so, they enable you to capture the Nod construction yard, power plants, etc. at a smaller cost.

Missions 10a and 10b: Although these missions feature different maps, the terrain is similar, and the way the missions play out is identical. Mission 10a is slightly easier.

Deploy your MCY immediately, then reconnoiter the terrain while you build your base. Don't get into any fights with any turrets—just find out the lay of the land. Then block off the Nod base entrance with sandbags—which is pretty easy to do in both missions—and start building helipads. Use Orcas to attack the turrets and drain the Nods of their money, which they can't recover since their base is blocked off. Once the Nods run out of credits, it's just a big mop-up job.

Mission 11: This is a difficult one. Move your MCY north and east, squeezing through behind the turret, then go north. Set up base just south of a small village, and some of the approaching Nods will attack the civilian houses instead of you.

Tiberium is scarce in this mission, and Orca helicopters come in really handy. You have to destroy all the Nods before the mission is over, so there's plenty of fighting to be done on a limited budget. Target selected SAM sites with your ground forces and then attack the defenseless power plants with Orcas. Once they're down, the Obelisks won't work.

Mission 12a: This is the easier of Level 12 missions. Money is very limited. A money crate near the eastern edge of the battlefield and just north of the northernmost river helps a little. Of course, you have to wipe out the Nods before everything's over, not just rescue the busy Doctor Moebius.

The key to victory lies in destroying the power plants in the northern part of the Nod base. Form two strike forces; send one along the western edge of the battlefield, and the other one north of the bridge closer to your base. Avoid fights unless they're inevitable—get those plants. If you haven't destroyed any Nod power-hungry turrets or SAM sites, this will put the Obelisk out of action. Then mount a base assault coupled with an engineer raid, get the Nod construction yard, and sell it.

Mission 12b: This is the harder of Level 12 missions. Money is short yet Asian, but there's a money crate. You'll find it next to the northernmost SAM site, on the cliff occupying most of the northwestern corner of the battlefield. Begin by taking control of all space west and south of the river that divides the whole battlefield. Attacking along the eastern edge of the map lets you destroy the Nod construction yard—its in the northeastern corner of the Nod base, which is in the northeast as well. After destroying the construction yard, you can safely set about destroying the SAM sites without them being rebuilt. Once all are gone, a chopper will arrive to fetch Doctor Moebius.

Alternatively, you may mount an assault coupled with an engineer raid through the western entrance to the Nod base, and capture the power plants/construction yard lined up against the northern base wall.

Missions 13a and 13b: These missions are identical, and quite difficult. They aren't completed until you've destroyed everything Nod along with the research center. Since the first of the two Nod bases is practically next door to yours, I suggest you employ sandbag barriers to block it off. Then extend the sandbags to block the entrance to the second Nod base further north. Once that's done, take a strong armored force to the cliff in the northwestern corner of the battlefield—your tanks will be able to destroy a whole block of advanced power stations lined just below the cliff. Following this, rush a strike force of armor and APCs with engineers through the gap created by the destruction of the power plants. Keep west to avoid the Obelisk, and north of the second Nod base. Enter it through the northern entrance—the Nod construction yard is in the northeastern corner of the second base. Its destruction/capture means the Nods wont be able to rebuild any power plants (the Obelisks are rendered impotent by the power shortage), and that wins you this mission.

Mission 14: This is a difficult and atypical mission. Start by getting rid of Nod artillery in your rear, to the northwest. Then cross the bridge to the north; line up as many tanks as you can fit in into the narrow valley, and destroy the Nod units sleeping on guard duty on a cliff northwest of the bridge. Following that, advance north through the narrow canyon until you come to its end. Defend at the canyons entrance with your vehicles in offensive formation. After the main Nod force is defeated, hunt down remaining Nod units—there are single artillery pieces and Stealths scattered around.

Mission 15a: This is the easiest of Level 15 GDI missions. At the start, things look bleak. The flame tank that menaces you at the beginning can be dealt with by using your MCY as a lure. While the flamer is chasing it, your Abrams can do its job. Its important you keep that Abrams healthy for the first part of the mission. Its all you've really got to fight with.

Locate your base near the northern edge of the battlefield, approximately midway east. Form a defensive perimeter, then expand your zone of control to the entire northern half of the battlefield. The entire southern half is taken up by a big plateau with numerous Nod structures all over the place. There are only two entrances to that plateau, and its easiest to just block them off with sandbags. Conquer the eastern entrance first. Capture the silos just south of the entrance, then attack the first Nod base from the east and the north at the same time. Use the ion cannon to hit the Obelisk as you launch your assault.

Use sandbags to block off the second Nod base. Destroy the small Nod complex in the southwestern corner of the battlefield, capturing the construction yard. By the time you've done that, the Nods will be running short of money. Mount a regular assault on the second base, hitting the first Obelisk with the ion cannon as your vehicles roll forward.

Mission 15b: This is probably the most difficult of Level 15 missions. Locate your base immediately north of the bridge which you cross at the start of the mission. Clean out the two round cliffs north and east of your base, and establish an advanced defensive perimeter between the two round cliffs— the long cliff to the north, and the small plateau at the battlefields southern edge. Attack in the south first. Many of the structures in the Nod base at the maps eastern edge can be destroyed by rocket launchers firing from below the cliff to the south. Capture that base, but leave barracks standing, or you'll get nuked. A Nod mini-base featuring an Obelisk may pop up on that small cliff plateau at the southern edge of the map. Don't be taken by surprise!

Having cleaned up the southern half of the battlefield and captured the first Nod base, stay on the defensive for a while and build up your forces. The Nods have two construction yards—one in the northeastern corner of the battlefield and one in their second base. The yard in the northeastern corner can be destroyed by vehicles firing from a position below the cliff. Destroying the southern of the two Obelisks in the second Nod base allows you to get at the second construction yard, at which point this mission is won—although you still have plenty of cleaning to do. Leave the Temple of Nod in the north-western corner of the battlefield for the very end. You get nuked for the second time when you attack it.

Mission 15c: This mission is a lot easier than it looks. You start off by capturing some Nod buildings, but don't set up your construction yard next to them—do so further south. Secure the western approach to your base, and watch out for airborne engineer raids!

Clear the eastern part of the battlefield first. There are huge tiberium fields south of your base, guarded by pairs of turrets. Controlling this area means practically unlimited cash.

Following that, extend your control over the northern edge of the battle-field. Two bridges lead south into Nod territory. If you strike across the one further west and turn west after crossing the bridge, you'll be able to capture a bunch of Nod power plants. Strike the Obelisk guarding that approach with the ion cannon as you begin the attack. Do not capture all the Nod buildings in the western half where the power plants are, or you'll get nuked with hor-rifying results.

Having captured the first Nod base, you'll have to endure some counterat-tacks and rebuild your forces. Use that time to make a Stealth (you can if you captured the Nod communications center) and reconnoiter the rest of the bat-tlefield. When the ion cannon is ready, take the road leading south, hit the Obelisk atop a round cliff with the ion cannon, and lay siege to the second big Nod base near the maps southern edge. There also is a water-encircled complex with a Temple of Nod in the southwest, and a construction yard in the southeast. Get the construction yard before the assault on the second

Nod base, but save the Temple for last—you get nuked when you start shooting at it.

Nod Missions

Note that the Nod army is especially well suited to employing the traveling sandbag tactic. The turret is a super weapon.

Mission 1: This is an easy one. Arrange everyone in formation with buggies leading, and move off to the south. Turn west when its possible, then go north through the village to find Nikumba hiding atop a cliff overlooking the village from the north. The opponent weak; retreat with your buggies upon encountering the enemy, and draw them into the fire of the minigunners that follow your buggies.

Mission 2a: This ones easy, too. Start the base where you are, establish a defensive perimeter to the northwest, then probe along the visible road until you come across the GDI base in the northwestern corner. A pincer movement—one column going along the southern road, another taking the northern route—is guaranteed to bring good results.

Mission 2b: This one's easier still. It's almost a carbon copy of Mission 2a, only the geography is a tad different. You start in the northeast; the GDI base is directly west of you. Again, a two-pronged attack—from the south and from the east—brings good results.

Mission 3a: This one's moderately hard. Deploy where you are, and secure the northwestern approach to your base first, then the southern approach. Stay where you are till you build some muscle, then push forward in the center of the battlefield, taking control of a pass marked by a convergence of three cliffs. This position is very defensible, and lets you build up a second, bigger strike force. The GDI base is in the northwestern corner of the battlefield, and the prison you have to capture is in the northwestern corner of the base. Attack with your big strike force from the south, keeping as far west as possible. Remember to give your engineer(s) a protective screen of infantry.

Mission 3b: This mission is easier than the previous one. The layout of the GDI base is different, but its still in the northwest, and the prison is in it's northwestern corner. This time, gather your strike force in a single column and strike along the shortest route possible, which is north by west.

Mission 4a: This mission is easier than mission 4b. Move off to the south, watching for a GDI ambush at the end of the canyon. Move fast—time is important. You will intercept some civilians at the foot of the canyon. The village is in the southwestern corner of the battlefield, and an empty GDI base is in the northeastern corner. You may destroy the whole base with a single motorbike, provided you know your firing ranges. The GDI convoy isn't much of a problem, either. Just be there in time.

Mission 4b: You get to confront the Abrams tank for the first time. Your first priority in this mission is to suffer minimum casualties, since the opposition is numerous. Use ambush tactics—let your fast vehicle lead pursuing GDI forces into your trap. Stage ambushes right at the start to get the tank, go south across a couple of bridges, then lay out an ambush between the river and the cliff to the southwest. Draw GDI hummers out one by one. The GDI village is in the northwest, and its full of GDI infantry. Be careful.

Mission 5: This mission is a big step forward. You get to make vehicles—and you'll need them! Set up base where you are, and don't budge until you've built up your forces. Strong GDI patrols in the area turn very aggressive upon exchanging fire. GDI has air strikes, too, so don't forget to keep a sacrificial gunner posted as a decoy north of your other forces/buildings. Best of all, lead the Warthogs onto their own troops by racing in among them with a motorbike when the air strike arrives.

You should form two teams of motorbikes. Take one along the eastern edge of the map, and the other along the western edge. The western group can destroy the GDI construction yard, and the eastern—the GDI weapons factory—it should strike second. The rest is a walk in the park. Just remember to build one required SAM site at the very end!

Mission 6a: This is the hardest of the three Level 6 missions. Your forces are split in two. The stronger one, to the west, actually plays just a supporting role. Use it to destroy GDI tanks and grenadiers atop cliffs as you move it south. The other force should move out second only after the first force has progressed to the center of the battlefield. Run it directly east, and you'll come across the GDI base. Blow a hole in the wall, dash in, retrieve the crate (you'll see it instantly), then rush out through the southern exit to make it to the embarkation point. Speed, speed, speed! That's what you need in this one.

Mission 6b: This is the second easiest of Level 6 missions. Go south, then east, through a narrow gorge. Turn north keeping as far west as you can, and travel along the curving cliffs till you reach a bridge leading northeast. The GDI base is just beyond. Rush in, get the crate, and leave by the other exit in the southeastern corner of the base. Continue south along the eastern edge to the battlefield to reach the embarkation point.

Mission 6c: This is the easiest of Level 6 missions. Strike out northwest (beware the grenadier in the tree south of the pass between cliffs), continue across the bridge you'll see, and turn west. GDI forces are pretty weak, and you can retrieve the crate without difficulty. Again, leave through the southern exit to get to the embarkation point. Avoid the GDI tanks west of the round cliff just south of the GDI base.

Mission 7a: This is a difficult one. Contrary to the briefing, GDI forces are very strong. The GDI base is in the southwestern part of the battlefield, on a large cliff. There's a hospital and a power plant on a plain west to the GDI base, and those are the buildings you have to capture to win this mission quickly.

Go roughly west from your starting point (there's no other way) and through the narrow gorge that leads to the GDI base. There's a village just north of the base, and that village contains a church, which in turn contains a money crate. Its close to GDI guard towers, but its still feasible to get the crate without sacrifices. Proceed west to find the above-mentioned hospital and power plant. If you capture them, you'll be able to sandbag the GDI inside their base with great ease.

You also receive a Nod base in the northeastern corner of the map the moment you make it to the bridge north of the GDI base. Defending this base is rather a pain because its often under attack. Make cleaning out the northern half of the battlefield a priority if you are going to use this base to an important extent. I recommend you build everything you need in the south, next to the captured power plant, *after* you've sandbagged the GDI in their base.

Mission 7b: The GDI in this mission grows strong quickly, so although your starting position is fairly good, things aren't so easy. You have two choices: Play it safe and inch down to the GDI base via the travelling sandbag, or rush the GDI base with a mobile force. Although your briefing speaks only of destroying the village of Bertoua, you cant get to it without going through the GDI base!

If you choose the second, mobile force option, don't stop to engage the GDI. Enter the base from the west, turn north, and keep the drivers feet on the gas pedal. You may be able to destroy the village quickly, especially if your second wave starts hammering at the western base door while your boys are busy up north.

If you go the safe, slow route, the GDI may destroy the village for you! Maybe its because of that single odd building you'll see if you get there first...

Mission 7c: This mission can be a piece of cake if you just sit back behind your sandbags. GDI will destroy the villagers for you. You should deploy right where you start, then take control of the river crossing to the south. Once that is done, you can just relax.

If you decide to take the active course, you should storm the GDI base in the southeastern corner of the battlefield, rush through to the northern exit, and set about the villagers. The village is only accessible through the GDI base.

Mission 7d: This is a difficult mission, though second easiest among those at Level 7. Your forces are split into two groups. The western group, containing vehicles, is in danger from the GDI gunboat; make sure you don't run into it once you move. The second group contains the engineers, who are vital to your success. It's actually the group that does the serious work. Move it south right away, keeping the engineers protected. A single guard tower is all that defends the northern entrance into the GDI base. Destroy it, and move in confidently. The Orcas in the southeastern corner of the base. Scout with a vehicle, then get the helipad. Use the other three engineers to capture the GDI construction yard, weapons factory, and refinery.

Beware the gunboat when you're destroying the village with the Orca. You'll also have to deal with the single bazookaman among the houses.

Mission 8a: The easier of Level 8 missions, but definitely not easy! Go east from your starting point to find the Nod base. Make at least three engineers, more if you can, and whatever infantry you can afford. The sale of your construction yard may net you an engineer.

Ferry four soldiers and one engineer to the abandoned GDI base—capture just one building to start with. Build a barracks or a Hand of Nod while you're bringing the rest of your guys over. Capture the enemy refinery while the Harvester is parked inside.

The GDI base is in the northeastern corner of the battlefield. Establish defensive positions on both sides of the big round cliff to the northeast, then start destroying GDI Harvesters as quickly as they are rebuilt. After a few GDI counterattacks and several Harvesters, GDI will be ripe for defeat. Mount a base assault, remembering that the GDI has two Orcas. Make sure you have enough bazookamen.

Mission 8b: This is the more difficult of Level 8 missions because your starting Nod base is in the north—which means its repeatedly bombed by GDI aircraft.

The initial strategy is identical to Mission 8a. However, after capturing the abandoned GDI base, you'll have to deal with a GDI gunboat that limits your access to tiberium. My advice is to build a turret using the traveling sandbag. It will destroy the gunboat on a consecutive pass.

You can use the sandbag method to assault the GDI base—its in the southwestern corner of the battlefield—or you can mount a regular assault. If you choose the latter, make sure you attack the enemy base from the north and east at the same time.

Mission 9: This mission is very difficult. Using your commando as the principal player, you must unite your starting forces into a single group. Lead your commando south, then northwest, shooting everyone along the way. Join with the rocket infantry first, provoke the hummer below the ridge your commandos on into attacking, and destroy it with the bazookas. After that, you can safely join up with the engineers.

Move southwest, keeping your eyes peeled for the river and the GDI gunboat—it can wipe out your group with a single salvo. Capture the base, then destroy the church in the village just north of your new home and retrieve the money crate it contains. Deal with the GDI gunboat using the turret tactic from Mission 8b.

COMMAND & CONQUER

Its best to assault the GDI base from the northwest—send a column along the northern edge of the map. Remember to fend off GDI air strikes with a decoy, or make the planes bomb the GDI base by leading them onto it with a motorbike.

Mission 10a: This is the easier of Level 10 missions. Gather up your guys and move off north. Turn east at the northern edge of the battlefield, then south onto a long peninsula. If you provoked south keeping to the east, you'll reach the end of the peninsula while avoiding the empty GDI base in its western part. In my experience, firing at the base brings other GDI troops racing to the scene, and while they are relatively easy to defeat, its easier still without the extra fighting.

Go as far east as you can along the peninsulas southern shore. You'll see the lab and the scientist. Both your artillery and your commando can kill him, and anyway, you'll receive a transport chopper when you get this far.

Mission 10b: This very difficult mission is one of the most challenging in the whole Nod career. Use your commando to reconnoiter and shoot any infantry, and your bazookamen to deal with enemy armor. Its important that they survive till the end of the mission.

Go east from your starting point, then north across the bridge. You'll have to deal with GDI tanks almost immediately, then with infantry supported by hummers. North of the river, turn west, and proceed westwards until you see a bridge leading south. Provoke the Mammoth south of the bridge into chasing your commando while the bazookamen finish it off. Proceed south, then west, cross another bridge leading south, and turn east. You'll see the GDI base.

The Mammoths you are supposed to destroy remain inactive as long as you don't fire on them with anything but your bazookamen.

Mission 11a: Very, very difficult. You must destroy the GDI gunboat traveling the river with your southern force. Use minigunners as decoys while you pound it with everything else you've got on the southern shore. Afterwards, go east with your southern force until you reach the bank opposite the GDI base, by the western edge of the battlefield. Use the artillery to destroy the GDI guard towers, and subsequently to bombard GDI infantry attacking along the river shore.

Your northern group should leave behind one minigunner to draw the

GDI air strike. Proceed south, but be careful—if any of your guys start shooting at the GDI Harvester, you've lost. Its essential that you arrive at the GDI base entrance without exciting too much attention.

After gaining control of the base, start by building a couple of turrets to help fend off numerous counterattacks. Consolidate control over the big tiberium field on the large cliff east of your base. The GDI base is just north of that plateau.

The GDI construction yard is in the northwestern corner of the base. You can slip a couple of Stealths by the patrolling Mammoth and destroy the yard before you mount the base assault. It will make things much easier.

Mission 11b: This mission is slightly easier than the previous one, because there is a money crate located in a church on the southern bank, near the western edge of the battlefield. As in 11a, start by killing the gunboat and moving your southern force east into position opposite the GDI base, so that your artillery can destroy the guard towers. As in 11a, destroy the GDI construction yard. The GDI base is in the northeastern corner, like in the previous mission, and the yard is in the northwestern corner of the base. GDI opposition is very strong, and you may want to use sandbag barriers to minimize trouble. Consider using the traveling sandbag to help with your assault on the GDI base.

Mission 12: Not nearly as difficult as the preceding ones, this mission nevertheless features a trying start. Your light forces have to defeat two Mammoths guarding the bridge you have to cross, west of your starting point. Use your dune buggies to draw Mammoths fire and destroy them with the bikes.

Cross the river and establish your base south of the round cliff that becomes visible. The GDI base is in the northeastern corner of the battlefield. Attack it from the east, through the village that lines the northern edge of the battlefield, with the help of a diversionary attack directed at its southern entrance.

GDI has Orcas. Ambush them with your bazookamen, and keep destroying the GDI Harvester. GDI will try to counterattack, but they get weaker with the loss of every consecutive Harvester. When you see the counterattacks are getting weak, mount a base assault.

Make sure you save plenty of credits for the next mission!

COMMAND & CONQUER

Mission 13a: You win this mission through the intelligent use of helicopters. You start in the southern part of the battlefield, at its western end; the first GDI base you have to deal with is to the east. Use sandbags and turrets to destroy patrolling gunboats and break the back of GDIs southern force, then assault the base, trying to capture everything worth the price of an engineer. You'll get a couple of transport choppers at this point.

Build a turret close to the waters edge in the eastern part of the map. It will expose a northern shore along with some buildings—a hospital and a power plant. Capture them by ferrying engineers and troops aboard the choppers. Quickly build up a base, and produce several engineers and bazookamen. The two GDI bases in this mission both have construction yards located in their corners. If you ferry your engineers and bazookamen aboard the choppers to chosen spots, the bazookamen can blow a hole in the right place and your engineers can capture the yards, which effectively wins this mission. Remember that your northernmost unit will be bombed. Post a decoy.

Mission 13b: Difficult mission—more so than 13a, but less than 13c. Your starting base in the northeast will be targeted by both GDI aircraft and airborne assaults, with transport chopper landing either in the middle of your base or west of it, across the river.

You receive a MCY with escort on the southern shore of the river as soon as you explore the northern part of the battlefield. Set up the yard, build barracks, and immediately set up sandbag barriers to help with the continuous GDI attacks on your newborn base. Then extend the sandbags to cut off approaches to your base as well as the GDI base in the southeastern corner of the battlefield. Build turrets by your sandbags to destroy the GDI guard towers, and capture whatever you fancy with your engineers.

Things are easiest if you continue to build sandbag barriers, advancing west along the southern edge of the map, then liquidating the GDI complex just across the river. Your final assault should include an attack on the last GDI construction yard, located in the southeastern corner of the second base.

Mission 13c: This is the least desirable of the Level 13 missions. Make sure you pick up the money crate from the church located on the island near the western edge of the map. Land your forces just south of that island, and concentrate on consolidating your defenses before you venture anywhere. Build sandbag barriers to isolate and take over the GDI complex just east of your landing point, as well as the big GDI base to the south. Deal with the GDI base in the south first, since its more dangerous—use the sandbags. Then go after the base in the northeastern corner of the battlefield.

THE COVERT OPERATIONS

C&Cs add-on disc, *The Covert Operations,* features fifteen standalone missions. You get to play with some of the weaponry hitherto available only in multiplayer games. The AI has been enhanced, no longer allowing its forces to walk blindly into every ambush, and the firing ranges have been tweaked in a rather inconsistent manner.

GDI Missions

Blackout: This mission is a pleasant introduction *to The Covert Operations.* Your two commandos start by stealing 2,000 credits from the church, then proceed south, west, and northwest along the road. At this point, you have to call in air support to deal with a flame tank, then destroy the complex of four Nod power plants. Start your base right there, inside the concrete enclosure.

Your next steps are to secure the approaches to your base—northwestern, northeastern, and eastern. The last two are easily closed off with sandbags. The Nods have a base in the northeastern corner of the battlefield, a complex with a Temple of Nod in the northwest, and a pair of Obelisks with guarding turrets along the road in the southwest. Your best bet is to sandbag off the western entrance to the Nod base, then destroy the power plants from the cliff overlooking the Nod base from the north. Mammoths are good for that purpose.

Save the Temple of Nod for last, as you'll get nuked when you touch it.

Hells Fury: This mission can be won in an unconventional fashion. After taking the Nod base in the south with your strong starting forces, you have to tackle the complex of Nod bases that stretch along the entire top of the battlefield. Fortunately, agent Delphi clears you a nice landing spot in the middle of enemy territory, and you receive a transport chopper the moment you build your first Orca. The transport chopper is good for just one flight to

Delphis landing spot, as it passes over SAM sites. Load engineers and grenadiers, and direct them east after landing. Destroy/capture the complex of power plants in the northeastern corner of the battlefield, and occupy the spot between the two SAM sites to the south. That's where Nod planned to build its Temple.

Following that, mount an assault/engineer raid on the Nod base in the center-north—the Obelisks are inoperational. Capture a building so that you may start building stuff in the enemy's own territory. The rest is easy.

Blindsided: This is the most difficult mission among *The Covert Operations*. Shoot the three Nods threatening your commando, then proceed west. You'll come to a Nod base containing soldiers and SAM sites. Destroying all of these will be rewarded with a transport chopper and engineers. You want to end up with all the power plants captured along with the airstrip and the Hand of Nod. Sell everything save for one power plant, but not before you produce an artillery, a couple of engineers, and a flamethrower. Attack the Nod base in the southeast by targeting the two power plants by its northern wall with your artillery, and ambushing the Nod infantry counterattack with the rest of your forces. Destroy the inactive Obelisk first, then capture the rest of the buildings—make sure you get the Harvester along with the refinery. The destruction of the last SAM site means the reappearance of the transport chopper. Use it to ferry troops to the other shore of the river, where a spot clears near the third Nod base. Capture the Hand of Nod just inside that base first, then clear it of enemy units. Use sandbags to secure the northern entrance, as well as to cut Nod off from the big tiberium field in the north-west. Then extend your sandbags into the third Nod base and destroy it from the inside. Build a Hand of Nod; make engineers to capture the two airstrips and set up turrets to deal with enemy structures and units. Afterwards, deal with the last Nod base in the northeastern corner of the battlefield.

Nods have choppers in this mission. Shoot them down by directing the bazookamen to stand under the attacking chopper *after* it has chosen its target.

Elemental Imperative: This is an easy one. Press east, then northeast until you see a village. Let your commando shoot all the infantry (especially all the bazookamen) in sight, but beware of the SSM launchers to the northeast. Advance northeast with your armor leading, and after defeating the Nods grouped around the SSM launchers, press on north across the bridge. You'll see the crates you're after among the village houses in the northeastern corner of the battlefield.

Ground Zero: This ones very difficult. First, you have to get to the conference center in the northwestern corner of the map. Go north, then west when you can't go north any further. Get rid of the Nod flame tank guarding the approach to the conference center by making it chase a grenadier the way you came, while you get the delegates. Afterwards, retrace your steps back to the starting point. Deal with that flame tank while bombarding it with grenades while its chasing the delegates. You'll be rewarded with extra units, and rewarded again when you clear the southeastern quarter of the battlefield of Nod troops. Go back to the conference center, and this time, turn south while you reach it; the moment you do, the conference center will be nuked, so hurry. There are sizable forces between you and the embarkation point, which will be marked at this point with a smoke grenade—its fairly far south—but given your reinforcements, you should make it easily. Hint: only one delegate need survive for you to accomplish this mission.

Twist of Fate: This ones difficult, too. Your first base will be nuked the moment you capture the Nod base in the center of the battlefield. From then on, you can only make Nod units—that's the advertised twist in the plot. Capture the small Nod complex in the northwest and build a new refinery nearby. Storming the main Nod base in the southwest is a protracted and messy affair—consider employing the traveling sandbag to block the rapidly-multiplying Nods inside their base, then destroy them in a methodical manner. You may have to attack several times before Nod resistance wears down. The northern entrance to the enemy base is the better choice for the main assault.

Infiltrated: This mission starts badly, but its easy. Just sell your refinery before Nod engineers can get to it, and rebuild it over the spot in the center of your base after you destroy the Nod turret that likes to pop up there. Build several Mammoths before you go after the Nod base in the northeastern corner of the battlefield. You should be able to destroy the Nod Harvester easily time after time, which means quicker victory.

COMMAND & CONQUER

Nod Missions

Bad Neighborhood: Locate your base in the southwestern corner of the battlefield, and sit tight until you've got good base defenses and a Stealth. Reconnoiter the area thoroughly, and recover the money crate north of the GDI base. Again, you should be able to destroy the GDIs Harvesters as soon as they venture out, time and again. This leads to conclusive defeat of GDI field forces, and makes taking the base easy.

Beware of the civilians—they'll actually throw a smoke grenade at your base to mark it for the GDI.

Hostile Takeover: This one features a difficult start and an easy ending. Move west with your starting forces, then turn north at the bridge guarded by a GDI tank. You'll come across a small Nod complex. Sell the communications center, make a few extra bazookas with the money, then sell the Hand of Nod. Get to the Nod base in the northwest before its destroyed completely. Repair it, get rid of the two guard towers to the north that are blocking access to tiberium, and build up a striking force. Retrace your earlier steps, exploring a little further to the east this time—you'll find an enclosure with three transport choppers. Capture them, and use them to ferry bazooka-men and engineers north of your starting point. Land them next to the church (it contains a money crate), then destroy the four guard towers guarding the river crossing to the north. Its possible to destroy three if not all of the towers without losing a single bazooka.

After this is accomplished, mount an infantry assault through the southern entrance to the GDI base and capture the power plants. This will make all advanced guard towers inoperational, which hands you the mission on a platter.

Deceit: This ones very hard. Take your commandos northwest until they come across a horseshoe-shaped enclosure with a money crate. Getting the crate is rewarded with a GDI transport chopper landing nearby. Capture it with your engineer, because its the only way you can get into the Nod base in the southwestern corner of the battlefield.

Build defensive barriers before anything else, and block off all the approaches to your base that are within reach—especially the ones east and immediately northeast. This is a long and difficult mission! Take over the western half of the battlefield first; capture the GDI communications center in the northwest. Try to recover the second money crate near the south-center of the battlefield by timing a transport chopper trip carefully. Then mount an assault on the GDI base along the northern edge of the battlefield. This is a mission in which the computer player has phenomenal production capabilities. You may want to build sandbag barriers throughout the mission, slowly conquering enemy territory in this manner till you're strangling them.

Under Siege: This one's easier. Start by selling unnecessary structures, such as the two southern SAM sites and the silos. Send your Stealth south to the village there (it can slip by the GDI units guarding the northern exit), and locate the church. Destroy it and retrieve the money crate it contains. Use the credits to build an Obelisk and otherwise beef up your defenses. Then nip at the GDI until its provoked into a full-scale attack. Destroy all attacking forces, then take the GDI base in the northwest by blowing a hole in the base wall right next to the western edge of the battlefield.

Death Squad: Use the two Stealths to make an opening in the western base wall, and all other forces to destroy the GDI communications center in the southeastern corner of the enemy base. While GDI is dealing with this, slip the Stealths in and go northeast. You'll find the second communications center further on, and if you position your two Stealths correctly, you'll be able to destroy it while staying out of the range of the nearby advanced guard tower.

The Tiberium Strain: This is one big lesson in the use of flame tanks and chemical troopers. Go south to the edge of the battlefield, destroying all GDI troops along the way, then retrace your steps and head east. The route has many twists and turns, and you must husband your resources. Keep your flame tanks healthy! Turn north after getting to the southeastern corner of the battlefield. The GDI base with three biochemical centers is in the northeastern corner of the battlefield. Remember that destroying any structures other than the research centers loses you the mission!

Cloak and Dagger: Despite appearances, this is one of the easier Nod missions. The MCY is in the GDI base in the northwestern corner of the battlefield. Be careful not to decloak the Stealth within range of any guard

COMMAND & CONQUER

towers, and you'll be fine. After blowing away the fencing around the MCY (you have to destroy it to make space, but don't damage the MCY), blow away the four power plants in the immediate vicinity—you can do so without endangering the Stealth. Build sandbag barriers throughout the GDI base, conquering it bit by bit. Destroy all power plants to start with, and capture buildings you need (weapons factory). Guard against GDI engineer raids from the north (an APC arrives from beyond the map). Finally, destroy the small GDI complex to the east.

Eviction Notice: This is possibly the biggest bloodfest among the Nod Missions. Start by moving your flame tanks north and dealing with a Mammoth just beyond the narrow gorge you'll see immediately. Turn east until you come to a village—the church and a nearby building contain money crates. Locate your base on the site of the village, and do not let the GDI see the construction yard throughout the mission. Otherwise, it will be destroyed. Build barriers to the north and to the west to block off strong GDI attacks, and gradually expand your control over the tiberium-rich eastern half of the battlefield. Finally, mount your big push in the center and storm the GDI base from the south. You may find sandbag barriers and offensive deployment of turrets and Obelisks essential to completing this mission.

CHAPTER 5

HEROES OF MIGHT & MAGIC

Publisher:	New World Computing
Platform:	PC MS-DOS
Release Date:	Fall, 1995
Multiplayer:	Yes
Rating:	

General Overview

Heroes of Might and Magic entered the game arena to compete with an old-time favorite, *Warlords II*. I was skeptical at first—it appeared to be yet another of those "me, too" games. Then I actually played a whole game, and was swept away.

Heroes of Might and Magic is among the best-executed games of all time. The visuals, the music, the sound effects are woven into the game to create a fabric of rare beauty. I thought the visual styling of the game particularly ingenious—the adventure screen reminded me of 15th century Flemish landscapes, and the armies on the battle screen, of medieval frescoes.

The premise of the game is familiar (these days, the premises of all the games seem familiar). Starting out with a single hero and a single castle, you must conquer all and subdue everyone. This goal is achieved through conquering neutral towns, turning them into castles, and then into troop factories by constructing the needed castle buildings. Everything costs gold, and structures almost always require resources—wood, iron ore, mercury, gems, sulphur, crystals. . . . Finding the necessary resources involves fighting your way past wandering armies (they're called wandering, but they are always stationary), some of which are very tough. Wandering armies also stand on guard over the many treasure troves scattered around the game world. Each map features at least a couple of swamps or valleys full of magical artifacts, chests of gold, and resources.

The process of of conquering the countryside, so to speak, is almost a complete game in itself. But each game also features three opponents (less, if you want, in a standard game or any single scenario). The computer-led Warlords in *Heroes* know things you don't, and this knowledge turns each game into a strong challenge.

Heroes offers a choice of a single scenario (standard game) or of a campaign consisting of several scenarios arranged into a sequence. Most 'campaigns' in computer games are designed in a learning curve, but that's not the case here. The only thing that changes in the difficulty is the map—things get more complex as you progress.

The battle system adopted in *Heroes* deserves high praise. At first, I thought it overly simplistic; after a few battles, I realized that the designers of *Heroes* scored a major coup. They came up with a battle system that looks simple and is easy to learn, but at the same time, offers great depth to any-one willing to take a second look. The same battle, with the same forces and the same enemy, may bring a convincing victory (10%–15% casualties), or a crushing defeat—depending on how your troops are arranged or which spell you cast first, and at whom.

Heroes of Might and Magic features four Warlord and troop types. The upcoming *Heroes of Might and Magic II* will increase that number to six, and introduce a larger battle screen. However, you'll find the advice on the pages that follow can be applied to both—the dynamics and the mechanism of the game are basically the same.

While choosing a campaign game means choosing a predetermined diffi-culty level, the standard games or scenarios can be customized to a large extent. You can opt to start the game at one of four difficulty levels, which determines how much gold and resources you start with. Your computer opponents can be anything from dumb to genius-level. This does not affect their production rates, as it does in most other strategic games. The big dif-ference is simply in how much information the computer players have, and how well they think things out. A smart computer opponent will spend more time on calculating its moves, and will only start battles it's sure it can win. However, this won't affect things as greatly as the other difference, the one in knowledge. At the Genius level, the computer players know everything about the map and about you—down to the last soldier in your castle!

Heroes features two separate Halls of Fame—one for campaigns, one for standard games. Your scores will be calculated differently for each. In the Campaign mode, the score simply consists of the number of days it took you to get to the end—the less days, the better. In the standard game mode, scor-ing is somewhat more complicated. It starts at 200 and then drops with each day or turn that you take to win the game. The first 60 days cost 1 point each, the second 60 (days 61-120)—half a point each. Days 121-360 (over two months, but under a year) cost a quarter of a point each, and 0.125 of a point thereafter for the next 360 days. They continue to halve in point value every 360 turns, but that's no longer of any real concern since most games end well before that.

Before your final score is calculated, your base score (the one that's deter-mined by the number of days) is multiplied by the game's final overall diffi-culty level, which is expressed as a percentage. This final difficulty is also influenced by your choice of scenario (some of the maps are more difficult than others). A game world rich in unguarded resources and mines, where all the opponents start far apart, makes for an easier game. The designers of *Heroes* allocated difficulty ratings to each of the maps based on their (and the playtesters') experience.

The winning conditions in all of the standard games are the same: Wipe out everyone else, down to the last hero. (Actually, it's enough to capture your last opponent's last castle/town, and then ensure they remain without one for a week.) In the Campaign mode, things are slightly different. The first 'mission' or scenario involves capturing a town, and the third, finding an artifact before anyone else does. The *Heroes*' campaigns are discussed in detail later on in this chapter.

The multiplayer feature makes *Heroes* all the more valuable. However, I, for one, found the wait between turns too much of a trial. In my personal opinion, the turn-based mode is a real downer in multiplayer games. Simultaneous play, such as offered in *Command & Conquer*, is the option of the future.

Golden Rules

- Explore as much as you can, as bloodlessly as you can. The smarter the computer opponents, the more they know about the game world—and that's their only advantage. You even the odds by exploring early on.

- Always choose to fight the other Warlords instead of wandering armies, no matter what the prize. By the same token, if you have the choice, always capture an enemy Warlord's town instead of a neutral one. Time your moves. Sometimes it's possible to easily acquire a freshly-built castle instead of a town.

- In the first stage of the game, aggressively acquire as much gold and resources as you can. Forget about the artifacts you have to fight for; keep increasing your holdings and income as a top priority throughout the game. The artifacts are there to help you defeat the enemy—they are not an end in themselves.

Keep attacking and defeating the enemy heroes. The battlefield is where human intelligence easily triumphs over the computer. You can lessen the impact the computer's greater smarts have on the game by waging a merciless war of attrition.

Remember that some campaign games have different priorities. The first mission involves capturing a town; do it and you've won, so don't bother about the other Warlords. The third one involves finding an artifact before anyone else, so concentrate on that. The final, King of the Hill mission in the Campaign game is easier (or less impossible) to accomplish if you concentrate on defense and capturing the Dragon Citadel instead of rubbing out all opposition. Otherwise, all *Heroes* games consist of wiping out everybody else.

Take every opportunity to boost your army strength. The game world features troops that can be hired—rogues, nomads, and genies. All are useful, particularly in the opening stages of the game, but watch morale. Mixing troop types can have bad consequences.

Know your priorities. Secure all needed resources, build up your castle, hire troops and heroes, expand your empire. The Sorceress, in particular, has to acquire mercury in quantity, Warlock needs sulphur, and both need gems. Humans and Barbarians need crystals. All of the above is in addition to exacting ore and wood requirements.

Study spells and use them wisely—they can win you many a difficult battle. Make a Mage's Guild a first-week priority in all your castles, not just ones belonging to a Warlock or a Sorceress. Increase guild levels at every opportunity—you'll also increase your castle ballista's attack strength. The most deadly spell in my opinion? "Teleport."

Remember to click on the Mage's Guild to renew the spells for a hero that has not moved out of the castle after a defensive battle; they won't be renewed otherwise! However, heroes that enter a castle following a field battle have their spells automatically renewed.

Winning Strategies & Options

The winning strategy in *Heroes* differs with the difficulty level you've chosen for yourself. If you're playing at Expert, for instance, your priority is to secure the resources and cash needed for troop buildup. At the Easy level, this can wait a while, and you often end up with enough resources for your immediate needs as you explore the map.

Almost all of the strategies discussed below were developed while playing *Heroes* at the Hard and Smart settings for human and computer players respectively. Some were played at Expert/Smart and Expert/Genius. As a result, I would recommend playing at the Expert/Genius level only in two instances: when you choose one of the easy maps, such as Claw or Squirrel Lake, or when you know a particular map so well, you know where everything is without even looking. The locations of the castles, towns, and mines on each newly-generated map stay the same, although their type may vary. Games played at Hard and Smart reward you with a high score, but present a strong challenge. If you want to go down a notch, give yourself better starting resources and gold instead of switching the computer players to Average.

Unless you've chosen the King of the Hill option (which has the computer players united against you) do not set the computer players' intelligence to different standards. If one computer player is weaker than the others, there's a strong chance he'll be vanquished early. This usually means another computer player gets very strong, for you rarely get to do the vanquishing.

The final choice you can make is the starting castle type. Although you are given a castle at random at the start of every standard game or scenario, *Heroes* restarts quickly, and it usually does not take more than a minute to be given the starting castle (and thus troop type) of your choice.

Towns, Troops, and Heroes

Someone's food is another's poison, and a troop type you hate may be your friend's favorite. It's hard to say one troop type is better than another in objective terms, so what follows is simply a rundown on each, with an indication of my own preferences wherever I felt they might be relevant.

Things are slightly different with the heroes of *Heroes*. Heroes of a given type (Knight, Barbarian, etc.) each come with certain powers. The Barbarian is perhaps the best of them all, with the Knight coming a close second. All are discussed in detail further on.

HEROES

The two best and versatile hero types are the Knight and the Barbarian, the Barbarian being, in my opinion, slightly better. The Warlock and the Sorceress are the lesser choices—although they do come into their own late in the game, when spells such as "Teleport," "Fireball," and "Lightning" become available with the development of your Mage's Guild.

All heroes come with a handful experience points (60 or so). Warlocks and Sorceresses also come with gratis spell books. Later on in the game, you may pick up an experienced hero who has just lost a battle, from the hero pool. Occasionally, you can get lucky and get a hero with a loaded spell book in addition to several thousand experience points, and sometimes (seldom!), the newly-hired hero carries an artifact.

- **Knight** heroes come with a bonus of +1 attack and +2 defense, which subsequently improves with experience. They are predictably good at defending your castles, and also perform well in the aggressive role. I favor combining them with Barbarian troops, which are good offensively but have weak defenses. The Knight's special bonus of +1 morale makes this hero particularly useful when combining troop types within a single army.

- **Barbarian** heroes come with +2 attack and +1 defense. They are invaluable for their speed. They lose no movement points in bad terrain—and *Heroes* features plenty of bad terrain. A Barbarian equipped with the Compass of Mobility is the fastest thing on four legs! I favor putting Barbarian troops in charge of human or plains-type troops. Their offensive bonus boosts the rather weak attack strengths of the human troops, and the extra defense bonus makes them still harder to kill.

- **Warlock** heroes come without attack or defense bonuses; they have increased spell power and knowledge instead—2 knowledge, 3 power. Presumably blessed with better eyesight, Warlocks have a superior scouting range, which is very useful for discovering what lies behind a range of mountains, for example.

Sorceress heroines, like Warlocks, have no attack or defense bonuses, but increased spell knowledge and power—3 knowledge, 2 power. A Sorceress aboard a ship can travel twice as far as other heroes, and this seafaring ability makes her a useful marine in maps that feature several land masses or islands.

The real choice you'll be making is between combat and spellcasting ability. For much of the game, Knights and Barbarians are more useful, since they provide your forces with a combat edge, especially against the wandering armies. However, if you take the trouble to carefully train a Sorceress or a Warlock from the early moments, you'll find those heroes very useful when you acquire "Lightning," "Fireball," "Meteor Shower," or any spell that inflicts direct damage on enemy troops in proportion to the casting hero's spell power.

Experience: The Making of a Superhero

Heroes vastly improve with experience. Advancing a level means an increase in their attack/defense bonuses or spell knowledge/power. Heroes are always most likely to improve in the area where their original talent lies. Thus, a Knight is most likely to improve in defense, a Barbarian, in attack, a Warlock, in spell power, and a Sorceress, in spell knowledge. However, the probabilities vary from level to level. The first 'promotion'—to Level 2—emphasizes the hero's natural talent, as outlined above. At Level 3, a hero is most likely to improve in his/her *complementary* talent (attack for the Knight, defense for Barbarians, spell knowledge for Warlocks, spell power for Sorceresses). Level 4 emphasizes the natural talent again. Level 5 and multiples (Level 10, 15, and so on) brings an equally big chance of improving either of a hero's primary talents (combat skills or spellcasting skills). The Knight is an important exception—at Level 5 and multiples thereof, the Knight has an equal chance (25%) of improving in any one of the four areas: defense, attack, spell power, and spell knowledge. Thus, overall, the Knight has the best chance of becoming a truly well-rounded hero through experience.

Of the four hero types, the Barbarian is the least likely to improve in spellcasting skills. His biggest chance is 10% at every fifth level. The Warlock and the Sorceress have the biggest chance of improving their combat abilities at Level 10 and multiples (20%), and between Levels 6–9, 16–19, etc. (10%). Otherwise, the Barbarian, Warlord, and Sorceress have just a 5% chance of improving in spellcasting skills and combat skills respectively.

Experience can be acquired in three ways. The first is through combat. A hero that wins a battle is automatically awarded experience points totalling the number of hit points destroyed. Defeating a hero or capturing a town or a castle brings a bonus of 500 experience points in addition to the hit-point total.

The second way of acquiring experience is pretty unspectacular. Each time a hero visits a temple for the first time, he/she gets 1,000 experience points. Subsequent visits to the same temple do not bring anything, so you may want to make a note who has visited which temple, or institute a routine where every new hero makes a round of the easily accessible temples (the Claw is a a perfect example of a game where this routine works well). Your standard hero itinerary can also include shrines (where a hero learns new spells), faerie rings, fountains, statues, and other destinations that improve the hero's performance in combat.

The third way to acquire experience is very true to life—your hero gets it through spending money. Every time a hero comes across a treasure chest, he has a choice of keeping it or distributing it to the peasants in exchange for experience points. (There are always 500 experience points less than there are gold pieces (1,000 gold equals 500 experience).

Some players value experience over money. My *personal* experience has been that there never is enough money, perhaps because I played all the games at Hard or Expert levels. Spending tens of thousands of pieces of gold every turn is not a problem when you've got many castles capable of producing expensive troop types. In the beginning, of course, you can use *every* penny you can get, provided you chose to play above the Easy level. I do choose experience over gold only if both of those circumstances occur at the same time—where I've got tons of money, and the newly gained experience gets the hero up to an important new level. However, the only times when I'm likely to have a surplus of money is when I'm incapable of building advanced castle buildings for lack of the special resources (gems, sulphur, mercury, crystals) that they require. In other words, the only times I've got extra money lying around are the times when something's seriously wrong, and even then, it's often wiser to hire an extra hero and send him off to look for the missing mines/resources.

Outfitting Your Hero

No hero should ever be without a fairly full spell book. That's requirement number one. Don't forget to buy one for your Knight/Barbarian heroes! It's easy to do so, as I found out on numerous occasions, and the best policy is not to hire a hero unless you have the money for both him and the spell book.

I concentrate on improving my Knight and Barbarian heroes before I do anything with a Warlock or a Sorceress. I like well-rounded heroes, so I always aim at improving the weaknesses in the first place. Thus, heroes with superior attack strength are given artifacts boosting defense, or put in charge of troop types that have strong defense. Heroes with better defensive strength are put in charge of troops that are strong on the offense, and given artifacts that increase attack strength. I distribute spell power and knowledge-enhancing artifacts to the heroes who need them most.

However, I must admit that I can see how cultivating a Warlord or a Sorceress to a high experience level, and then outfitting them with all the artifacts possible, could result in an invincible superhero. If you have the patience, you should try that approach, for it's potentially very rewarding. I must admit, I prefer creating superheroes out of Barbarians more than any other type of hero. Their ease of movement is the decisive factor in their favor.

Note that you will always have the choice—to create one superhero, or create several decent heroes. I always opt for the latter, and circumstances invariably conspire to elevate one of the decent heroes to a superhero level of experience. Quite often, I end up with two superheroes instead of one, which proves to me the superiority of this approach.

Towns and Troop Types

There are four types of towns, and subsequently, of castles and troops. (Just to remind you—an investment of 20 wood, 20 ore, and 5,000 gold turns any town into a castle.) There are some far-reaching differences between the various castle types, as explained below:

Farm towns evolve into Knights' castles and produce human troops. The building costs of the five troop-producing structures (the Thatched Hut is always there for free) total 13,000 gold, 30 wood, 35 ore, and 20 crystals (required for the Cathedral only). Farm or Knights' castles (they're referred to both ways in the manual) are pretty easy to build up, and since the human troops they produce are both good and cheap, they are the safest choice. The strong defensive abilities of human troops (perhaps reinforced by a Knight in charge) make holding onto a Knight's castle relatively easy. If you have a straight choice (where other considerations such as location aren't really important) between conquering a farm town/farm castle or one of another ilk, go for the farm town.

The requirement for the ore and the wood needed to build up a Knight's castle is relatively easy to fulfill. It's possible to construct all the possible structures without ever owning any mines, just through collecting resources, although it's hardly the recommended course. (At any rate, you always have more than one castle in a winning game.)

Plains towns evolve into plains or Barbarian castles. The total cost of all troop-producing structures equals 12,800 gold, 15 wood, 50 ore, and 20 crystals (needed for the Cyclops' Pyramid). furthermore, each Cyclops costs one crystal in addition to the sizeable amount of cash.

Barbarian castles can be a bit tricky to build up beyond a certain point because of the high ore requirement. If you only have one ore mine, it may be a very long wait before you can build both the Troll-producing Bridge and the Pyramid, which call for a total of 40 ore! Since the Trolls and the Cyclops constitute the best Barbarian troops, and are necessary to winning any game of *Heroes*, this means you must put a very high priority on securing a good supply of ore early on, and a steady supply of crystals later on in the game.

Forest towns turn into forest or Sorceress castles. The troop-producing structures cost a grand total of 18,000 gold, 15 wood, 40 ore, 10 gems, and 30 mercury. As is immediately obvious, selecting a Sorceress castle for your starting point puts a lot of financial strain on your (capable) shoulders. You'll have to have those heroes buzzing to and fro like nobody's business just to acquire all the resources you need. However, the forest-type troops are probably the best single troop type in the game, so acquiring a Sorceress castle is a fortunate development. Just be prepared for the cost and the trouble involved in putting up all the castle structures, and then make sure you've got enough gold to hire all those great troops.

Mountain towns turn into mountain or Warlock castles. The total cost of building all the troop-producing structures is a whopping 25,000 gold, 40 ore, 30 sulphur, and 10 gems. The troops aren't the cheapest, either, so if you're a Warlock, make sure you're a rich Warlock. The rewards of owning a mountain castle are considerable, however. You get no less than three flying units, and this trio includes two relatively decent and inexpensive types (Gargoyles, Griffins), as well as the most powerful troop type in the game: the Dragon.

If you choose to start the game with a Warlock castle, you must secure a steady supply of sulphur and ore as quickly as you can. In addition, early acquisition of other sources of income (towns, gold mines) becomes a very high priority. Finally, mountain castles become relatively easy to defend once you've built a Swamp—the hydra is a tough unit that can outlast many attackers, allowing the garrison's ballista to do its lethal job.

Similarly, there are deep-reaching differences between the various troop types. While you can combine troops of many types into a single army, such combinations can prove counterproductive because of the loss in morale. A Knight hero, preferably equipped with a morale-raising order or two, is the only leader capable of effectively leading a mixed army. Note that mixed armies perform better in castle defense than in the field. The presence of a Tavern helps raise morale.

As a rule, you'll want to form strong and homogeneous armies, both for reasons of morale and ease of assembly. Therefore, take the time to read the brief descriptions below, then check out in practice which troop type best suits your style.

Knights or human troops are the easiest to both make and lead in battle. They are very strong on the defense, and have good attack strengths. In addition, all human troops are relatively inexpensive, and do not demand any special resources to make.

Peasants are the cheapest unit in the game. Some will also say they're most useless one. Pitiably weak on attack and defense, and with just a single hit point, the Peasant is not well suited to become the spearhead of your army. Still, Peasants have their uses. First of all, you can acquire a lot of them for free from the huts scattered throughout every game world. Secondly, Peasants cost just 20 gold each. This means you can easily assemble a couple of hundred, and a couple of hundred Peasants can inflict considerable damage. The problem lies in protecting them from a preemptive strike by the enemy—they are very vulnerable. Put them next to Archers and other ranged-attack troops to provide close protection. That's where they work best. If you cast "Haste," your Peasants can rush across the battlefield like a bunch of budding sprinters, and pitchfork a not-too-strong enemy into extinction. They rarely last for more than a couple of turns when in combat, even if you cast "Protection."

Archers are the best of cheap ranged-attack troops. Their attack strength of 5 is better than that of the Elves or the Orcs. However, since the computer player always targets ranged-attack troops before anything else, your Archers are often reduced to the role of cannon fodder. Use "Protection" to make them last as long as possible. Since they are ranked as "slow" troops, you won't get to move them until after the slo-mo Peasants! Archers work well when safe behind castle walls, but they must be sufficiently numerous to survive a couple of enemy attacks and still retain some hitting power.

Archers are a lifesaver early on in the game, when a pack of slow troops such as Peasants, Dwarves, or Ogres often blocks you from a mine, from resources, or simply from a pass leading to unexplored territory. Just keep them firing arrows at the enemy troops while carefully assigning target priorities, and no slow troop will ever reach them and engage them hand-to-hand. However, don't enter battles with Archers alone. Always bring along a protective screen in the form of another troop type, even if it's only Peasants.

Pikemen are cheap troops with a fairly poor attack (5), but excellent defense (9), which helps compensate for their limited hit points (15). They come in pretty handy in the opening stages of the game since they cost just 200 gold each. They are the natural choice when it comes to garrisoning your castle with a number of troops, and perform adequately on the offense thanks to their medium speed. A Barbarian hero with good offensive ability can turn a Pikeman into a deadly killer!

Swordsmen are, to my eye, the most solid troop type in *Heroes*. They're inexpensive, have good hit point total (25), and are good both in attack and on the defense (7 and 9, respectively). Employ them as the core force of your early armies and the standard foot-soldier type in later, better ones. They are predictably good in castle defense, and make a dangerous foe even when they're not led by an enemy hero, but simply constitute a wandering army. Make sure you have the muscle to take them on!

Cavalry is the second best human troop type after Paladins. Unfortunately, the 20 wood required to build a jousting arena is often needed to turn a freshly-conquered town into a castle. You reach the stage when you can build one at about the same time as you conquer your first town, so this dilemma is quite frequent. My advice is to build the jousting arena first. Cavalry is a great unit, faster than Swordsmen or Pikemen, and can reach mounted or four-legged troops across the battlefield in a single turn. Its only drawbacks are the relatively weak hit points (30), but at 300 gold a throw, it's still a good deal.

Paladins are the ultimate human troop type. As fast as Cavalry, they also get to attack twice every turn. Their attack/defense strengths are an impressive 11/12. Again, the main drawback is the low number of hit points—just 50. Still, Paladins are cheap at 600 gold each, and a dozen of them can turn your human army into an unbeatable force. Make sure you get your money's worth out of them by using them in attack rather than in defense (although a few Paladins always do wonders for castle defense).

When fighting Paladins, don't let them execute that double attack often. Once you engage them, engage them from as many directions with as many troops as you can. You can't count on hurting them badly with ranged attacks because of their speed and high defense, so make sure you have the muscle before you set out after any artifacts guarded by Paladins.

Barbarian Troop Types

Barbarian troops are perhaps the best troop type for the experienced player. They're cheap and easy to acquire, which makes building up a strong army a snap.

Goblins are the Barbarian equivalent of Peasants, only much better (and twice as expensive). Medium speed, strength 3 attack, and 3 hit points make them much more versatile than their human counterparts, and like them, they are freely available from the huts present in every game world. Led by a Knight, Goblins become quite a force thanks to the instant tripling of their weak defense (from 1 to at least 3). Use them as a strike force that eliminates threats to your ranged troops, or in a supporting offensive role. Their vulnerability makes Goblins a poor choice as a troop carrying out the main attack.

Wandering armies composed of Goblins demand more careful handling than those of Peasants. Medium speed means Goblins can close the distance quite fast!

Orcs are the Barbarian archers. They have the same number of hit points (10), better defense (4), but worse attack (3 instead of 5). Just like Archers, they need to be present in your army in numbers to be of any real significance. The initial handful of Orcs in the retinue of a Barbarian hero isn't enough.

Like Archers, Orcs are a slow troop, which means they only get to fire at the very end. Use "Protection" (it increases their defense to a respectable 7) and curse on the enemy ranged-attack troops to make your Orcs survive as long as possible.

Many wandering armies are composed of Orcs. The procedure for dealing with them is laid out further on in this chapter.

Wolves are among my favorite troop types. Fast speed, 6 attack, and 2 attacks per turn make them a potentially devastating weapon when used with care. The care caveat is necessary since Wolves have a pretty weak defense (2). Use a Knight hero to boost this rating and further improve their impressive attack. The 20 hit points aren't enough to limit losses in the event of an enemy counterstrike, so make sure your Wolves always attack first!

Wandering armies composed of Wolves are dangerous opponents. You should have along at least two stalwart troop types that can take punishment, plus at least one other such as Goblins or Peasants. It bears to remember Wolves eat Peasants alive. You must make sure your Peasants have the strength to wipe out the entire group of Wolves they're targeting with their attack. Otherwise, the retaliatory Wolf attack will decimate them.

Ogres are the simplest Barbarian troop type that has a respectable defense (5) coupled with high hit points (40). Unfortunately, they're agonizingly slow, and so can only be effectively used defending ranged-attack troops such as Orcs. Use them for counterattacks, or cast "Haste" or "Teleport" to make full use of their impressive strength 9 attack.

Ogres are a feature of all my Barbarian castle garrisons; their staying power makes them invaluable in that role. Like other tough but slow troops, they're often the last troop to remain on the battlefield after a particularly bloody encounter, and that fact best illustrates their worth. They can't get into combat quickly, but have staying power.

Wandering armies composed of Ogres aren't that much of a danger once you include enough ranged-attack troops in your lineup. Their glacial speed means you can thin their ranks out with arrows and rocks before they get anywhere near.

Trolls are among the best ranged-attack troops in the entire game. Strong attack (10), and medium speed mean they start throwing their boulders around relatively early in the battle, and with good effect. Their weak point is traditionally Barbarian—only 5 defense. However, Trolls have 40 hit points. What's more, a damaged Troll fully regenerates between turns. Make a Troll Bridge a high priority on your building list!

Wandering armies composed of Trolls aren't as dangerous as it may seem because they never number very many. Use flying troops or fast troops such as Wolves or Cavalry to break the Trolls' ranged attacks. Remember that any Trolls you want to kill have to be killed before the turn ends; otherwise, they return in full health! If the only troop of yours that can engage the Trolls is a half-dozen Archers, they're better off shooting at a different target—one that they can actually harm.

Trolls are particularly useful in castle sieges. A dozen or two makes the battle go much smoother and faster! Remember to protect them from the castle's ballista with spells; they're likely to be its first target.

Cyclops are the ultimate Barbarian unit. They cost 750 gold and 1 crystal each, and the Pyramid that provides them requires 20 crystals. Yes, you got it, a crystal mine is a necessity! Medium speed, 80 hit points, and a 20% chance of paralyzing enemy troops in the aftermath of an attack make Cyclops a good troop type to have and a lethal opponent. Their defense rating is as high as that of good human troops (9), and their strength 12 attack has a range of two spaces! Take full advantage of this by planning accordingly.

Once you've acquired the spell "Teleport," Cyclops become a great troop to use during castle sieges, where the defenders are often hopelessly crowded. A single space within the castle walls won't allow a Phoenix or a Dragon to do their hot, dirty work, but a Cyclops can be teleported in there with ease.

Fortunately, Cyclops wandering armies tend to be on the weak side. A strong ranged attack followed by a charge from fast troops is the best way to start the proceedings. Usually, the prize is well worth the required effort—Cyclops armies guard fairly substantial treasure troves.

Sorceress Troop Types

Sorceress troops are truly exceptional. In my opinion, they're simply the best in the game. Unfortunately, they're fairly troublesome to acquire (you won't get beyond Dwarves and Elven Archers without ore and mercury), and are fairly expensive.

Sprites appear to be a very flimsy (2 hit points, 2 defense) and expensive (50) form of flying Peasant, or rather Goblin. In reality, they can be very useful when employed in large numbers. Their ability to fly anywhere on the battlefield is invaluable, particularly since it's coupled with a strength 4 attack and the fact that the target cannot retaliate. Sprites are great for tackling large wandering armies composed of weaker ranged-attack troops (Orcs, Archers), and can be very useful in castle sieges and castle defense. Conserve their numbers by attacking and then withdrawing them to a safe, cool place. Less subtle tactics will result in your losing the entire Sprite force time and again, which means their numbers will never grow large. And as mentioned, a large (50+) group of Sprites can be positively lethal.

Dwarves are the the grunts of the forest army. Cheap (just 200 gold!) and slow, they have respectable hit points (20) and a decent attack and defense (6 and 5, respectively). They usually form the bulk of the garrison in a Sorceress' castle, and are good to take along on offensive forays because of their staying power. Like Ogres, Dwarves often are the last troop type to be left standing on a bloody battlefield, both for reasons of slow speed and inherent toughness.

Dwarves have a very useful special ability: They have a 20% chance of resisting any enemy spell aimed at them. However, any Dwarf wandering armies are generally easy meat. Just keep your cool and the arrows flying, and all the Dwarves will die before they can reach your Archers.

Elves are the Sorceress' take on Archers. They have more hit points (15 instead of 10), and fire two arrows per turn in combat. However, they are slightly weaker on the attack and identical to the human Archers in all other respects except price; at 250 gold a head, they're almost twice as expensive. Given their low growth rate, however, the price is not a problem.

Elves aren't as important in the Sorceress' lineup as they might be because Druids are a far better troop type, and are available relatively early. However, I always hire all the Elves I can, since ranged-attack troops are always in short supply. The 15 hit points do provide the Elves with a slightly longer lifespan, as you'll find out when tackling one of the Elf wandering armies. The best way to deal with Elves when they're on the other side is to tie them by attacking them with flying troops. Apart from losing half their attack strength when engaged in hand-to-hand combat, they also lose the extra attack per turn.

Druids are the ultimate ranged-attack troop type. They're fast, so they get their shots off before anyone else when on the attacking side. A strength 7 attack and the ability to inflict up to 8 points of damage make Druids as deadly as the Trolls. They're easier to kill, of course (25 hit points compared with the Trolls' 40), but are just as good on the defense, and cost significantly less—just 350 gold. The all-important thing, especially in big battles, is that the Druids shoot first—and when their defense is boosted by a hero with a good defense bonus, they can become very dangerous indeed.

Steer clear of Druid wandering armies until you have clear superiority, and even then, be prepared for the loss of all your ranged-attack troops (the Druids will target them first). The best solution? Tie them down with flying troops strong on the defense (Gargoyles are ideal), and move up to them as fast as you can.

Unicorns are among my favorite troop types. Their attack/defense stats are identical to human cavalry—10 attack, 9 defense. However, they have more hit points (40), and can be absolutely deadly (in addition to being able to inflict up to a whopping 14 points of damage, Unicorns have a 20% chance of blinding the enemy with every attack). They may cost 500 gold each, but they're worth every penny!

Wandering armies of Unicorns are fairly dangerous. Fortunately, they're almost always pretty limited in numbers. Bring lots of ranged-attack troops with you, and at least two troop types that can take damage and mete it out, too.

Phoenixes are the ultimate Sorceress troop type. They're fast, they fly, and their blistering strength 12 attack has a range of two spaces. Given their strength 10 defense, Phoenixes aren't easy to destroy, either.

Getting a Sorceress' castle to the Phoenix stage isn't easy, though. You have to construct Stonehenge (Druids) and Fenced Meadow (Unicorns) first, and each of these makes its own special demands— 10 mercury, then 10 gems in addition to a lot of cash. Both Druids and Unicorns aren't cheap, and so you may find yourself constantly short of the 10,000 gold needed to build a Red Tower (to say nothing of the ore and mercury requirements). In addition, each Phoenix costs you mercury in addition to 1,500 gold.

Are Phoenixes worth the trouble? I've completed many games of *Heroes* where I didn't build a single Phoenix or even a Red Tower at any of my forest castles. However, if a game goes on beyond a hundred and twenty turns or so (eight weeks to the *cognoscenti*), you should look into the Red Tower business, because any longer game sees the computer opponents filling their armies with top-notch troops. The Phoenixes prove to be very useful then. They provide the punch you need to knock out a stronger enemy.

Wandering armies of Phoenixes are rare, and if they're guarding something, you can bet your nelly it's something really worth fighting for. Approach them with care and caution, and don't forget to disperse your troops in a manner that will minimize the damage from the Phoenixes' two-space attacks.

HEROES OF MIGHT & MAGIC

Warlock Troop Types

Warlock armies are the most unusual in the game. For example, three out of the six troop types can fly, but only one has classic ranged-attack capability (the Centaur), and then, is next to useless in battle. All this makes for interesting battle tactics!

Centaurs are a sort of a ranged-attack Peasant. Their strength 1 defense makes them early casualties in any battle in spite of their 5 hit points. Low attack strength (3) and minimal damage (1–2) mean that you have to have lots of Centaurs in an army if you want them to truly make an effect, and not just serve as a target for enemy ranged-attack troops. They're not overly expensive (60 gold), but since they get targeted first in almost every battle, it's pretty hard to accumulate a substantial number.

Wandering armies composed of Centaurs are a cinch. Usually, you need to use less caution than when fighting any other ranged-attack troop type. Since Centaurs are a four-legged unit, they occupy two spaces on the battle screen, which means your fast troops can cross the battlefield and attack them within a single turn.

Gargoyles are among the best value-for-money troops in the game. They're fast, they fly, and their 15 hit points hide behind a strength 7 defense—not bad for a unit that becomes available very early in the game. Their main drawback is the weak attack strength (4) and limited damage (2–3). Because of that, don't count on your Gargoyles to take the role of killer first-strike troops; they work very well as spoilers, but won't wipe out any but the weakest of enemy troop types.

Wandering armies composed of Gargoyles are relatively easy to deal with. Just make sure the units you send in have good attack and defense, as the Gargoyles will attack almost immediately (they're fast, remember?).

Griffins are a fire-breathing variation of Gargoyles. Basically, they're a notch better in almost every area—more hit points (25), better attack (6), more damage (3–5)—except defense, where they have a 6 to the Gargoyles' 7. However, Griffins are unique in that they enjoy unlimited retaliation capability. They can retaliate against every enemy unit that attacks them in a given turn. They're far from tough. I found the best way to use them was in large packs bolstered by a hero's defense bonus. Just fly the Griffins right into the middle of the enemy lineup, and watch them weaken all neighboring troop types by retaliating each time they're attacked!

Despite all their talents, Griffins don't last long in combat. This fact is helpful when planning assaults on wandering Griffin armies. Just make sure your army includes at least one tough troop type, capable of surviving multiple attacks per turn for several turns.

Minotaurs are among my favorite units. Good attack and defense (9 and 8 respectively), 35 hit points, medium speed, and the capability to inflict up to 10 points of damage all add up to one powerful unit. Led by a good hero, Minotaurs are powerful enough to form the spearhead of your army, even though they can be acquired relatively early on. Their price isn't bad either; at 400 gold each, they're not much more than Cavalry or Ogres.

The only problem you may have with getting Minotaurs is the gem requirement for the Minotaur Maze. You should make the Maze a priority, however, because Minotaurs provide a much-needed hard-hitting element to Warlord armies. After you engage the enemy with Gargoyles and Griffins, you need some kind of troop to come up with the second, knockout punch. The medium speed means Minotaurs cannot cross the battlefield very quickly, but they can still get there in time to prevent your flying troops from getting swamped.

Wandering armies of Minotaurs require the same degree of caution as Cavalries. While they are slower, they have more hit points.

Hydras are lethal—75 hit points coupled with the ability to hit all adjacent enemy troops, plus the fact the enemy cannot retaliate against attack, make the Hydra the cornerstone of castle defense. It's often the last troop left standing on the battlefield. Its strength 8 attack and strength 9 defense make it comparable with tough human troops, except it has more hit points.

The Hydra's big weakness is its low speed. Use "Haste" or "Teleport" to employ your Hydras to their full potential. If attacked by Hydras, try to outlast them; attack them with one troop at a time while peppering them with arrows and rocks. When defending against Hydras in a castle, don't engage them; keep running away and let the castle ballista do the dirty work. All this will take place after other enemy troops are dead—the hydras last a long, long time. . . .

Be very careful when attacking wandering armies of Hydras. They often guard gold mines (guaranteed if the gold mine is in a swamp) and other very desirable objects, so you'll go after them sooner or later regardless of their strength. Include plenty of ranged-attack troops in your army!

 Dragons are the game's most powerful unit—200 hit points, flying ability, and a two-space, strength 12 attack (and strength 12 defense) make the dragon a very formidable opponent. Throw in a total immunity to spells of any kind, and you've got one fearsome creature.

In order to get Dragons, however, you must spend quite a bit of cash and resources. The Dragon Tower costs 15,000 gold plus plenty of sulphur and ore. In addition, each dragon sets you back by 3,000 gold and 1 sulphur. As the game wears on, you'll have no choice, because after a hundred and twenty days or so, one of the computer players is almost guaranteed to get the Dragon Tower. Intense pressure may prevent him/her from hiring any dragons—or it may not.

Dragons are always the guardians of the Dragon Citadel, which is a feature in many maps, and whose capture provides you with an extra 1,000 gold a day. Unless you have troops coming out of your ears, leave the Citadel alone; the defending Dragons number six to nine, and can easily overwhelm a medium-sized army. Tackling Dragons guarding a treasure trove is another matter. The treasure chests you gain will probably make up for most of your losses, and there is other stuff to be gained, too—artifacts, resources, etc.

It's useless to count on ranged-attack troops when fighting Dragons. The only solution is to include several tough troop types of medium speed or better. Slow speed means high probability the Dragons can kill two groups of yours with one attack.

The Ultimate Soldier

So, what's the best troop type? Given all the options, my personal preference is for the Phoenix.

Phoenixes have half the hit points of Dragons, but they cost half as much, which means you can build two Phoenixes for every Dragon. They are just as good in attack and do only slightly less damage, so your two Phoenixes will actually do more harm than a single Dragon. The slightly weaker defense (10 to Dragon's 12) is not a serious drawback. Being the cunning commander, you will, of course, anticipate losses and bolster precious troops like Phoenixes with heroes strong on the defense.

The only truly great advantage the Dragon enjoys is the immunity to magic. However, that is a sword that cuts both ways since you cannot cast any positive, performance-enhancing spells on it, either. By contrast, increasing the Phoenix's defense is as simple as casting "Protection."

First Steps

Each game of *Heroes* falls into two distinct stages. In the first stage, it's a race to acquire all the resources and gold needed for expansion. The second stage begins the moment you fight your first battle against an enemy hero. From then onwards, you'll face a varied and seemingly endless procession of enemy heroes bent upon capturing your castles. If you set the computer opponents to Smart or Genius, this second, difficult stage of a *Heroes* game can start disconcertingly early, well before you're ready.

You begin each game of *Heroes* in an identical manner, regardless of whether you've chosen to play a standard game or a campaign. A single hero corresponding to your castle type sits astride a horse at the castle gate, and where you then send him/her is of great importance.

Before sending your hero off, however, you should always enter your castle and build a structure (that has to wait at the Expert level, where you start with no money and no resources). You can only build one structure per castle, per day, and quick buildup in the early days is the best course of action.

FIRST BUILDINGS

The jury's still out on whether it's better to kick off the construction work by building a Mage's Guild or a troop-producing improvement. I'd definitely recommend building the Mage's Guild first if you started the game as a Warlock or Sorceress. A Sorceress or a Warlock with an empty spell book is nothing more than an icon on the computer screen; they don't benefit your army in any way, other than allowing it to leave the castle.

If you started the game with a Knight or Barbarian castle, it's usually better to start off by building something that will yield extra troops. I favor structures that produce ranged-attack troops, as the addition of a few Archers or Orcs in the opening turns allows you to tackle wandering armies composed of relatively weak troops—Peasants and Goblins for the most part.

Whichever castle you start with, by the end of the first week you should have a couple of troop-producing structures, a Mage's Guild, and a well and/or Tavern. I recommend you always build the Mage's Guild within the first week. The early acquisition of some spells can save you money by saving your troops; a Cursed enemy will inflict lesser losses, and a Protected troop will suffer fewer casualties. Innocent-sounding adventure spells such as "View Mines" can provide you with a vital advantage: As your opponents capture their first mines and the map icons take on their colors, you can approximate the location of their starting castle (it's always nearby), and monitor their progress. Of course, there are the obvious advantages, too (all "View" spells basically tell you where to find something) and ensuring a steady supply of resources necessary for castle buildup is your highest priority.

The choices involved in building structures beyond the first three or four are very straightforward: Build whatever you can afford, as soon as you can. Each building contributes to the damage done by the castle's ballista—that miraculous "Bolt of God" that strikes the troops besieging your castle at the beginning of every turn. It's important to remember that the ballista's attack skill, or strength, is increased with the building of the Mage's Guild, and each extra guild level thereafter.

Do not neglect to build both the Tavern and the Thieves' Guild fairly promptly. The Thieves' Guild provides vital information about wandering armies right away, and the Tavern greatly helps castle defense—you're almost guaranteed a couple of extra attacks provided your garrison doesn't mix too many troop types.

EXPLORING THE MAP

Many players love sending their newly-hired heroes into battle right away. The computer players like doing that, too—even more than humans. I don't. (Does it make me inhuman, subhuman, or any other prefix-human?) I believe in conserving my strength as long as I can, and do all the bloodless exploring possible before getting into any armed tussles. There are exceptions, of course. If there are Peasants guarding a chest of treasure, I'll take them out.

I cast a "View" spell before starting to explore beyond my immediate surroundings. It's a total waste of time to clear a path in one direction through fairly tough wandering armies, and then find out that the resources you require are elsewhere. I concentrate all my troops into a single army under my exploring hero. I've found out it's safe to leave your castle empty for the first few turns (unless you're playing with the computer guys set to Genius level. At the Genius level, anything short of sleeping with a machine gun under your pillow isn't smart). While my first hero is off exploring with his big army, I start acquiring extra heroes. I consider three to be an optimum number for the opening stage of the game when I own one castle, and increase that number by one for each castle I acquire.

By the time I've secured the resources necessary to continue construction work at my castle, I invariably manage to find a neutral town or two, and bump into the first of the enemy heroes. From then onwards, the game takes on a very predatory character. Therefore, it's vital that you concentrate on finding all the resources you need during those few peaceful initial turns.

BUILDING AN EMPIRE

Upon entering the second stage of the game—after contact first with enemy heroes—I suggest you focus on acquiring another town or towns. Conquering towns immediately gives a small boost to your finances (250 gold a day), and, of course, all towns can be turned into castles. However, do not engage in any castle building when there are unhired troops waiting at your first castle. Army first, castle second; that's the firm rule. Remember, the castles are there to provide you with more troops and more cash to hire the extra troops—a castle has no other purpose than to help your war effort. Don't start thinking about castles as city-style centers that should be petted instead of exploited for maximum benefits. The moment there are no troops to be hired and you have what it takes, go ahead and turn a town into a castle.

Concentrate construction expenditures on your first castle for a few turns, following the same pattern as with your first castle. If you happen to conquer a third town in the meantime, hold off with turning it into a third castle until your second one is on solid footing.

At all times, avoid the situation where all your heroes are stuck guarding newly-acquired castles. It's a total waste of the heroes, and if you simply have no other choice, it means you've made some unwise moves in the meantime (don't feel bad—this is a difficult game, and it happens to everyone). I do not guard newly-captured towns at all. Should a computer-led hero capture a town from me, it's always fairly easy to take back, and often, it makes sense to wait until your opponent has shelled out the 5,000 gold, 20 ore and 20 wood needed for a castle before moving in. Freshly-built castles are very vulnerable and not much harder to capture than towns (unless, of course, there is a huge army inside the walls. However, this seldom happens in the opening stages of the game).

Continue making expansion a priority. Keep acquiring all the new towns you can while remembering that it's better still to acquire a town from another player. As a rule, always choose attacking another player over battling a wandering army or the garrison of a neutral town. This game is about vanquishing your opponents! It's a common mistake to get sidetracked into pursuing artifacts with all the necessary military effort, and then find out that your experienced and artifacted hero has but a small army to lead, while the enemy hero that's menacing him is leading half the population of China.

More troops. More heroes. More towns. More castles. More money and resources. More troops. More heroes. These are the priorities, in that order.

What the Computer Thinks

The AI in *Heroes* seems very cunning. In reality, that's because the computer players have something you don't: *information*.

To put it simply, computer players know where stuff is. The higher the intelligence you set them at the start of a standard game, the more they know. At Genius level, they often manage to find the Ultimate Artifact within the first month. Whatever the level, they always know where all the mines are, and which wandering armies will join theirs instead of fighting. You can also expect them to have at least an idea of your garrison strength; if they think they can overwhelm it, they'll try, and at the higher intelligence levels, you'll have to work hard to prove them wrong.

Victory Is Good Administration

Many players, who are initially successful, fumble when they reach the point where they have an empire of some size and stature. This is almost always because of poor administration, and nothing else. If you are a thoughtful Warlord, you'll find that there's always plenty to do, almost every turn. If you aren't, you'll find yourself with a lot of cash, and at a constant loss as to what to do next.

Make it a rule to have an ongoing plan, and stick to it without being inflexible. After adding several castles to your empire, you should immediately begin paving the way for the final victory. In the middle game, this is best achieved by hitting the computer players whenever you can.

Always make it a point to demolish any enemy heroes that dare appear on the map. Go after them mercilessly and hunt them down. If you can't, set an ambush. Build a big army around your best hero in your best castle, then move it out. The computer players will flock to the empty castle like vultures to carrion, and then your superhero can just erase them one by one.

I usually take out an insurance policy when following this course of action. I have a second hero with next to no troops standing relay duty. If my first hero's movement points are exhausted, hero number two can move in, take the army over, and demolish another enemy hero within the same turn.

The Buddy System

I found that the most effective way to conduct an offensive is by using heroes in groups rather than individually.

In the opening stages of the game, this often takes shape as the troops relay. Your exploring hero is usually a few turns away from the castle, battling wandering armies to clear the way to a desired resource. A second hero stands roughly midway between the first hero and the castle. Finally, there's the resident castle hero. The moment fresh troops are available, the resident hero takes them to the second hero, who in turn transfers them to your first, fighting hero. In this way, you can save plenty of valuable time. Of course, if your first, fighting hero has used up his spells, it's best to let the second hero take over the leadership of the army.

Later on, the buddy system is invaluable in deep-probing offensive operations. By using two heroes working in tandem, you can explore a much bigger area much faster, and you also stand a much better chance of winning every battle you choose to fight. Whenever you run into strong opposition, combine the two armies under one hero, sending the other hero home for reinforcements or installing him as resident at a newly-conquered castle (this last course of action is my favorite).

WINNING BATTLES

In the end, the acid test of you as a Warlord comes with battle. The first rule here is very simple: don't get into battles you're not sure you can win. Thieves' Guilds, spells such as "Identify Hero," and your own hard-won experience will help you avoid losing propositions. To help you further, here's a brief explanation of how computer terms for army strength correspond to actual numbers:

- **Few** means five or less.
- **Several** means between five and ten.
- **Pack** means between ten and twenty.
- **Lots** means between 20 and 50.
- **Horde** means between 50 and 100.
- **Zounds!** means over 100.

HEROES OF MIGHT & MAGIC

To start with, make sure your troops are arranged the way you want them. Their position on the battle screen corresponds to their position in the hero's retinue (from left to right). Put ranged-attack troops at the bottom and top (far left and right), slow-moving but strong troops next to them (near left and near right), and the fastest troops in the middle. Remember to make room for exceptions: Hydras often work best in the center because of their ability to strike all adjacent enemy troops.

If you're fighting enemy Archers, Trolls, etc., and have flying troops, consider flying them over to prevent the enemy from executing any ranged attacks. You'll have to compare hit points, attack and defense strengths before reaching a decision here.

Start each battle by clicking on the enemy tent and finding out more about the enemy. Then you should scrutinize each enemy troop in turn. It may turn out that a troop you've been eyeing as a priority target is, in reality, not very dangerous, while something else is.

Anticipate enemy attacks. The computer always picks your ranged-attack troops as the first target. By putting slow but hard-hitting troops next to your Archers/Orcs/Elves/Trolls/Centaurs, you can quickly destroy some of the enemy's best soldiers.

Try to compose each army well, including troop types that help each other. Aim for including ranged-attack, tough (many hit points), and fast (flying) troops in every army you form. You'll find you can do so much more with it on the battlefield.

Finally, you can drastically influence the course of a battle through skillful spellcasting.

Casting Combat Spells

Broadly speaking, combat spells fall into two categories:

- **Spells that you cast on enemy troops:** It's usually best to cast these right at the beginning of your turn.

- **Spells you cast on your own troops:** Usually, it's best to wait with those spells until the troop you want to enchant is ready for its turn. This is because the enemy hero may decide to cast a spell upon the very troop you want to enchant. Your spell will automatically break the enemy enchantment.

Heroes features a number of spells that allow the hero to strike the enemy directly—"Thunderbolt" and "Firebolt" are more common, "Meteor Shower," "Storm," or "Armageddon" are fairly rare. Use "Storm" and "Armageddon" only if you know math—these spells inflict damage on all troops, so make sure your losses aren't greater than the enemy's. Calculate the spell's power (basic power times spell power of the casting hero), and apply the result to each troop in your army to see how it will fare. Of course, if you're losing the fight anyway, "Armageddon" is a good way to make your enemy's victory a Pyrrhic one (Pyrrhus was a Greek general who specialized in winning battles while losing so many soldiers that he lost the war).

Don't underestimate the power of such mundane spells as "Slow." I've won many desperate castle sieges because my surviving Peasants kept running away from the pursuing Hydras, while the castle ballista kept firing.

Finally, never send your hero into battle with an empty spell book. It spells only one thing: disaster!

THE CAMPAIGN GAME

In the Campaign mode, you assume the mantle of one of the four Warlords, and proceed to play through eight missions as that character. Therefore, I suggest you play a couple of standard games first, to see what troop type you really like.

The strategy you follow in a Campaign does not differ appreciably from the ones you can successfully pursue in a Standard game. Nevertheless, as pointed out below, the objectives of some Missions are refreshingly different—no need to bash everyone's head in—and so you may want to adjust your moves accordingly.

Missions 5, 6, and 7 are played out against the opposing warlords on a one-to-one basis. Thus, if you choose Lord Ironfist, you'll find yourself battling the Barbarian Lord Slayer in Mission 5, the Sorceress in Mission 6, and the Warlock in Mission 7. If you're Slayer, then you'll fight Ironfist in Mission 5, the Sorceress in Mission 6, and so on.

HEROES OF MIGHT & MAGIC

The final Mission pits you against all the other Warlords—they unite against you. Good luck—you'll need it. I certainly did, more than once. Here's a brief rundown on the Missions:

Mission 1: You have to capture the town of Gateway, located in the middle of the small island you and the other Warlords are on. Don't battle the other Warlords—sit tight and assemble troops until you can defeat the Gargoyles, the single Dragon, and finally the defenders of Gateway in one quick blitzkrieg. The Mission is accomplished the moment you get to Gateway, which can take anything from a week to three, depending on your skill.

Mission 2: This time, you have to rub out all opposition. Everybody starts on an island of their own. Colonize yours quickly, defeat any armies that land on your shores, then use the ships the enemy heroes came in to go after the other Warlords. You may also use the stone lith for quick transportation between islands, although the results can be somewhat unpredictable. Whichever way you go, don't waste money and wood on building ships. The Knight and the Barbarian tend to do best on this map.

Mission 3: This time, all you have to do is find the artifact—the Eye of Goros. Your mission's over the moment you do, so focus on that. Nevertheless, one good army comes handy in clearing the path for your searching heroes and defeating the enemy heroes that are looking as hard as you—they usually have pretty weak armies.

Mission 4: This is a major bloodfest. You have to eliminate everyone else in a protracted campaign. Concentrate on maximizing your income (capturing and holding onto towns, turning them into castles) and of course securing all the needed resources—don't go hunting artifacts until everything's going well with the conquest. Use a single superhero with a strong army standing outside an empty castle (he can cover two) to lure enemy armies and defeat them. In the meantime, you should continue with your offensive—for maximum effectiveness, pounce on enemy castles with a strong army the moment they are built.

Mission 5: Depending on whom you chose at the start, you get to fight Lord Ironfist or Lord Slayer. In both cases, the other guy occupies the other side of the map, and the two of you are separated by a barrier—a river in the Knight's case, a desert in the Barbarian's. You have to build a strong little empire before you can mount your assault, and in the meantime you'll be confronting a steady stream of enemy heroes rushing to their doom (of course). Stay on the defensive until you maximize your resources and gold, then take the war to the enemy. The Dimension Door spell is very helpful in both cases.

Mission 6: This time, you fight against the Sorceress Lamanda. If you are Lamanda, you fight Lord Slayer.

As mentioned, Lord Slayer resides behind a big desert. Lamanda resides in a castle far away—you have to travel all over the place before you get there, and that travel involves navigating through a forest maze full of strong armies. First, use the only stone lith on your piece of ground to teleport a hero to an island that has a coastal town—you need it to build ships. Then sail north until you find Lamanda's land. It's a slugfest from then onwards.

Mission 7: The last one-on-one mission is against the Warlock (unless you are the Warlock, of course—then it's against Lamanda). This time, you have to negotiate a maze of mountains to face your adversary. You're given a nice little piece of ground to get started— make sure you develop it fully before you get going in earnest, as the Warlock is enormously strong! He'll just sit there and wait, building up armies, while you lose a significant part of your military battling through the maze. Once you clear the way, be prepared— you're up for one tough fight. You cannot hope for victory without using heroes strong in spellcasting!

Mission 8: Since you got this far, everyone's united against you. Fortunately, you do not have to exterminate everyone to win this mission, and with it, the Campaign. You "only" have to conquer the Dragon Citadel, located on an island in the center of the map. This involves battling a lot of Griffins, then quite a lot of Dragons—twenty, to be exact. The Griffins aren't a problem, but they may inflict losses which could prove decisive in your second battle.

Before you can take the Citadel, you have to keep your empire from crumbling in the face of enemy onslaught, and even expand it—you have no hope of becoming sufficiently powerful on the strength and income of a single castle. However, don't even try rubbing everyone out—go for the Citadel. Depending on who you chose to be at the start of the Campaign, you may get to wipe out one of the opposing Warlords in relative ease, but don't let that fool you—the remaining ones are more than your match. Get your act together, and get the Citadel!

Publisher:	Impressions
Platform:	PC MS-DOS
Multiplayer:	Yes
Rating:	🏇🏇🏇 1/2

General Overview

Lords of the Realm is unique in that it is the only truly successful strategy game set in medieval times. It garnered several awards and honorable mentions from computer gaming magazines following its publication.

The premise of the game is somewhat predictable. Starting as a Sheriff of a single county, you must expand your rule until your supremacy is recognized with your being crowned the King of England (or Germany—the CD version of the game offers you that option).

What's not so predictable is the amazing accuracy with which the game's creators have managed to duplicate medieval economics. Your first responsibility is to feed your people, and this is no easy task. Sowing and harvest time means greatly increased demand for field labor. At the same time, there's wood to be gathered, iron to be mined, stone to be quarried, weapons to be built—not to mention actually raising armies from the population of your county or counties. In addition, *Lords* accurately reflects the cost of war in the Middle Ages: A charger (a trained horse of the size and stature needed to carry a man in full armor) costs the equivalent of two villages. While you won't be selling any of your villages to the other nobles in the game, the proportions are there—you can feed several hundred people for a year on what it takes to equip fifty armed men.

In addition to administering your county, *Lords of the Realm* makes you responsible for building its defenses in the shape of castles. The business of castle design is a fascinating mini-game in itself; however, it can be entirely bypassed if you don't feel like doing it—building good castles is not a prerequisite for victory. You'll also deal with itinerant traders, you'll form armies from the troops you've raised, give them their marching orders, and command them in battle. This last function is perhaps best left to the computer; it is also the weakest part of the game. Featuring animated soldiers that execute movement and combat orders, the battle screen in *Lords* is nevertheless quite crude in comparison with those found in more recent releases—including Impressions' own *Caesar II*.

The option to actively lay siege to castles is another feature introduced by *Lords of the Realm*. Like the battle screen, it's only a partial success. It's interesting to organize your army into foragers, sentries, and builders of such siege implements as ladders and catapults. It's exciting to divide your men into groups storming individual stretches of the castle wall, and to time their assaults with a barrage from your catapults and trebuchets. However, it is also made very frustrating by the complex interface, and that you have to wait until the beginning of a new turn to see your army storm the walls.

All these concerns will doubtless be resolved in the inevitable *Lords of the Realm II*. In the meantime, the original *Lords* remains a charming and interesting foray into the world of feudalism. It's a particularly nice game in the multiplayer mode, where the inadequacies of the AI are replaced by human cunning.

Golden Rules

Get your county's economy on a solid footing before attempting any expansion. Make sure everyone's happy and well fed. Acquire a herd of cattle and a flock of sheep as soon as possible. Don't order your serfs to gather wood, mine iron, etc., until you have the food supply situation under complete control.

Keep your taxes at fifteen gold a head. This is low enough to make a county's happiness increase by a heart each turn (given normal food rations). Increasing taxes is an option if you're experiencing explosive population growth with starvation looming down the road, and want to slow down the growth rate.

Don't build castles and don't storm castles. A good army in the field is all you need to keep danger at bay. Stormed castles are damaged and fall into ruin unless repaired promptly. It's better to starve the defenders out, especially since your besieging army does not suffer any losses.

Go to the Raise Army screen each turn, in every county. Mercenaries for hire appear at random in random counties, and you don't want to miss the chance to hire them if you've got enough gold in your coffers. Mercenary swordsmen are always a good bargain; knights aren't, so don't hire any unless there's nothing else, you desperately need armed troops, and are wallowing in gold.

Take every opportunity to trade with visiting merchants. At first, you'll mostly be buying--grain, cows, sheep. Later on in the game, the only item you'll regularly buy should be arms. You will buy food or live-stock only to quickly prop up a freshly conquered and ailing county.

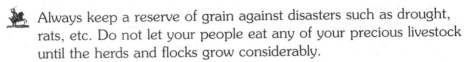 Always keep a reserve of grain against disasters such as drought, rats, etc. Do not let your people eat any of your precious livestock until the herds and flocks grow considerably.

When you've got sufficient field labor to deal with the harvest, start assigning serfs to mining iron and manufacturing weapons. If you have a floating pool of free labor and all the county fields are in tip-top shape, you may consider ordering the serfs to gather wood or quarry stone on a temporary basis, and sell the fruit of their labors when a merchant comes along.

Keep aloof and distant from the other Lords. They're far too busy fighting each other to be concerned about you—at least throughout the opening stages of the game! Don't enter into any alliances as a rule; concentrate on paddling your own county—er, canoe—and doing it well.

Never raise armies of unarmed peasants unless you're absolutely desperate. Fifty armed men are enough to conquer the majority of neutral counties. Two hundred armed men are enough to deal with most of the computer Lords' armies, and five hundred armed men constitute an invincible force.

Winning Strategies

The secret to winning at *Lords of the Realm* is very simple: Be a good Lord, and keep your peasants fat and happy. Once you've achieved that, the rest follows naturally. Fail to do that, and the happiness of your subjects will drop steadily until it hits the level of five hearts. Then you'll have just five turns in which to improve things. After that, you'll be deposed as sheriff of that county.

Achieving a happy state of affairs isn't easy, and the difficulty varies with the pre-game options you have chosen. The strategy outlined by me has been developed while playing *Lords* at the highest difficulty, with expert economy. Since much of the game is about medieval economics, it's more exciting to present yourself with a strong challenge.

THE GOOD LORD, OR MANAGING COUNTIES

The peasants inhabiting every county want to be well-fed. Their main priority in life is to keep their stomachs full. It's rather basic, but then things in the Middle Ages tended to be that way.

The happiness of your peasants is of utmost importance. If it drops to five hearts or lower for five consecutive turns, you're out as Sheriff, and will have to re-conquer that particular county. The mood of your serfs is swayed by two considerations: One is the amount of food they're getting, the other is money—more precisely, taxes.

I found that setting the tax to fifteen gold pieces per hundred people is the optimum solution. Fifteen gold is the maximum tax rate at which a county's happiness grows steadily at the rate of one heart per season, or turn.

Setting the food rations at below normal decreases happiness, setting them higher increases it. A county's happiness must be over ten hearts before any of its serfs will agree to join your army. County happiness also affects the morale of the armies that are raised within its boundaries; well-fed soldiers are spoiling for a fight, undernourished ones tend to desert.

As a rule, I keep the tax at fifteen gold and the rations at normal. This guarantees steady growth; sometimes, it even has to be checked with a slight tax increase. Do not let your people get too happy and cozy with the way things are, or they'll start multiplying very quickly. The result can be a sudden food crisis that disrupts everything and forces you to painstakingly rebuild and re-balance that county's economy. Beware especially of immigrants from neighboring counties. At first welcome, the new arrivals may swamp you as they grow in numbers!

As a last resort, you may improve the mood of the population by getting them drunk. This happiness boost has very sharply defined limits, and you won't get more than three hearts as a result. The improvement is proportional to the size of your county's population. A tiny county will get quite merry on a single cask, bigger ones will want more before they even start to smile.

Who Eats What

The dietary possibilities of your serfs include these mouth-watering options: grain (bread), cows (beef), sheep (mutton), and dairy products. Dairy products are obtained by letting the cows live instead of turning them into beef. Since cows are quite expensive to acquire, buying them in order to put them on your serfs' tables is extremely wasteful. You may let them know what a good roast tastes like once you've got a big herd of cows (which reproduce at an alarming rate, and you want to cull them a little).

As a rule, it's good to build up your herd to a size where dairy products can feed the entire county if it's put on half rations. The same applies to sheep: Don't turn them into mutton until the flock is very large. However, bear in mind that sheep breed just once a year, unlike cows. I tend to keep my peasants mutton-less, and only let them slaughter a sheep or two in an emergency.

That leaves us with grain. Expert husbanding of grain stocks is a skill required of every Lord! Grain is subject to all sorts of misfortunes, whether stored or planted and growing. One of my top priorities in every game of *Lords* is to build a nice surplus of grain that can be used both in emergencies and upon acquiring a new county—usually, it's pretty ravaged by war when you take it over.

At the very start of the game, however, you won't even be able to think about a reserve because you won't have enough grain to feed your people. Remember, you always have to put aside a certain amount for sowing in the spring. As your farms grow more efficient in tandem with the number of reclaimed fields, harvests will grow more bountiful. Setting aside grain for the spring will become less of a problem, also because by that time, you usually have a fairly sizeable herd of cows.

When playing at the expert economy level, you have no choice but to put everyone on half rations right away, and a disaster may even force you to issue quarter rations. This will mean a decrease in happiness and health among your people. Take every opportunity to buy cows and more grain from visiting merchants, as well as the occasional cask of ale.

Tilling the Country Fields

Your first priority is to improve farm productivity and save some grain for sowing. Allocate all surplus labor to field maintenance—forget about mining or quarrying for the moment. Extra field labor will result in fields being transformed from rocky, barren ground into fertile meadows, dramatically boosting crop output. When you start the game with expert economy switched on, the average yield you can expect from your fields is three to four sacks of grain for each one sown. With several fields reclaimed and lying fallow, you'll see it rocket to ten sacks for each one sown within a reasonably short time.

The biggest problem you'll encounter is at harvest time. Different seasons bring different requirements for field labor; harvest time is the busiest. If you don't allocate enough serfs to do the harvesting, precious grain (and you'll quickly see how precious it is) will rot in the fields.

The best solution I've developed is to keep a pool of free labor in each county, and keep them busy with field maintenance. The extra labor they put in means that at harvest time, you can transfer all the serfs from field maintenance to harvesting. You may lose a field sometimes, but the extra field maintenance means it will be quickly reclaimed.

You can also allocate your labor pool to other tasks, such as quarrying or cutting wood in between the busy periods. However, temporary help is notoriously inefficient, and overall, it's best to concentrate on maintaining very high farm productivity than risk a famine for the price of a single cartload of wood.

If you have more than sufficient labor in spite of allocating some to non-farming activities, go ahead and raise an army. Details are discussed later on in this chapter.

Managing Resources

Lords of the Realm features four types of non-farming activity: cutting or gathering wood, quarrying stone, mining iron, and manufacturing arms.

The four above-mentioned activities are very labor-intensive. Furthermore, you cannot expect a serf that has spent all his time fooling around in the mud to become a skilled miner or armorer overnight. Increased productivity can only be gained through experience on the job. A hundred serfs who have been mining iron for ten years will be more productive than a thousand freshly put to the task.

You need wood and stone to build castles, iron to make weapons, and weapons to equip armies raised from your serfs. All of these are also traded by the itinerant merchants, although a particular merchant may not trade in some of them—he'll buy and sell wood and iron, for instance, but not stone or arms. Of course, the buying and selling prices are vastly different, and arms are extremely expensive—in the neighborhood of a thousand gold pieces for fifty items in any weapons category.

To win at *Lords of the Realm*, you'll have to both manufacture arms *and* buy them. You don't really need to build castles, so you don't need stone and wood.

Since building castles also involves additional labor, employing serfs as builders is, in my opinion, the hard way to victory.

Raising and Forming Armies

Basically, *Lords* features three kinds of soldiers.

 Peasants: Armed with pitchforks, peasants are the most ineffective troop type there is. Fifty swordsmen can defeat five hundred peasants—that's how weak they are. Don't ever form armies out of unarmed peasants; they are much more useful for tilling the fields, quarrying stone, etc. The computer players like to do just that, and you'll score many brilliant victories over them with your armed men.

 Armies raised locally: To raise a troop of armed men, you must have the weapons in your arsenal. They can be manufactured locally, or bought from a merchant. You'll have a choice of many kinds of weaponry: axes, spears, swords, crossbows. The armament determines the troop's attack and defense strengths and its upkeep cost. For instance, swordsmen are of the most value in battle, but they cost the most to maintain.

Whatever the maintenance costs of armies raised locally, they are peanuts compared to what you'll have to pay for mercenaries. Bearing this in mind, I arm my new recruits with either swords or bows/crossbows, depending on what kind of troops I already have in service.

 Mercenaries: From time to time, a group of mercenaries will offer their services in exchange for gold. The bad thing is, mercenaries are hellishly expensive. They come in several varieties—Norman crossbowmen, Danish swordsmen, Aquitanian knights—and some are better value than the others.

I found mercenary swordsmen to be the best value. For starters, there are two hundred of them, which means a single mercenary unit can be employed as an independent army. They're reasonably priced—six hundred gold for two hundred men ain't bad, especially compared to the eight hundred gold you have to shell out to hire fifty knights. Although knights are the best military unit there is, they're simply outrageously expensive.

Most of the time, you'll be combining the troops you've raised into armies. Remember that no two mercenary units can serve together in the same army! You cannot hire two hundred Norman crossbows and combine them with two hundred Danish swordsmen, for example, which is a great pity because that would have been one hell of an army. Instead, you have to combine mercenaries with troops raised locally.

As a rule, I always combine ranged-weapons troops with others. For instance, if I have been fortunate enough to hire two hundred swordsmen, I will purchase crossbows/bows from the merchant or have my armorers make them, then raise a troop of bowmen to accompany my swordsmen. The same logic applies in reverse: If I've just hired Norman crossbows, I try to provide them with at least a minimal protective screen in the form of swordsmen (or even, in an absolute emergency, pitchfork-equipped peasants).

You'll find that an army of two hundred armed men can deal with most of the computer players' armies, and five hundred armed men are sure to outmatch almost anything the computer throws your way. The computer-controlled nobles have the same financial problems as you have. They try to circumvent them by sending peasants into battle. Your armed men, of course, can deal with them any time, even if they're outnumbered ten to one.

Once you've raised and formed an army, try to avoid having to feed it—send it just across the border into a neighboring county. If that neighboring county is neutral, you'll hear a protesting bleat from the local sheriff. Ignore it. If the county in question belongs to a computer-controlled noble, he/she will send out an army to deal with your incursion. If you've followed my advice and armed your guys, you shouldn't have any trouble.

The Politics of the Lords

The diplomatic system in *Lords* is pretty rudimentary. Basically, you can be neutral, allied, or at war. My suggestion is: Don't ally yourself with anyone—it's best to get involved only in wars of your own making. Since your aim is total domination, and the computer isn't very good at raising and forming armies, you shouldn't be too troubled about provoking the other nobles. Once you've put your county economy on a solid footing, you don't really have anything to fear; that's when you're playing against the computer, of course. Other humans are a different story! You'll have to be on your guard, be very active on the diplomatic scene, and carefully consider any potentially provocative steps.

Fighting Battles

The battles in *Lords* are also pretty rudimentary. If you're playing against the computer, you can skip that bit altogether—unless you're hopelessly outnumbered and want to make sure you won't be defeated. The computer troops almost always attack without hesitation. It's pretty easy to outmaneuver them by leading them into a swamp, attacking them from the flank or rear, etc., all of which significantly increase your chances of victory.

Laying siege to castles is another form of doing battle in *Lords of the Realm*. The mechanics of preparing a siege and an assault on the castle walls are pretty complicated, and in themselves, the assaults are not worth the trouble. This is because any castle that has been stormed is invariably damaged when you finally take it over, and damaged castles fall into ruin if they're not promptly repaired. Repairing them, of course, requires wood, stone, and builders. In a freshly-captured county, all your efforts will be focused on getting its economy and population back on its feet. You usually don't have the serfs to spare for repair work, even if you have the wood or the stone. It's much better to starve the defenders out. The castle falls into your hands absolutely intact.

The key to armed success in *Lords* is simply maintaining several two hundred-plus strong armies in the field. I recommend using two armies to capture a county with a castle—one to lay siege, the other to fight off the relief forces that will attempt to break the siege from time to time. After a few turns, the castle will fall. You should immediately move your troops out of the newly-acquired county, as its economy is too weak to support your soldiers. Simply move them into the county that's next on your to-be-conquered list, and start the siege process again.

Throughout it all, keep raising new armies and sending them off to conquer new lands. The Lords in *Lords* are a warlike lot, and fight among themselves all the time. By the time they realize what a danger you've become, it's usually too late!

CHAPTER

7

MASTER OF MAGIC

Publisher:	Microprose Software
Platform:	PC MS-DOS
Release Date:	Fall, 1994
Multiplayer:	No

Rating:

General Overview

Master of Magic was the second hit from Steve Barcia, the creator of the record-breaking *Master of Magic*. In a nutshell, it could be described as *Civilization* with magic and tactical combat replacing some of *Civ's* economics.

In *MOM*, as it's popularly called, your goal is to become the top Wizard, either through casting the spell of "Mastery" (which takes a long time to research and an even longer time to cast), or through eliminating all the other competing Wizards. To achieve this, you must build an empire, *Civ*-style, by founding cities and developing them into strong production centers. Developing cities involves building numerous city improvements, assigning labor (the choice is between farmer and worker) and, perhaps most importantly of all, holding on to them—it's easy to lose a city to marauding raiders, monsters, or enemy armies.

The world of *MOM* is actually composed of two worlds: Arcanus (an earth-like world) and Myrror. Myrror is basically a mirror of Arcanus; the general geography is similar, only there are different races and monsters, and plenty of additional mana—which is explained in the manual. You can start the game on Myrror if you're willing to forfeit three spell book choices, but be warned. Myrror is a tougher world than Arcanus, and at the higher difficulty levels, it's much tougher. It's usually easier to start on Arcanus, and then find your way to Myrror.

The economics of *MOM* are fairly simple. As in *Civilization,* city improvements have certain maintenance costs that have to be paid each turn. Also, the upkeep of every unit costs gold and food (spearsmen, who are the most basic unit, demand only food, no gold). Fantastic creatures summoned to serve in your army do not cost gold or food; instead, they cost a certain amount of mana, or magic power.

This bread-and-butter side of the game is complemented by a rich array of magic spells that have to be researched or traded before they can be used. Since a combination of spells can turn the most frail unit into a nearly invincible one, your knowledge of magic and spell-casting skills are as important as the size and strength of your army.

The armies in *MOM* are composed of three kinds of units: regular army units, fantastic creatures, and heroes. The heroes are particularly important, since they pass on various benefits to the troops they're grouped with. They can also carry a variety of artifacts that can turn a hero into an invincible superman/superwoman.

Regular troops and heroes greatly improve with experience. Each turn that a unit/hero is in existence means extra experience points. Fighting battles boosts a unit's experience by one point per troop in an opposing army, or two points per fantastic creature. In other words, a hero that has won a victory over an army of four Swordsmen supported by Hell Hounds will receive six experience points: four for the Swordsmen, two for the Hell Hounds (plus the standard point-per-turn, for a total of seven points more on the next turn). Note that fantastic creatures serving in your armies do not receive experience points.

Your progress is determined not only by your military might and number/size of cities, but also by your magical powers, which, in turn, are determined by your mana resources. Mana is the currency of magic; it's produced by magic nodes and certain city improvements. You can change gold into mana and mana into gold at a 50% loss (or none, if you've picked the Alchemist special ability). Mana is not only used to cast and maintain spells, but also to improve your spell-casting skill and research new spells.

Word of caution: When first released, *Master of Magic* was so buggy as to be virtually unplayable. If you come across an earlier version of the game, steer clear. The bugs were eradicated in subsequent releases; version 1.3 is widely acknowledged as the definitive one.

This chapter is based on my experiences while playing *Master of Magic*, version 1.3 at the Hard and Impossible levels. I recommend that you play *MOM* at the Hard level for an interesting and challenging game. At the Impossible level, the gameplay becomes unbalanced, and the computer player's behavior becomes boringly hostile.

I would also suggest you set the Magic to Normal, and choose Medium land size. The gameplay feels most balanced with these options.

Golden Rules

 Try to keep the tax rate at 30%, unless unrest gets absolutely out of hand. As most other strategic games, *MOM* is in a large part about husbanding your resources, or mana and money.

Increase mana production as early as possible through building mana-producing city improvements, conquering magic nodes, and casting appropriate spells ("Dark Rituals" is almost obligatory for every Death Merchant).

 Expand fast. Conquer nearby neutral cities and start new ones with careful consideration given to your choice of race. Although *MOM* is about magic, you can make magic truly happen only if you've got a big economical base.

 Assemble armies thoughtfully, especially if you have several races in your empire. For example, it makes no sense to build Orc Swordsmen if you can build Barbarian Swordsmen, because the Barbarian unit is much better, and costs the same in upkeep (building costs may be higher, but that doesn't matter as much).

 Balance building new units with improving your settlements. You won't be able to support many units, anyway, if you neglect to ensure sufficiently high food production, and you need granaries and farmer's markets for that. Marketplaces are a must, as are unrest-quelling institutions such as shrines and temples. Libraries allow you to speed up research or divert mana to improving your spellcasting skill. Build up every settlement you have to the farmer's market/shrine/library level, and improve selected ones beyond.

 Cultivate your heroes and all your military units. Both heroes and military units improve, beyond belief, with experience. You can get an idea of how much by casting the "Heroism" spell on a green unit and watching its performance in combat.

 Practice common sense in diplomacy, and try to keep everyone happy with you until you're ready for action. Offer tributes of spells, but think twice before signing any Wizard's pacts—you'll be seriously restricted in your exploration efforts. Avoid alliances unless you're absolutely, one hundred percent positive that's the thing to do. The last thing you want is to be dragged into a new war by a belligerent ally.

Use your magic wisely. Make sure you have a nice comprehensive set of battlefield spells (increase attack and defense, direct attacks such as "Fire Bolt" or 'Psionic Blast"). Also, ensure you have the magical power to counter global enchantments cast by other Wizards ("Disjunction True" is the best) as well as battlefield spells ("Counter Magic" is best). "Web" is invaluable in the early stages of the game, as is "Giant Strength" and "Stone Skin." I always include a couple of Nature spell books on every Wizard's bookshelf.

 Explore all the ruins, keeps, and so on that you come across, and make capturing a Tower of Wizardry an early priority. If you start the game on Arcanus, Towers of Wizardry become especially important; conquering one gives you access to Myrror with all its races and mana without having to forfeit three spell-book picks.

Winning Strategies

You must have a good idea of your strategy even before you start playing the game. Yes, that's right. *MOM* features an amazing array of pre-game options. In my experience, more than any other game I've ever played. At the same time, those choices—made before you've even seen your starting city—determine your strategy to a decisive extent.

CREATING YOURSELF

The persona you assume is of utmost importance, especially if you're playing *MOM* at a higher difficulty level. While *MOM* features a number of 'pre-set' Wizards, these compare to custom Wizards the way an off-the-rack suit compares to a tailor-made suit.

This is where you make your first and most important strategic decision. Are you going to be a Nice Guy, within limits, of course, or are you going for the throat? Very many players (including myself) prefer the Nice Guy approach, which means choosing Life magic over Death (remember, Life and

Death magics are mutually exclusive). If you choose Death, you more or less commit yourself to a very warlike course. Owning Death books penalizes diplomatic relations, as explained in the manual. At the same time, Death magic features tons of good, cheap combat spells. The spell "Dark Rituals" is a cheap (if not horrible) way to boost mana production in your cities, thus increasing the mana available for casting all these deadly combat spells.

Picking Spell Books

There are five kinds of magic in *MOM:* Life, Nature, Sorcery, Chaos, and Death. Life and Death magic are mutually exclusive, so the first choice you must make is the one between Life and Death. Both are very powerful magics, with Death spells being slightly more advantageous in the military sense. Whatever Death gains on the battlefield, however, is more than offset by its negative influence on diplomatic relations!

It's very important to remember that the other Wizards will like or dislike you depending on what magic you specialize in. They'll also compare the spell books you own with theirs, and like you more if you share spell books of a certain color. Owning books in Life and Nature magic always makes you a likable character, while Chaos, Sorcery, and especially Death cause alarm. At higher difficulty levels, where the computer-controlled Wizards are very forgiving of each other's transgressions but hostile towards you, choosing Death over Life makes things rather difficult. The other Wizards need constant stroking, and even then, are prone to declaring war on you for no reason.

Whether you choose Life or Death, I suggest that you acquire at least one spell book in all of the remaining possible magic realms: Chaos, Sorcery, and Nature. If you do not own any spell books in a given magic, then you won't learn *any* spells from that magic realm. Although you may be lucky and retrieve a spell book from one of the dungeons, monster lairs, etc., you can't count on it, and I've found that covering as many bases as possible is a good approach.

As a rule, it is good to own four or more spell books in a single magic, because you need some specialization in order to acquire rare and powerful spells. The number of spell books you own determines how many spells of that magic type you can learn, and also how powerful they are. Spells range from common to very rare, with the common ones being the weakest (but often very useful!) and the rarest ones being the most powerful. I suggest specializing in Life or Nature magic, since the pleasant vibes these magics generate mean a lot at the higher difficulty levels. If you choose to specialize in Chaos, you will know a lot of good combat spells, but other Wizards will be rather hostile.

You may want to try playing with just two or three kinds of magic in your arsenal (the maximum permissible number of colors on your magic bookshelf is four). If you chose Life magic and own three or more white books, Nature magic becomes slightly redundant; if you chose Death and own three or more purple books, Chaos is the first choice for a discard.

If you want to play with just two kinds of magic, I suggest you always keep Sorcery or blue magic as your second option. Sorcery is the 'magic of magics'; it allows you to break the other Wizards' magical powers (at higher difficulty levels, it just helps even out the odds a little).

Special Abilities

You can round off your Wizard's persona by choosing from one of *MOM's* wide range of special abilities. All special abilities carry a cost—you forfeit, one, two, or even three spell book choices.

The most expensive choice is starting the game on Myrror—that's three spell books to you, my friend. The cost of starting the game on Myrror is heavy for a reason. It provides a great boost in your magical powers, right from the very start. Also, the Myrran races have plenty of good military units.

I would recommend choosing Myrran if you decide to go for the throat, and choose Death magic to give direction to your Wizard's career. You'll need tons of mana to furnish you with the means of executing your deadly policies, and a Myrran race can give you just that. I am against choosing any other extra abilities in addition to Myrran—you'll forfeit an extra spell book or two from your measly total of eight. However, some experienced players may find Channeller useful.

Myrran is the only choice that costs three spell book picks. However, there are several that cost two. Warlord deserves special consideration. Essentially, Warlord gives your troops an extra experience level. They start as regulars and go on to become ultra-elite. When coupled with the right race—fast-growing, with good military units—Warlord can be a very good choice in spite of its stiff price. If you want to have a really deadly special abilities combination, combine Warlord with Alchemist. All your great troops will be equipped with magical weapons.

The second two-pick choice that merits consideration is the Channeller. Combat spells are a part of every battle, and when the battle takes place relatively far from your Wizard's fortress, the casting costs can get high (they increase with the distance). The Channeller eliminates that distance surcharge on the casting cost of combat spells, thus enabling you to use them more often. Also, you pay half the usual mana maintenance costs on fantastic creatures and overland spells, so all this makes Channeller a useful ability. However, it can only be exploited to its full potential if you have considerable spell-casting powers in the first place. That's something you acquire as the game goes on. But on its own, it's not as safe nor as good as the Warlord.

The other special abilities costing two spell book picks are Infernal/Divine Power, which increases the effectiveness of all religious city improvements (shrine, temple, etc.), and Famous, which starts you with +10 Fame. Divine/ Infernal Power are two sides of the same coin—one applies to Life magic, the other to Death magic, and both aren't worth the two-pick price. You can increase your mana production by other, cheaper means, and can minimize unrest by carefully siting your cities, as discussed later on in this chapter.

Famous provides you with a boost at the start of the game; +10 Fame means you pay 10 gold less per turn in army upkeep, plus you have a better shot at recruiting heroes, buying magical artifacts, etc. It's simply not worth two spell books—it barely merits the cost of one—since Fame is something you acquire anyway as the game unfolds.

In my opinion, Warlord is the only two-pick special ability that offers good value for the price. The Channeller's advantages only become full-fledged after you've built a sizeable empire, and if you've managed to do that, you have a good shot at victory anyway, Channeller or no Channeller. Most of the battles you fight early on are close to home, and often your initial mana income is too low to allow maintaining any fantastic creatures beyond the time it takes to do battle.

In contrast, the one-pick abilities contain several very tempting choices. The Alchemist, which gives your troops magical weapons with a +1 To Hit bonus, tops the list. Basically, it's like casting "Holy Weapon" on every military unit you produce. Additionally, you can change gold into mana (it almost never makes sense to change mana into gold in any *MOM* game) at a one-to-one ratio. You'll find this ability very useful. It's fairly easy to achieve a steady gold surplus, so in practice, the Alchemist means a lot of extra mana, thus providing a lot of the benefits offered by the twice-as-expensive Channeller!

Archmage is a very attractive ability that provides you with an instant spell-casting edge. You'll find it very useful throughout the game, starting with early battles where the ability to cast "Stone Skin" three times instead of only twice may just save yours. Later on, you'll benefit greatly by the fact that your spells are more difficult to dispel.

Node Mastery removes one of the greatest early bugaboos—the fact that spells don't work in magic nodes (except for spells that belong to the same magic realm, of course). Node Mastery also increases mana production, thus providing some of the Channeller's benefits at a lower price.

Finally, Charismatic is a good choice if you've opted to play at Hard, and almost obligatory if you're playing at Impossible. The lift generated in your relations with others by your charming personality is cheap at the price of a single spell book pick.

In my opinion, the only remaining one-pick ability that has any merit on its own is Sage Master. Acquiring new spells is crucial to winning the game, and anything that makes it easier really helps. Chaos, Nature, and Sorcery mastery obviously makes sense only if you decide to concentrate heavily on a particular type of magic. This is somewhat limiting, although it does make for an interesting game. Of course, they may make sense given a specific combination. For instance, Runemaster combined with Archmage gives you tremendous wizardly clout; whether you cast a spell or destroy spells cast by others, you have much better chances of success.

Finally, you should remember to select your special abilities in the context of other choices—the type(s) of magic you specialize in, and most importantly, your starting race. For instance, Warlord works much better when you start with a militaristic race like Gnolls, Klackons, or Barbarians than if you pair it with Halflings.

Selecting a race in *MOM* is perhaps even more difficult than choosing the kinds of magic you will use, or special abilities. Each race has its own military units, city building capabilities, and an inherent ability to get along with the other races.

The Racial Dilemma

First of all, your choice of race is dictated by whether you chose the Myrran ability. If not, you are automatically limited to the Arcanus races as a starting choice. In a good game of *MOM,* you get to rule many other races in addition to the one you start with. However, your initial choice greatly affects your success; it determines whether you'll get to rule any other races in the first place. If you fumble things right at the outset, you won't.

Before you settle on a race, remember to check on its likability. Every race featured in *MOM* is liked by some and disliked by others. If you happen to choose a starting race that is unpopular with others, you will have to deal with higher rates of unrest in your cities. Theoretically, you can move your Wizard's fortress to a city owned by someone more *simpatico,* after you've acquired the necessary spell. In practice, I found it much easier to simply pick a starting race that is endowed with lots of talent and is also liked by others. Barbarians are a very good example. They're made for fast, aggressive play partly because other races don't mind coming under Barbarian rule. For details, please refer to the appropriate section in the manual.

All Myrran races and one Arcanus race (High Elves) have a special feature. They produce mana just by existing—which makes me suspect some sort of spontaneous internal combustion. The rate is half a mana per person, or citizen on the city display screen; thus, a town of ten Dwarves will produce five mana per turn all on its own (mana from city improvements is extra).

The following list discusses briefly each of the races featured in *MOM,* and their usefulness both as starting choices and later additions to your empire. I have decided not to include all the stats for the sake of brevity. You can find them in the game manual (if you own version earlier than 1.3, you should also glance at the README.TXT file for stat updates).

 Barbarians are, in my opinion, the best race to start with on Arcanus. Barbarian cities grow very fast, making early expansion easy. Barbarian military units cost 50% more to produce; however, they are still a bargain because of their special ability to execute a thrown attack before engaging in melee (or hand-to-hand) combat. This allows common Spearsmen and Swordsmen to attack flying units, and makes them generally fearsome in attack. Remember—

always attack first with the Barbarians! They aren't as good on the defense.

Barbarians can construct warships, which helps compensate for the fact that they don't have any flying units. Their biggest drawback is that they cannot build roads. When starting out with the Barbarians, your first priority is to conquer a settlement belonging to a race that can make engineers, and thus build roads.

The Barbarians' natural strengths are enhanced if you choose the Alchemist and/or Warlord special abilities. Nature (green) and Chaos (red) magic complements them nicely, and so does Death magic. "Dark Rituals" are a useful way to limit explosive Barbarian growth that tends to result in unrest.

 Beastmen are the closest that Myrran races come to Arcanus races—they rather resemble Barbarians. They don't have a thrown attack, but have a To Hit, melee strength, and resistance bonuses. They are the right choice if you want to start the game on Myrror but otherwise want to keep things as 'normal' as possible.

Unlike Barbarians, Beastmen can build roads. This is important insofar as only two Myrran races can do that (Dwarven are the other). If you start your game with Beastmen, always try to conquer the other Myrran races as quickly as possible—especially Dark Elves.

 Dark Elves are the killer race in *Master of Magic*. All units have some form of ranged attack—Spearsmen, Swordsmen, and Cavalry can execute a strength 1 magic ranged attack four times. Strength 1 may not seem like much, but remember that there are several figures attacking at the same time! The downside is that like other Myrran units, Dark Elven soldiers are very expensive. Also, Dark Elves are perhaps the most disliked race of them all. You may want to consider moving your fortress as soon as feasible to a city inhabited by a more amiable people.

 Draconians are another Myrran race, but these boys can fly (except for settlers—too weighed down by the housebuilding tools?). The Draconians that hurl fireballs or shoot arrows have a fiery breath attack, and all military units enjoy increased defense and resistance. However, you pay through the nose for all these wonderful things, and coupled with the relative fragility of Draconian units, this definitely makes them a second-drawer choice—at least as far as I'm concerned.

 Dwarven are the other Myrran race to make engineers (roads are an especially important consideration on Myrror since all of them are enchanted, making for supreme ease of troop movement). Dwarven are very tough (3 hit points, or hearts), very productive, and very resistant to magic (inherent +4 bonus against enemy spells). On the flip side, Dwarf cities grow very slowly (as they should), and all the units are frightfully expensive. Also, they cannot build several important city improvements. Almost every race cannot build this or that, but the absence of a Parthenon is a serious drawback. Because of their slo-mo growth, Dwarves are definitely not the best choice for a starting race. However, later on in the game, you'll greatly appreciate both their high productivity and super-efficient engineers, plus such cool weapons as the Steam Cannon (unfortunately, not that powerful).

 Gnolls are a rather primitive Arcanian race who can't even build libraries, but feature good basic units (albeit at a slightly higher price). The +2 attack strength gives Gnoll units an advantage in the very early stages of the game; however, they are pretty weak on the defense. The Gnoll army features Wolf Riders, who can move three spaces on the battlefield; however, it's fairly quickly outclassed by the armies of other races, capable of developing more sophisticated units.

The one Gnoll positive attribute is that they are well liked by other races. However, if you choose Gnolls, make sure you pep up their racial qualities by selecting warlike types of magic and special abilities. If you do not press home the Gnoll advantage early on in the game and add several other races to your empire, you may be in trouble. For that reason, Gnolls are not my favorite race.

 Halflings seem to be a benign counterpart to Myrran Dwarves. While Halfling citizens do not generate any mana, their farmers are better than anyone else's, generating an extra loaf per turn per farmer. Since one of the biggest problems in *MOM* is finding sufficient food for all those armies, this sounds like great news. Unfortunately, the Halfling military units aren't much. The only ones that really deserves notice are the Slingers. Given several experience levels, Halfling Slingers can be lethal; the computer-controlled Halfling city garrisons often exclusively feature Slingers in the defensive lineup. It's a pity that the rest of the army isn't up to par, as Halflings are very likable folk, they get along with everybody, and can build most of the important city improvements. This lack of military muscle is the reason why Halflings aren't among my favorite starting races. They make a great addition to your empire, though, because of the mentioned farmer productivity, which, of course, can be applied to maintaining armies formed out of other races.

 High Elves are a favorite Arcanian race of mine. First of all, High Elf citizens produce mana, just like the Myrran races. Secondly, they have one of the best conventional ranged attack units. Longbowmen and the mounted Elven Lords closely resemble High Men's superb Paladins in their battlefield performance, although they are weaker. High Elves also have flying units—the Pegasi. Although all their units cost slightly more, I think they're worth it—especially since they have the Forester ability (forest does not cost extra movement points).

The biggest drawback to High Elves is that they cannot build roads or Parthenons. As with other races that are somewhat handicapped in their capabilities, the right strategy is to conquer a city owned by a race that can produce engineers.

 High Men are humans proper. More sophisticated than Barbarians, they can build anything with the exception of flying units. High Men also boast one of the best units in the game—Paladins—whose resistance to magic means you can depend on them in the most vicious tussle with a powerful Wizard. Priests and Magicians complement the High Men's military array with pretty potent magical ranged weapons.

The problem with High Men is that the basic military units— Spearsmen, Swordsmen, and Cavalry—are relatively weak and unexciting. It takes some time to bring High Men up to their full potential, and in the meantime, things can get pretty shaky. However, they still are a much better starting race than many of the others. The ideal situation is when you start the game with a race like Gnolls or Barbarians, which feature good military units, and acquire a High Men settlement right at the start of the game. Then you have the best of both worlds, or rather, both races.

The other big advantage to starting the race with High Men is that they are among the most liked races. Interracial unrest is at its minimum.

 Klackons are a race that got transplanted into *Master of Magic* from *Master of Orion*—a previous game from Simtex/Microprose, discussed elsewhere in this book. Like their prototype, the Klackons in *MOM* enjoy a productivity bonus. However, Klackon units cost a whopping double the normal amount, so you can hardly count on any savings there, and the rather limited range of city improvements they can build (no temple, Sage's Guild, or shipyard) is one of the poorest available to any race. Add to it the fact that Klackons are generally disliked by the races they conquer, and the productivity bonus hardly seems worth all the extra hassle. However, do not hesitate to acquire a Klackon city at any point in the game, especially if you've started the game with a race that has no road-building capability; Klackons can make engineers.

 Lizardmen are, as the name indicates, a rather tough but primitive race with the inborn capability to swim. You don't have to build any ships, which is just as well because Lizardmen cannot construct the city improvements required for that purpose. Lizardmen units have double hit points and enjoy a defense bonus, but the more sophisticated ones cost double the normal amount. Since basic units such as Swordsmen are available at regular prices, Lizardmen are great for early expansion, which is very necessary. Since Lizardmen are primitive folk (they can't build Parthenons and most Guilds), you need to acquire a race that's more sophisticated in order to win a game at a higher difficulty level.

 Nomads are basically High Men without the roads, ships (triremes don't count for reasons given later), and Magicians. The absence of engineers is compensated for by a 50% gold bonus for Nomad cities, so when you eventually do build roads, Nomad cities become very profitable.

The Nomad army features flying creatures (Griffins) that aren't particularly strong, a variation on Cavalry called Horsebowmen, and Rangers. Horsebowmen become a good unit once they've progressed at least to Veteran level, but the best Nomad units are the Rangers, whose performance with bows and arrows is quite impressive. What's more, attaching a Ranger unit to an army stack makes it able to move through difficult terrain without movement penalties.

Nomads are certainly a viable alternative as a starting race, even though their lack of shipbuilding skills can be a serious handicap. However, they are a relatively bland and unexciting race, so they do not rank among my favorite choices.

 Orcs appear to be *MOM's* most privileged race. They have no restrictions at all on city improvements, can build relatively good flying units, and generally make a good starting race. If you don't choose Orcs yourself, you may have to wait a long time before you see them in a game of *MOM*, because the computer seems to dislike them. In close to a hundred games of *MOM*, I've encountered computer-created Orc settlements only a couple of times.

The Orc similarity to High Men also means it takes some time to develop their full potential. I do not choose to play them as a starting race very often for just one irrational reason: The unit icons are rather ugly. Also, other races don't like Orcs as much as they do Nomads or High Men—two races that are very similar.

 Trolls are another Myrran killer race. They have the most powerful units in the game—and also the most expensive ones. You pay three times the standard amount! However, they grow very slowly, are disliked by other races, and are severely limited in their range of available city improvements. The Trolls' unique feature is that damaged units can regenerate between attacks. Although they have fewer figures per unit (four instead of standard six), Troll units make excellent garrisons, particularly if ensconced inside city walls. However, the high price of these marvellous units means that by the time you build your first one, the computer players will have built three—and that's at Normal game difficulty.

The better you get at playing *MOM,* the less important your choice of starting race (however, it's never totally unimportant). If you aren't used to playing at higher difficulty levels, I would encourage you to try one of my recommended choices.

THE GROWING OF A WIZARD

As in most strategic games, the first steps you take in a game of *MOM* are especially important. A little empire is not as good as a big empire, and greatly reduces your chances of winning the game.

My standard opening moves are almost invariably the same—it's the sequence they're played in that changes from game to game. I build a granary, a second Swordsmen unit, and raise the tax rate to 1.5 gold per person. This last move invariably results in a quickly growing gold surplus, which can be used to speed up the building of the granary. Having secured my second Swordsmen unit, I send out the Spearsmen to locate a suite suitable for my second city. In the meantime, with the granary supplying the extra loaves needed for troop support, I build still more Swordsmen—one or even two.

The next step depends on what the wandering Swordsman has uncovered. Sometimes, the guy you send exploring comes across Raiders composed of units belonging to another race (as opposed to monsters etc.). This is always a sure sign there is a neutral city nearby—a city that you ought to take over.

Capturing a city is always better than building it from scratch, and can provide you with the precious bonus in the shape of a new race. Building a multiracial empire is beneficial, as it allows you to capitalize on the strengths of each race and form invincible armies using the best units from each one.

As pointed out earlier, if you've started out with a race that does not make engineers, it's an absolute priority to find and conquer a race that does.

If your exploring unit hasn't come across any signs of foreign presence, I suggest you activate the Surveyor (F1 key) and scan the uncovered terrain for good city sites. Do not ignore sites right next to unexplored blackness! Occasionally, you'll get the message that cities cannot be built less than three squares from any other city, even though your starting settlement is more than three squares again. What this means is that there is a foreign city in unexplored territory less than three squares away, and you should proceed from there.

If your survey does not uncover any surprises such as the above, start making settlers. Let your explorer do some more exploring around the most promising city sites while you're waiting for the settlers.

SITING CITIES

The average *MOM* world is very Earth-like in that it has a lot of water. You invariably start the game on a medium to big island or small to medium continent. Given the three-squares-between-cities rule, this means space is limited.

Your first and only consideration when siting your cities is to space them so that you can start the maximum number of cities possible. You should make sure that you have at least two cities that can grow to a huge size (the Surveyor will provide you with a population forecast), and thus build all the city improvements and turn out expensive military units in a swift and efficient manner. However, beyond that first couple of super-cities, don't worry too much about maximum city size, i.e. don't worry about overlapping city radiuses. Medium-size cities have a big advantage over big cities: Keeping peace is easy. Besides, as you progress in your spell research, you can acquire spells that boost city size. The Nature spell "Change Terrain" is particularly useful and quite easy to acquire, provided you have at least one Nature spell book and can trade spells with other Wizards.

Once you've established what's the maximum number of cities you can fit into your initial land mass, so to speak, you can fine-tune the location to your liking. I try to spread the benefits fairly evenly, and make sure every city has some sort of production/trade bonus. The square containing deer (game) is a sort of a wonder square because of the extra food. If there's a conflict, I always try to put it under the control of a fairly promising city instead of propping up a weak one.

Whatever you do, make sure you have a port on every coast—north, south, east, and west.

WHO LIVES THERE?

If you have more than one race under your control, you'll also have to decide which race gets to start the new settlement. This will largely determine your new city's character, so choose wisely! Don't make mistakes such as starting a port city with a race that can't build good ships, for instance, if you do have another race that can. Remember that Merchant's Guilds are only a possibility in cities that have a shipyard.

Your choice of the new city's racial profile should also include inherent racial characteristics, and not just city or unit-building capability. For example, Lizardmen are always better starting off a city on the shore or close to the shore rather than further inland; that location capitalizes on their inborn swimming ability. Nomad cities should be founded in locations where they can maximize their trade bonus—Klackon cities, where they can take full advantage of the Klackon production bonus; and so on. Know your races! Read the manual and *MOM's* README notes carefully.

EXPANDING YOUR EMPIRE

During your initial phase of empire-building, you will have to deal with visits from rampaging monsters. These appear particularly frequently when you're playing at the higher difficulty levels, so it makes good sense to make sure every single settlement of yours has a garrison of at least four units, and large cities, six or more.

Growing Good Cities

This means you'll have to put quite a lot of emphasis on food production and increasing your revenues. The two go together, since a farmer's market requires a marketplace be built first. You should make these two structures priorities in any settlement you start, along with a shrine (keeps peace and, depending on the race, provides Shamans), Barracks (lets you make military units other than Spearsmen, Shamans, Priests, or Warlocks), and a library (you can speed up research, or divert the extra mana into improving your casting ability).

At this point, further city development can take several directions. Your subsequent choices will vary from city to city depending on the races involved, their strategic position, and your plans. However, there are still some general guidelines that are good to follow:

 Try to build all the unrest-quelling institutions you can in any given city. In addition to keeping your townsfolk productive, these city improvements produce mana, which is always welcome.

 Build improvements that boost food supply everywhere you can. Food tends to be a constant problem because of the need to feed your ever-growing armies, and supplies can get dramatically short when a rival Wizard specializing in Chaos casts "Great Wasting"—which is almost guaranteed to happen, sooner or later, at the Impossible level.

 Build improvements boosting production according to the city's importance. A city that's not particularly productive should get all production boosters it can if it is under danger and likely to become a point of conflict. A big city can *always* use all the improvements affecting production. Remember, you cannot build sawmills and subsequently Forester's Guilds in cities without forest squares ("Change Terrain" can fix that).

 Build expensive military structures only in cities with high production levels. The Armory is a must for *every* race that has Halberdiers or Slingers (Halflings). Some races, which do not gain any immediate benefits from an Armory, need a Fighter's Guild to make Pikemen. Beyond that, build Armorer's Guilds and War Colleges only in big cities with high production levels.

 Your capital (the city containing your fortress) should always have city walls. Same goes for border towns that are likely to become points of conflict. The remaining cities should have walls only if their contents (in the shape of precious city improvements) warrant the trouble.

Important Note: Remember to put a high priority on unrest-quelling institutions (shrine, temple, etc.) in all cities that are likely to come under pressure. Sieges mean city garrison casualties, and since the military units help keep peace, losses may result in rebels among the townsfolk. This is the last thing you need in a besieged city!

Conquering Towers of Wizardry and Magic Nodes

Conquering a Tower of Wizardry and thus gaining access to Myrror is an absolute priority if you start on Arcanus. The many benefits of starting the game on Myrror—the ones that cost three spell book picks—can be yours the moment you've captured a Tower of Wizardry.

Unfortunately, at higher difficulty level, Sss'ra, the Myrran Wizard, casts "Planar Seal" as soon as possible (which is pretty quick). If you've managed to conquer a Tower and start a Myrran settlement before he does, congratulations! You're well on the way to winning the game. However, the armies that guard Towers are extremely strong, and it costs valuable time to assemble a killer army that can vanquish them.

As soon as your cities can support all the necessary units, form one strong army under the leadership of a hero, and start exploring the various ruins, dungeons, temples, etc. As your army and hero gain experience, send exploratory squads into Towers of Wizardry and Magic Nodes to find out the strength of their defenders.

As mentioned, Towers of Wizardry are particularly tough nuts to crack, often tougher than Nodes. The presence of guys such as Sky Drakes or Death Knights makes some Towers virtually impossible to conquer unless you have an experienced hero carrying a couple of artifacts, leading an army that includes top-notch troops such as Elite Berserkers or Paladins along with good ranged-attack units (Elite Priests are best because of their capacity to

Important Note: Never make explatory squads bigger than three military units. Losing four units or more together with the battle means loss of fame; losing three doesn't cost you anything beyond the units. Besides, even only three units can inflict meaningful losses on the defenders of a Tower of Wizardry or Magic Node if they are supported by skillful casting of battle spells (note that in Magic Nodes, the only spells that work are those of the same kind as the Node— Nature spells in Nature Nodes, Chaos in Chaos Nodes, and so on). Personally, I found Sorcery Nodes easier to conquer than others, particularly when equipped with the "Phantom Warriors" spell.

cast the "Healing" spell). However, the rewards from conquering a Tower are great, and you shouldn't be afraid to sacrifice some troops in order to prevail. Just make sure you don't sacrifice your best guys. Keep them grouped around your best hero for the final assault.

The one big plus when tackling Towers of Wizardry is that you have recourse to your whole spell book. Even a simple spell like "Web" can take a lot of air out of a Sky Drake!

MEETING OTHER WIZARDS

At some point in your expansion, you're going to start running into the computer-controlled Wizards. When playing at a higher difficulty level, these Wizards will be almost invariably much stronger than you are, with enormous reserves of mana and great spell-casting powers. Don't despair. They may have all the mana in both worlds, but they don't have your brains.

The computer-controlled Wizards all have distinct personalities. Their initial attitudes towards you are shaped by two factors: the personality of the Wizard in question, and a comparison of the spell books each of you own. If you own

MASTER OF MAGIC

Chaos magic (red) or Death magic (purple) spell books, each of these exerts a slightly negative influence, Death being slightly worse than Chaos.

The influence of a Wizard's personality on his/her attitude towards you is pretty self-explanatory and shows itself in the wording of the initial greeting. Wizards such as Merlin and Oberic tend be fawning; don't expect the same from Kali.

The current state of your relations with another Wizard is shown by the color of the eyes of the Gargoyles on the diplomacy screen. Red is bad, green is good, and yellow means neutrality (the scheme is identical to *Master of Orion's*). Your actions affect your relations, of course. The manual discusses diplomatic dealings in sufficient detail, so I'll concentrate on the strategy here.

I've found that the most effective diplomatic strategy is to be nice to everyone while stabbing them in the back whenever possible. It calls for strength of character to be consistently false—but it pays dividends. In *Master of Magic,* of course; don't take this advice any further. Offer spells as gifts upon meeting another Wizard. Think of it this way: Sacrificing a spell or two is a good way to guarantee that the other Wizard will trade spells with you. Making the other Wizard like you is also a necessary prerequisite to making them declare war on someone, and provoking fights among computer Wizards is the surest way to victory. *Divide et imperam*—divide and rule—should be your motto. Try to implement this policy promptly; after turn one hundred, the computer-controlled Wizards become quite forgiving of transgressions on each other's part and tend to vent their spleen at you. The designers incorporated that feature because otherwise, the grievances of the first hundred turns would keep the computer Wizards constantly at war with each other, thus making it easy for you to win the game. This design feature is probably the best proof that the divisive, scheming strategy outlined above really works well!

If you've started the game loaded with Death magic and are playing at a high difficulty level, you may find everyone is feeling uneasy about you when you first meet them. Offer spells as tribute, and generally smooth ruffled feathers until you feel ready for an armed rumble. At a high game difficulty level, you'll have one coming your way soon or later, whether you like it or not.

> ### Special note for players who opt for the Impossible level:
>
> Pay attention to city garrisons; the absolute minimum is four units, preferably five. The Impossible level has Raiders and rampaging monsters coming at you in numbers every few turns. Capture all neutral cities in your area to get rid of the first problem; clean out all the lairs, keeps, ruins, etc. to get rid of the latter.

MILITARY *MOM*

Military matters are a very important part of *MOM*. You can choose to win either through banishing all the other Wizards, or by casting the spell of "Mastery." Either option involves plenty of warfare, because once you've started casting the "Mastery" spell, everyone will gang up on you.

Given this, you'll understand that your prowess as a military administrator and leader is crucial to winning the game. In order to be good both at administering your army and leading it in combat, there is something you should keep in your mind at all times: Experienced units are far better than green ones.

THE MEANING OF EXPERIENCE

The stats you'll find in *MOM's* README file and manual all apply to units in their green, inexperienced state. However, they are very different when the same unit reaches Elite or Ultra-Elite status.

For example, High Men's Spearsmen start as Recruits with a strength 1 attack, 2 defense, 4 resistance (resistance is basically defense against spells), and 1 hit point each. At 20 experience points, they turn into Regulars—their attack strength increases to 2, and their resistance to 5. At 60 experience points, they become Veterans, improving to strength 3 defense, and 6 resistance; 120 experience points result in Elite units, which is as good as most units get, and your Elite Spearsmen have 3 attack, 3 defense, and 7 resistance. Also, they receive a +1 bonus to hit, and an extra hit point. Compared with raw recruits, your Elite Spearsmen are three times as strong, four times as tough, and nearly twice as difficult to put under a spell.

If you choose the Warlord special ability, or cast the spell "Crusade," your units can progress a level further—and that's when you find out why Warlord costs two spell book picks. Ultra-Elite marks a dramatic increase in a unit's capabilities. At that level, the above-mentioned Spearsmen will have a strength 3 attack, +2 bonus to hit, 4 defense, 8 resistance, and 2 hit points. If you choose Warlord *and* cast "Crusade," your units can progress yet another level to become Champions. Champion Spearsmen have a strength 4 attack, +3 bonus to hit, 4 defense, 9 resistance, and 3 hit points. Compare that with the raw recruit at 1 attack, 2 defense, 4 resistance, and 1 hit point, and you'll see a unit's experience is worth its weight in gold.

A word about the extra levels added through the Warlord or the spell "Crusade": The bonuses mentioned are applied the moment the unit is recruited, not when it reaches Elite status. Thus, under a Warlord, a brand-new unit starts out as Regular. With Warlord and "Crusade," it starts out as a Veteran, and reaches Champion status at 120 experience points.

Strength in Numbers

You'll notice that various units have various numbers of figures; for instance, Spearsmen have eight figures, Swordsmen have six, and Cavalry four. This is a very important difference, since all unit stats (attack and defense strengths, hit points, etc.) apply not to the unit as a single entity, but to each and every one of its figures. Thus, the eight figures in a Spearsmen unit go a long way to compensate for this unit's relatively low attack and defense values.

You should also remember that any unit's base chance to hit the enemy when attacking is just 30%. Again, that 30% applies to each and every figure in that unit. It's better to have eight chances of 30% each than four chances, as is the case with Cavalry! In this light, it's also easy to see why bonuses To Hit are truly important.

THE USEFUL UNIT GUIDE

Master of Magic features a multitude of military units. In fact, there are so many that chances are you'll be feeling very confused at first. Every race has at least one, and often several units that are unique. On top of that, standard units like Swordsmen or Cavalry have different attributes from race to race. I've listed the most common types of units below, together with comments on the possible variations.

 Spearsmen are the most basic unit found in *MOM*. They do not cost any gold to maintain—just food. They can be built in any settlement the moment it becomes a hamlet, and can produce anything. Their standard stats are 1 attack, 2 defense at the recruit stage.

In spite of the fact that they have eight figures to a unit, Spearsmen are generally a weak unit. The exceptions are Barbarian and Dark Elf Spearsmen. The former have a thrown attack, the latter have a magical ranged attack, and both are quite deadly.

 Swordsmen are among the best value-for-money units found in *MOM*. They're pretty cheap, have a basic 3 attack and 2 defense, and come with a large shield. This last fact is very important: A large shield means the unit defends better against Bowmen and Slingers.

Experienced Swordsmen can be a very valuable unit. I use them as the core of my city garrisons, and usually include at least one unit in every army. Barbarian and Dark Elf Swordsmen are outstanding for the same reason as the Spearsmen—thrown and ranged attacks.

 Cavalry is a highly mobile unit whose main strength is in attack; do not use it for passive defense—charge! Recon squads of three Cavalry units combine mobility with sufficient strength for armed probes into ruins, keeps, nodes, etc. I recommend you form at least one roving squad like that to explore territory.

Cavalry units have 3 hit points per figure, which helps compensate for only four figures to a unit. Cavalry has First Strike capability—it gets to inflict damage before the defenders strike back. But be careful who you charge; some units, such as Pikemen, negate First Strike capability.

Nomads have a variation on Cavalry called Horsebowmen. Their ranged-attack capability is meaningless at first, but becomes useful at the Elite level. Barbarian Cavalry have a fairly lethal thrown attack that, coupled with their First Strike capability, makes them very dangerous.

 Bowmen are your basic ranged-attack troops. They are pretty useless as green recruits, and have to reach Elite status to become useful. It's a complete waste of time to send them into battle before they turn Veteran.

Make a couple of Bowmen units early on, and keep them as part of the city garrison until they reach the desired experience level. Special note: High Elves have a variation called Longbowmen who are absolutely lethal, but pretty pricey too. Halflings have Slingers, who become frightful killers with experience. Nomads have Rangers, who are deadly with a bow and also endow armies they're stacked with with great speed and ease of movement. Lizardmen have Javelineers, which are really good—strong attack, extra hit points, and naturally swimming capability.

 Shamans and Priests are mutually exclusive. If a race has Shamans, it doesn't have Priests, and vice versa. Shamans are weaker than the Priests, but they are cheaper; both units have four figures to a unit.

Shamans and Priests share several important qualities. First of all, both are capable of four ranged magical attacks per battle—the Shamans' ranged attack has a strength of 2, and the Priests', strength 4. Both types of units are Purifiers, which means they can clean up corruption from land squares (the result of a "Corruption" or "Great Wasting" spell). Both are Healers, which means damaged units stacked together with them in a single army will heal more quickly. Finally, Priests can cast the "Healing" spell once per battle, which is very useful.

Not surprisingly, Shamans and/or Priests are an important part of every army and city garrison.

 Halberdiers and Pikemen are two variations on the same theme. As with Priests and Shamans, they are mutually exclusive. Many races have Halberdiers; only Nomads and High Men have Pikemen.

Halberdiers have better attack and defense strengths than Swordsmen, but do not have a large shield, which makes them more vulnerable to ranged attacks. Most Halberdier units negate First Strike capability, but some don't—it depends on the race, so make sure you check out the ones you can make. In addition to negating First Strike, pikemen are armor-piercing; they automatically cut a target's defense in half when attacking. Since Pikemen require a Fighter's Guild, all units you make are automatically Regulars, adding to their value.

 Catapults can be made by all races that can build a Mechanician's Guild. It takes some time before you can build that Guild, and Catapults are both pricey and useless at the Recruit stage, which may make them seem not worth the trouble. However, they become a very good unit at the Elite level, and their ability to hit flying units makes them particularly valuable. If you can make them at all, do so, and make sure they've got at least a couple of experience levels before sending them out to battle.

 Super Cavalry is what I'd term units such as High Men's Paladins, High Elves' Elven Lords, Beastmen's Centaurs, Gnolls' Wolf Riders, and Trolls' War Trolls. Each of these units has a host of special qualities coupled with impressive attack and defense strengths and a movement of two. Make sure you include a couple of Super-Cavalry units in every army you send out to actually conquer something!

 Magicians are a feature of all the races that can build Wizard's Guilds. In addition to a fearful fiery ranged attack, they can cast the "Fireball" spell once per battle, and are immune to conventional ranged weapons (bows, slings). Their ranged attack is very powerful, so you should include at least one Magician in every army and garrison, but do not replace Priests with them entirely! Priests have the "Healing spell," which is more valuable than a single "Fireball."

 Flying Units are a feature of races that can build the Fantastic Stable. High Elf Pegasi, Nomad Griffins, and Beastmen Manticores are good examples. Most flying units have some sort of special attack capability, such as the ability to fire missiles, fiery breath, or poison attacks. Flying units are a great addition to any army you send out, but usually they're not necessary in a city garrison, whose ranged-attack troops should be sufficient to deal with any attacking enemy fliers. If you can afford it, try composing an army of flying units headed by a flying hero (you'll have to cast the "Flying" spell). A good army like that is perhaps the ultimate army, especially if it has ranged-attack capabilities.

In addition to the above, there is quite a lot of race-specific units that defy easy categorization. Unfortunately, a chapter does not offer sufficient space to discuss them all. You'll find stats for all *MOM* units in the game manual and README file. If there's a difference, remember that the stats in the README file are the ones that apply.

Heroes

Heroes are the ultimate units. They're not easy to come by, and initially, they are very easy to lose. What applies to all *MOM* military units applies all the more here. Experience counts! As you can see in the game manual, heroes can also advance by more levels than other military units, and thus can reach incredible heights of excellence. A Demi-God or even a Grand Lord can mow down several enemy units without any trouble!

Heroes come in all shapes and sizes, with tons of various special abilities. However, they can be categorized into just a few basic types:

 Spellcasters and Sages are invaluable when kept next to you, in the city with your Wizard's fortress, because 50% of their skill is added to yours when casting/researching spells. However, Spellcasters are also very useful on the battlefield. They can cast spells with no drain on your mana resources, or execute ranged magical attacks. I usually wait till I have two Spellcasters among my heroes before I send one out, though. Early examples include Valana the Bard and Zoltran the Sage.

 Ranged Attack heroes come equipped with a bow. They make excellent leaders for your field armies; with experience, and given a magical item, a bow-sporting hero can take down a Sky Drake. Do not keep them in a city—let them roam and conquer. B'shan the Dervish will offer his services in almost every game of *MOM* you play.

 Battlefield Killer heroes have impressive attack/defense strengths, and are obviously made for leading your field armies. Brax the Dwarf and Gunther the Barbarian are good early specimens of battlefield killers. Given lots of experience, a couple of spells such as "Flying" or "Invulnerability," and a couple of magical items, battlefield killers can become pretty nearly invincible.

The caliber of the heroes that offer their services depends on your fame. The more famous you get, the more/better heroes will come knocking at your door until you have the maximum number of heroes permissible. However, do not shy away from hiring weaker, early heroes because you want to wait for someone more talented. Heroes greatly improve with experience, and the earlier you get your hero, the more experience he's likely to get!

Try to outfit all your heroes with magical items that improve their performance on the battlefield. You'll find a few of these when exploring ruins, keeps, temples etc. (sometimes, you may even find an imprisoned hero as well!). If you want to create a magical item, time your move carefully because it's an enterprise that involves considerable mana and time. Make sure you outfit every hero with the right item. For instance, a hero with high attack strength but poor defense needs protection more than he needs extra strength in attack.

Fighting Battles

It's always better to be the attacker for the simple reason that the attacker gets to move first. This includes casting spells, and at the higher difficulty levels, casting "Counter Magic" at the very beginning of every battle is often the

MASTER OF MAGIC

only way to avoid defeat. The opposing Wizards are almost invariably more powerful than you are; however, they usually aren't as good at actually leading the troops on the battlefield.

The computer-controlled armies always target your ranged-attack troops first, so you may want to protect them by casting "Stone Skin" or equivalent before you even go into battle (it's a bit expensive, being an overland enchantment, but that can't be helped). Priests, Magicians and Shamans are at the top of the enemy hit list, along with Slingers, Bowmen, etc. Swordsmen tend to come second because of their extra protection against ranged attacks. Other troops and heroes come next, depending on their relative importance in the computer's electronic mind.

Your first step should be to right-click on all enemy units in turn to see what they're worth, and identify the worst threats. Then cast whatever spell is appropriate. You cannot do that after you've moved your last unit, and it's easy to forget once you start moving units around. After that, it's a question of setting target priorities for your troops and maneuvering them on the battlefield in the optimum manner. If you enjoy a big superiority in ranged-attack weapons, stand still and let the enemy come to you. If the reverse is true, get moving as fast as you can. Always move forward with all speed when attacking a city with city walls—Cavalry or Super-Cavalry is very useful.

If you're fighting another Wizard, always try to take out the enemy hero if present. Computer-controlled Wizards are very dismayed to lose any heroes, and immediately put a lot of effort into replacing them.

CHAPTER
8
MASTER OF ORION

Publisher:	Microprose Software
Platform:	PC MS-DOS
Release Date:	Summer, 1993
Multiplayer:	No

Rating:

General Overview

Master of Orion is the classic space strategy game. It was a hit the moment it appeared, and the updates to the game balance and AI continue to make it a contender against much fancier, newer variations on the space-strategy theme. Its basic premise is a familiar one. Starting out with one space colony and a couple of spaceships, you must become the ruler of a united galaxy. This can happen only through winning the elections held periodically by the Galactic High Council, where representatives of all the galactic races cast votes according to the size of their populations and personal political preferences. You do not have to be the biggest to be the best. In fact, since other races tend to mistrust and dislike a race that has grown too strong, the second-strongest contender often emerges the winner.

MOO, as it's widely called, is famous for having a truly playable diplomatic system—it's possible to win through diplomacy as opposed to brute force. But even brute force has many sophisticated aspects in this beautifully balanced game. Technological advances are essential to maintaining a military edge, and the intricacies of space ship design are a mini-game in itself.

The only major flaws in *MOO* are its graphics. They smacked of the fifties even when the game first appeared, and cannot compete with a visual feasts like *Ascendancy.* However, *Ascendency* is a bad game, and *Master of Orion* is a great game.

The best strategy for winning *MOO* changes with the game's difficulty level. Oddly enough, it's not dictated by the choice of your race to the extent you'd expect. While some races are clearly better than the others because of inherent production advantages, there's not that much significance in having other special racial advantages. They do add nice spice to the game, though.

Like most truly good strategy games, *Master of Orion* will keep you busy on a variety of activities.

The foremost of these is planetary management. You must strike the right balance in spending on new spaceships, planetary defense, and technological research. This is not a matter of setting the production bars to an 'ideal' ratio, but constant re-adjustment. On the average, you can expect to fiddle with a planet's production bars once every five turns, although sometimes, things have to be changed three turns in a row. All this can be avoided on the easier difficulty levels, where your opponents are somewhat forgiving.

However, on the Hard and Impossible levels, constant tinkering with the production bars is necessary to reduce the computer opponents' inherent production advantages.

(Please note that throughout this chapter, I'll be referring to *MOO's* star systems as 'planets'. Since each star system is represented by a single planet, I think this simplification makes sense.)

The second major activity is conducting diplomacy and trade with the computer players. Diplomacy and trade are very important in *MOO,* and the player who neglects the Races screen is headed for defeat. At the Impossible level, the only way to have a stab at victory is by offering a technological advance as tribute upon meeting anyone! Once everyone likes you, you'll find it easy to stir up trouble among other races by talking them into breaking alliances and fighting one another.

The technological advances in *MOO* are mini-games in themselves, and you'd be wise to spend some time with the Technology screen every few turns. You should consult it anyway every time you intend to trade technological advances with other races. If you're in a hurry to discover a particular technology, you can greatly speed up that discovery by continuously adding credits to its research. It goes without saying that you have to learn what these technological advances really mean, and some of them have far-reaching implications that aren't evident at first glance. *MOO's* technologies are discussed later on in this chapter.

You'll make use of many newly discovered technologies while engaging in *MOO's* fourth major area of activity—spaceship design.

Spaceship design becomes particularly important at the higher difficulty levels, where your space fleet is almost always numerically inferior. However, even the easiest difficulty levels won't excuse a failure to update your space fleet, and although it may have gotten really big over many turns, it may not be able to deal with a single enemy ship.

Golden Rules

 Expand fast. Build medium-sized, long-range armed ships to claim planets out of your colony ship's range, and concentrate initially on researching propulsion technologies. Unless you're playing at a very easy game difficulty level, the colony ship with reserve fuel tanks isn't worth it.

- Help newly founded colonies grow quickly by sending regular, small numbers of transports rather than one big chunk. This won't hurt the donating planets as much.

- Start building a space battle fleet as soon as you can fit a computer and a laser aboard a small hull. Update your space fleet with new models regularly; precede each new design with a round of technology trading.

- Make sure everyone likes you—even when playing Darloks. Give technological tributes to everyone you meet—and keep running your hand up their collective leg until they're at least Relaxed.

- Formulate a diplomatic strategy on the basis of the alien leaders' personalities. It rarely pays to enter into any big trade deals with an Erratic leader; they're the worst of the bunch. Even military-minded Xenophobes respond favorably to repeated leg-stroking; Erratics like it too, but punch you in the face anyway.

- Don't start wars with anyone; make *them* start a war instead. An honorable reputation goes a long way when doing diplomatic deals. Avoid using biological weapons.

- Choose a race with the production advantage that best suits your style of play. Nearly all the races in *MOO* enjoy some sort of direct or indirect production bonus—Klackons through productive workers, Meklars through better factory controls, Psilons through reduced research costs, Humans through trade. Silicoids look great. They can live anywhere and don't need to clean up pollution, but their excruciatingly low 'birth rate' is a big handicap.

- *Divide et imperam*—divide and rule. Keep the computer players fighting each other, and guess who will be the winner . . . you. Be on the lookout on temporarily uninhabited planets; computer players like to wipe each other's planets population out. They give you a chance to expand your empire without starting a war (although it's likely you'll have to fight a couple of battles over the planet you covet).

- Keep your self well-informed throughout the game. This means regularly reading up your spies' reports on the other races— checking on their diplomatic state of affairs as well as their technologies.

- Make regular technology-trading rounds. Always precede them with a visit to your own Tech screen, and a read-up of the Report. If you aren't offered what you wanted, think whether you can't trade it to another computer player for something you can really use. Do not *give away* technologies that will lose you the game. For instance, giving advanced terraforming technology to a race that's already leading in the galactic elections is like putting a gun to your head.

- Use your spies for espionage rather than sabotage. It's relatively safe to spy on someone, provided they already like you a lot. This is yet another benefit of early technology tributes.

- Remember being biggest doesn't win you the game; having the most votes does. Since other computer players feel threatened by size, having many friends and being the second-largest race is often better.

- By the middle game, make sure you've always got at least one very good friend in the galaxy—preferably two. Having someone declare war on any of your enemies at your request, almost whenever you want, goes a long way towards winning the game.

- The election can only be won by a huge majority. Abstain if you can; voting for one candidate always makes the other quite angry. On the other hand, voting for someone you are at war with can be very helpful in bringing peace—sometimes very desirable, too, for you are fighting one of the two biggest races in the galaxy.

- When you find yourself a candidate for the throne of Orion, double your efforts to make some good friends. Never wage war on anyone who has voted for you in the election, unless you're dealing with a madman that keeps attacking you anyway.

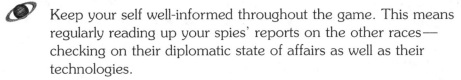

MASTER OF ORION

Winning Strategies

Every game of *MOO* begins in the same fashion. You are given a fairly large planet with forty (million) colonists, two scout ships, and a colony ship.

FIRST GALACTIC STEPS

Your first priority is to use the colony ship wisely. You can't do that if you don't really know where you are, so I recommend you begin by going to the Map screen first and finding out more about the galaxy. If you have selected a high number of computer players (I heartily recommend going for the maximum—it makes the game much more fun), it's likely your first planet is near the galaxy's edge. Note the location of promising-looking stars (yellow, green, red) relative to that of your home star/planet. Plan to keep part of the galaxy reserved for your own use. If you keep control of the stars that can serve as stepping stones to reach other stars, then the other stars are yours—that is, as long as you develop the planetary landing technologies before your rivals develop propulsion ones that will extend the range of their ships.

Having done some galactic planning and crystal-gazing, return to your home star. Make sure you send each of your ships to a different star (of course, your colony ship has limited range). Do not start a new colony until you have reports about all of the stars/planets within a three-parsec radius.

You want to settle as many planets as quickly as possible, because so do the computer players. However, it's counterproductive to spend credits on another colony ship right at the beginning. Concentrate on building new factories for the first ten turns or so. Then, devote three mouse-clicks' worth to technology research. Do the same for your other colony the moment new factory construction hits three or more per turn (or 'tuan', as *MOO* imaginatively calls it). This lets you quickly discover the first set of technologies, and concentrate almost all of your research spending on propulsion. Do not cut spending on other technologies, however; allocate a small amount to each one.

You will have to start sending colonists to your second planet as soon as it's settled. I recommend you do so in small increments every other turn (the first wave can be bigger). I found that sending eight to ten percent of the new planet's total population in the first wave and two percent in four-to-five subsequent waves (every other turn) considerably speeded up the new colony's development without slowing the growth of the mother planet too badly.

Finding Extra Funds

Sending off colonists results in an important phenomenon: The construction of new factories hits maximum well before all the factories have been built. The 'max' indicator means that you don't have enough colonists to operate additional factories. If you continue building them, they won't produce any credits for a few turns. *Whenever you see the 'max' indicator appear, you should instantly see whether you can transfer some credits into technology research.* You'll often find out that as many as 50 BC per turn are wasted on building factories that don't produce. Allocating these funds to research greatly speeds it up in the opening stages of the game, where a discovery may cost just a few hundred (billion) credits.

The ABCs of Galactic Expansion

If you're playing at the Hard or Impossible level, you cannot afford to wait till your second colony ship is ready. The computer players might start colonizing planets on your doorstep even as you're still building factories on your mother planet.

You may prevent this sad occurrence by building a dozen or so armed medium-size ships with reserve fuel tanks, and using them as scouts/claimants. I recommend you arm them with lasers—some of the ships they'll fight off will be armed only with rockets. You'll find details on spaceship construction further on. For now, just note that armed long-distance ships can help you secure a good-looking planet for your own use—at least initially. It is usually a good idea to let your second planet make these armed explorer ships while the mother planet builds new colony ships.

Remember that all planets aren't equal. Those that are very small, poor or ultra-poor, or with hostile environments, aren't as good. However, each planet you can colonize is a planet you can colonize, and your aim is to colonize every planet you can before they run out.

Sometimes, a less-attractive planet occupies an important strategic position. To use an obvious example, it serves as a stepping stone to a big, rich planet. When a situation like this occurs, do not be afraid to revise your priorities. Denying new colonies to other races is as important as starting new colonies. At higher game difficulty levels, this may be taken further. If you don't deny planets to your competitors, you won't have any yourself.

Whether you've just colonized planet number five or number ten, sooner or later you'll come into contact with other inhabitants of the galaxy.

CLOSE ENCOUNTERS OF THE NERD KIND

My advice is this: Unless you play at a low difficulty level, go out of your way to be nice to the snakes, bears, lizards, and other creatures of the galaxy.

Whenever you encounter another race, you'd do well to follow a certain routine. First of all, go to the Map screen and examine the real estate held by your newly encountered opponent. Then check the Status on the Races screen. At high difficulty levels, you'll almost invariably be much weaker than the computer player, especially in the space fleet department. Don't despair or gasp for air. Just note the number of planets the other guy has, then check on the leader's personality by asking to view the Report on that race. If you intend to exchange technologies, you should also refresh your memory by going to the Technology screen. Ask for an audience only after you've prepared yourself in the manner described above. Otherwise, you'll find yourself trading valuable technologies in exchange for something your scientists were about to discover on their own.

Once the audience begins, my first move is always to offer a technological tribute. If the newly encountered race doesn't like my face, I offer two. The only exception to this rule is when the computer player is quite weak, which rarely happens at the higher difficulty levels. What's more, at the higher difficulty levels, computer players who haven't been treated to a tribute often declare war on you a couple of turns after you've come across each other.

It may seem like a waste to offer any technologies free of charge like this that are good for an exchange. However, at higher difficulty levels, the computer players will likely refuse to trade technologies with you unless you give them one or two to start with. This does not apply when you're playing Humans. All bets are off when it comes to those guys . . . you know . . . *people,* regardless whether you're playing as them or coming up against them. Of course, we're only talking about *Master of Orion* . . .

The happy-to-meet-you-here's-a-free-technology approach pays dividends for the rest of the game. Even if you go to war with the party in question, you'll find it easier to make peace—and making peace is part of war. It's stupid to continue fighting someone who has ceased to threaten.

To Trade or Not to Trade

Unless you're absolutely sure you and the newly met computer player are going to war at short notice, you should also make your first trade deal. Trade starts paying dividends only after some time has passed, and the longer it goes on, the bigger the profits. If you're playing at a high difficulty level, however, you should think twice before offering a trade deal to a powerful . . . er . . . Human computer player. The Human computer player makes immense profits from trade (higher difficulty levels mean an extra bonus to the already sizeable Human trade bonus), and you may be helping Humans win the game.

You should also reconsider agreeing to new trade deals if your Trade is currently showing a deficit. If you keep offering or accepting new deals every few turns, you'll severely limit your own trade profit. Make one deal, wait, make another, wait—that's the correct tactic. Inevitably, this advice does not apply when you're playing Humans.

If you are the biggest and best in the galaxy, you don't really need trade. Trade helps the others more than it helps you, so if you continue trading, make sure there's the appropriate payoff. It's counterproductive to trade with the guy competing with you for the galactic throne, for example. However, trade deals with races that support you at election time are all to the good.

Spying is Believing

Before you exit the Races screen after your first inter-galactic meeting, you should allocate funds to setting up a spy network within the computer player's domain. Your very first spy will provide you with an updated Report on the other player's technological knowledge, and I'd suggest you wait for that before you start making any technology trades (that does *not* mean you should wait with your initial technological tribute). You'll quickly see that computer players often refuse to trade technologies even though they could use one, especially at the higher technology levels. They'll also never offer to trade their top technology in a given field, and generally will drive a hard bargain, especially on the higher difficulty levels. The only way to make them offer sweeter deals is by making them like you more, which is dealt with in detail in a separate section.

You shouldn't keep more than one spy per race unless you intend to go on a major spying offensive. Until then, all you want is an updated Report detailing what wars and alliances the computer player is involved in, and what technologies they have. The information contained in the racial Report has far-reaching importance, and if you use it right, it becomes a very dangerous weapon—more so than any technological advance on its own. Use it to play the diplomacy game, decide between war, peace, and trade, and finally to design spaceships that exploit the gaps in your opponent's technologies.

PUTTING YOUR EMPIRE INTO SHAPE

Sooner or later, the borders of your galactic empire will become defined. There will be no more planets to colonize—at least not until you've discovered how to make planetary landings in some pretty hostile environments. If there are several of those especially hostile planets within the frame of your galactic border, make every effort to acquire the technologies needed for colonizing them—through research, technology exchange, and even spying. Until that happens, guard them with your spaceships.

The Territorial Imperative

As you'll notice, there are no real borders between the competing empires. Computer players colonize planets without paying any attention to their location, as long as they're within range. It's pretty disconcerting to find two or three foreign colonies springing up right in the middle of your part of the galactic sandbox.

If you can land on the planets the computer player(s) claimed from right under your nose, you should consider whether a quick war wouldn't be to your advantage. If you aren't sure you can win, you should mark the offending computer player for special treatment. Ask other players to declare war on him, refuse any trade deals, and take every opportunity to make his life misery without provoking a full-scale war. This is relatively easy to achieve at the lower difficulty levels. At higher difficulty levels, this is where (paradoxi-cally) your initial technology tribute will help you. The mistreated computer player will be much more forgiving of your belligerent stance. Without the ini-tial tribute, there's a strong chance of war, and an unwanted war at high diffi-culty levels often spells disaster.

In the meantime, concentrate on building a strong economy and your first star fleet. I found it's better to hold off with building missile bases until all fac-tories have been built, but there are occasional exceptions to the rule. For instance, a poor or ultra-poor planet takes so long to build all the allowable factories that you'd do well to start construction of missile bases earlier. Of course, if you are under a direct threat, priorities will shift as well.

At this point, you should also be scrounging credits wherever you can and pouring them into research. At the higher difficulty levels, the computer play-ers are very quick to acquire tons of new technology before you do, and it's essential you keep up in at least two areas: Computers and Weapons.

THE TECHNOLOGY RACE

The manual discusses the types of technology available in some detail, so here I'll focus on identifying research priorities and benefits. I'd also like to note this point: You begin every game with a certain list of technological advances to discover, and this research list is by no means comprehensive. It features just part of all the available technologies (the Psilons' research list is a little more comprehensive, but by no means complete). You have to trade and/or steal the technologies that are missing, yet important; that is a given. This is why establishing good relations with at least part of your galactic com-petitors is so crucial.

Also, it pays to remember that small increases (a single click's worth) in funding the research of any technology are matched a roughly equivalent bonus, courtesy of the game designers. When you walk around distributing banknotes, scientists feel much encouraged and work harder, I suspect (it would have that effect on myself).

At the start of the game, you should concentrate almost all your research credits on propulsion technologies (but do leave some spending in every other category. Future research in any category is penalized by a complete cutoff). Of course, if there are three rich tundra planets on your doorstep, you may want to switch priorities. However, I usually find it's more expedient to guard planets like that with space fleets, and concentrate on propulsion anyway.

The first benefit there, is increased space ship range, which will let you expand your galactic empire. Almost every single new game of *MOO* features a couple of really nice planets just out of reach, and the sooner you can reach them, the better. I tend to concentrate on propulsion until my ships have a range of five parsecs (deuterium fuel cells), then go after better engines. At the time of the switch from range to engines, I also re-allocate research credits—about fifty percent continues to go into Propulsion, but other technologies are now given increased funding.

In my experience, Propulsion is extremely important in the first part of the game for two reasons. One is that more planets will come within your ships' range, and your ships will be able to get to them more quickly. The other is that nuclear engines (or any other better engine, for that matter) increase your ships' defense rating (as long as you remember to give them the best maneuvering capability available). In the first stage of any *MOO* game, computer technology levels are fairly primitive. Many of the ships built by the computer players have an attack level of zero or one. A defense rating of two means you cut the danger to your ships by fifty percent.

Having acquired better engines and longer range for your ships, you should allocate a meaningful amount to weapons research. Your first priority here is better missiles for your missile bases. Missiles can also give you important tactical advantages in spaceship combat.

Apart from the above, I tend to concentrate on technologies which increase production in any way possible. Terraforming +10 is a cheap technology to acquire, but the extra ten colonists plus the additional 20 factories they can operate make a lot of difference. You'll immediately feel the effect of the extra credits. Reduced Industrial Waste and better Eco Restoration release credits previously used to clean up pollution, so *de facto,* they provide you with increased production. Each new technology in planetology makes your colonists more productive, and may also allow you to colonize previously inaccessible planets.

Note that technologies that seem innocent can result in deadly battlefield applications. Propulsion, for instance, gives you the Warp Dissipator, High Energy Focus, and the somewhat less useful Energy Pulsar. Force Field technologies provide you with Repulsor Beams (invaluable when you have to combat hordes of enemy ships equipped with short-range beam weapons, bombs, or biological weapons). Finally, Computers give you an all-important edge in battle. If you fail to upgrade the computers of your space fleet and missile bases, sooner or later you will be unable to score a single hit on fast-moving enemy ships bristling with electronic defenses. Advances in Computer technology also significantly improve your espionage and anti-espionage capability.

Technology Milestones

MOO is a beautifully balanced game, and as such, all technologies are important. That importance may vary according to your specific situations. Here are some general notes on each technology type, and advances which mark a big qualitative jump forward.

 Computers. The better your computers, the more accurate your weapons (your spies get better too). ECM jammers are less important at the beginning, more important as time goes on (you'll need to put them on bombers tackling enemy missile bases). Space scanners are always very important. I often choose the Deep Space Scanner ahead of other, simpler Computer technologies, because it helps me prevent the computer players from colonizing planets before I do. Similarly, the Improved Space Scanner is invaluable in providing you with the destination and ETA of enemy space fleets.

Automatic Robotic controls are obviously super-important, since they enable you to increase production. Further on in the game, Hyperspace Communications let you re-direct fleets en route to a destination; Oracle Interface greatly increases the effectiveness of beam weapons; and Technology Nullifiers let you grapple with a much more sophisticated enemy with a hope at victory.

 Construction. All Construction advances have a strong effect on cost of building ships and the amount of space they offer. Better armor is extremely important. It gives both your ships and land troops an edge. Reduced Industrial Waste has the same effect as increasing production. Specially constructed armor for your ground forces, starting with Battle Suits, will help you in colony assaults.

Force Fields. The innocent-sounding Force Field technologies are extremely important. Every improvement in your shields means better protection for your ships and missile bases. This is especially valuable in the opening stages, when weapons are relatively weak. A ship protected by a Class II shield can avoid a lot of damage from weak laser weapons and early rockets! Planetary shields tremendously boost planetary defense. Their protection is added to that offered to your bases by conventional shields. The Repulsor Beam can render useless whole fleets of ships equipped with one-square range weapons, and they're also good for keeping enemy bombers away from your planet (as long as you position ships equipped with Repulsors correctly). Zyro and Lightning shields are a must for bombers, negating a lot of the danger presented by enemy planetary missile bases. The Cloaking Device is particularly well-suited for special fighting ships, such as torpedo launchers and dedicated bombers (bombers whose only purpose in life is to bomb, not shoot). Finally, the Stasis Field and the Black Hole rank among the most lethal equipment available. The Stasis Field immobilizes a whole group of ships, and the Black Hole Generator is absoslutely devastating to both ships and missile bases. Finally, a short series of increasingly sophisticated shields provides your ground troops with extra protection.

In my opinion, Force Fields is the single most-overlooked research category. At higher levels of difficulty, where the computer players routinely field fleets numbering thousands of ships, Force Field technologies are essential to close the quantitative gap.

 Planetology. This technology type has several sub-types, so to speak. Terraforming technologies increase your population, resulting in bigger production and more votes at the Galactic elections. They can become very important if you are one of the two contenders vying for the top office. Controlled Landings enable you to colonize increasingly hostile planets. Eco Restoration brings big benefits (the credits you save on pollution can be instantly applied elsewhere). Biological Weapons antidotes are extremely useful at higher difficulty levels, where computer players reach for biological weapons whenever there are any available. Soil Enrichment, Atmospheric Terraforming, and Cloning enable you to grow new colonists faster. Cloning becomes especially useful in the endgame, where you may be conducting a new planetary assault every turn.

The one category to avoid here, especially if playing at higher difficulty levels, is Biological Weapons. Don't ever use biological weapons or trade them away. The benefits are not worth the consequences.

 Propulsion. The most important technology type early on in the game, Propulsion remains quite important throughout every *MOO* campaign. This is especially evident at higher difficulty levels, where the computer players' space fleets almost invariably outnumber yours. Your only solution is to be there "fastest with the mostest," and fast ships enable you to do that. They also boast increased defense (as long as you've also given them the right class of maneuver), and allow you to fight space battles in a more sophisticated manner.

Not all Propulsion technologies have to do with speed and range. High Energy Focus is invaluable in ships armed with beam weapons, and Sub-Space Teleporters are the perfect addition to any ship equipped with a Stasis Field or Black Hole Generator. Displacement Devices offer a lot of extra protection from the lethal weaponry featured in the endgame.

Nevertheless, Propulsion does feature a couple of dogs. Pulsars sound great, but are quite impractical. They are too big to be fitted on smaller, cheaper ships, yet are only effective if used in numbers. Furthermore, they do not distinguish between friend and foe, which ties your hands on the battlefield. Star Gates are expensive to build and maintain; if you've got one of those compact empires and ships with good engines, you don't need Star Gates. Build them only if your far-flung empire features outposts too precious to lose to the enemy, even temporarily.

 Weapons. This is probably the most exciting area in research, as it features a great number of cool items with corresponding visual and sound effects. Basically, the weaponry falls into two categories—

missiles and beam weapons—although there are also bombs and Stream Projectors which strip a target of its armor.

In the initial stages of the game, your priority is Propulsion; nevertheless, you'll be spending some credits on Weapons, too. If your research list allows it, get Hand Lasers first, especially if playing at a higher difficulty level. If you happen to run into a hostile yet cocky computer player, you may have transports landing on your weak, newly-born colonies before you have the time to form a semblance of a space fleet. Your other priority is Hyper V/Hyper X missiles. Nuclear missiles are absolutely useless, as they are ludicrously slow and have short range; any ship equipped with Class II maneuver can dodge them. After you get the Hypers, things get less urgent in the missile department, but you should make sure you acquire Merculites/Stingers by the middle game.

Neutron pellet guns are cheap to research, and compact in size. I choose them whenever they are available because I can usually re-arm my small ships with that weapon within a short time. The neutron pellet gun is much more lethal than the laser. However, if you are confronting an enemy equipped with huge numbers of small ships, you should probably look into the Gatling laser before you do the neutron pellet gun.

Your military might takes a huge jump forward when you get the ion cannon. Heavy ion cannons are my armament of choice for much of the early middle game. They are largely useless for planetary attacks, but at higher difficulty levels, the first half of the game consists of worrying about defense more than offense. Acquiring Merculite missiles and ion cannons marks a transformation of your space fleet and planetary defenses. This is usually the right moment to design your first large ship, more of which comes later.

You should be improving your missile and beam weaponry regularly, even though the ion cannon and Merculites are adequate for a long time. This is because of the miniaturization process; every advance you make reduces the cost and size of older weapons. Thus, your first large ship may be able to take only a quartet of heavy and a single missile launcher (after you've added other necessary features). However, given a few discoveries, you'll be able to double its warload. Ship-building details are discussed in a separate section.

The next ripple of change through the battlefield comes with the discovery of anti-matter torpedoes. Unlike missiles, torpedoes do not run out, although they may be fired just every other turn. Given their destructive power, torpedoes are important players on the battlefield, and you should immediately design a ship around them. Use torpedo-equipped ships firing from a standoff position in all your battles, and you won't be sorry. As with other weaponry, new and better torpedoes become available with time.

You may have well discovered the Fusion Bomb along the way. It's cheaper than the ion cannon. You don't really need to discover any more bombs if your torpedo technology is recent. In long games, the acquisition of the Omega-V or neutronium bombs is sometimes necessary; more often, it isn't necessary, and you get the bombs anyway as a result of a half-hearted technology exchange.

Weapons for ground troops do not deserve as much consideration as weaponry that can be used aboard ships. If your space fleet is good enough, your colonists won't have to do much fighting. Of course, you may opt to research a ground weapon simply because it costs much less than the next item on your research list, and because its acquisition will take the weapons miniaturization process another step forward. Of course, you may have to revise this strategy in certain situations—like being next door to unfriendly Bulrathis with their ground combat bonus. Otherwise, ground weapons should be passed by in favor of other technologies. In any case, acquiring new armor (Construction) and personal shields (Force Fields) can give your ground forces a boost as strong as researching ground weapons.

Defeating the Guardian and colonizing Orion mark the beginning of the endgame (there may be games of *MOO* that may end with Orion still uncolonized—it's all up in the air at Galactic election time). Whoever gets Orion gets a big technological shot in the arm. In addition to several technologies that appear on players' research lists, the conqueror of Orion also acquires the Death Ray, an awesome, if bulky, beam weapon. The Death Ray, mounted on ships equipped with High Energy Focus and Oracle Interface, is the game's most lethal weapon.

However, the player that gets the Death Ray hasn't automatically won, because other beam weapons available later in the game are quite lethal, too. The Disruptor and Stellar Converter are long-range beam weapons that do heavy damage, and aren't as space-consuming as the Death Ray (meaning you can fit more of them onto a ship). The Mauler Device is the most lethal of research-list beam weaponry, although it's short range.

MOO features a small range of so-called streaming weapons (Graviton beam, Tachyon beam). Personally, I don't like them much. The amount of damage they can cause is unpredictable, and while 200 small fighters armed with Tachyon can do a lot of damage, on the average they do just as much when armed with other weapons, but much more predictably.

SHIP DESIGN

Designing a space ship in *MOO* involves making many choices. The later in the game, the more choices you face. However, no matter how expert you are at fitting out ships, the key to successful ship design lies in intelligence, intelligence, and once again, intelligence.

I don't even think about designing a new ship without going through the following exploratory motions:

- An assessment of ongoing research. If I'm just a few turns from acquiring new armor, weapon, or any technology that can affect ship design to a significant degree, I always wait, boosting research of the key technology by adding a click of credits every turn.

- An attempt to trade technologies. Before I start construction, I make rounds of the races, and see whether I can pick up something to improve my new ship. More often than not, I do! If you anticipated designing a fighter with a heavy laser and you suddenly get the ion cannon . . . that changes things.

- An evaluation of the space fleet. A look at your fleet can point out the need for a certain weapon or special equipment.

MOO features four sizes of ships—small, medium, large, and huge. Having spent uncountable hours in front of *MOO's* ship design screen, I have these droplets of wisdom to offer.

The first thing that's important about a ship is its price. Yep, price. You can design all the huge or large ships you want in the opening stages of the game, but by the time you will have managed to produce any . . .

My tried-and-true-stratagem is to kick off starship production by building perhaps a dozen medium ships equipped with reserve fuel tanks and weapons. With these, I lay claim to any planets I intend to colonize. If the distances between my planets (or stars) are short, I also build a short series of primitive fighters—small ships armed with a laser.

Invariably, the colony ship comes next. I always equip it with the best engines I have, and some cheap beam weaponry. A colony ship armed with a single laser, but with 100 points of damage, is worth several other ships in combat, even if it doesn't have a computer (computers are costly). As soon as my ships' range reaches five parsecs, I design a serious small fighter. Since small fighters rely on their maneuverability for defense, I always give them the fastest engines and highest class maneuver I can. Also, as a rule, I give them the latest in computers that will fit (often, the newest computer is too big to allow space for any weapons). I may also choose a computer a class below if that will let me install a much better weapon—say, a neutron pellet gun instead of a laser.

Finally, as the last model in my initial ship series, I design a dedicated medium-sized fighter. If there are no other weapons available, I'll equip it with a heavy laser and a Gatling, or possibly a couple of ordinary lasers. However, I always make sure my medium fighter has at least a Class II shield. If there are other weapons available, I arm the ship with multiple neutron pellet guns, or possibly Gatling/neutron pellet combinations. I found Gatling lasers very useful in the opening part of *MOO,* because that's when the computer opponent is most likely to build large numbers of small ships.

The big revolution comes with the ion cannon. The medium fighter becomes the most important ship in my fleet. It's usually armed with a heavy ion cannon, it has the best computer I have, and the strongest shield that will fit. I always build ships with the best armor available (even though it takes up a little more space) and good engines.

The engine problem in *MOO* is this: The better your engines, the more space they take up. While this difference is negligible in small and medium-sized ships, it becomes a real consideration with bigger designs. Generally, I recommend you always install the best engines you have until you move beyond Sublight Drives (warp speed 3). Once you've got Ion engines, which push ships around at warp 6, any engine improvements to large and huge ships should be carefully re-assessed. Installing a Hyperthrust (warp 9) engine on a huge ship instead of an Ion dramatically increases the ship's defense levels, true—and you could argue that the few huge ships you build should be fast enough to get to any trouble spot within a turn. However, the sacrifice in hull space is very painful, and in my experience it is possible to plan things so that your fleet rarely has to travel more than six parsecs to an emergency situation. When you get to the point where your planetary empire measures 20 parsecs from one end to another, you usually can afford two strong fleets.

All my large ships have battle scanners. This adds to the ship's attack level, and also allows you to evaluate your opponent when fighting over a planet on which you have no missile bases. Battle scanners are very, very important! Later on in the game, when there are a great many devices you can install in your three Special slots, you may sometimes ignore the scanner if you have lots of other ships with scanners.

I always equip my large and huge ships with the best of everything: best armor, best engines, and maneuver, computer, and shield. If I intend to use the ship in offense as well as defense, I also add ECM jammers and/or Anti-Missile rockets (later on, Zyro or Lightning shields) to protect my big investment from enemy missiles.

After installing all that, there's not that much space left. Usually, on my first big ship model, there's just enough space to fit in four heavy ion cannons, one or two short range weapons (pellet gun, ion cannon, etc.) and a missile launcher. This may seem like a waste of space—a missile launcher is good for a maximum of five shots, and takes up a lot of space. However, I found that the computer players are terrified of missiles. Even if the approaching projectile cannot do much damage, they tend to move the threatened ship(s) back, and that often means tactical freedom.

As the game goes on, the slight improvements on the ion cannon (blaster, fusion beam, phasor) give way to a new generation of lethal beam weapons: Disruptor, Stellar Converter, and Mauler Device. These are strong enough to penetrate planetary shields, especially with the Oracle Interface, and effectively push the missile-armed ship firmly into second place. While it's still important to feature missiles in your battle lineup for tactical reasons, you should concentrate on acquiring the new beam technologies and designing new ships around them. The computer players sometimes respond to your interest in beams by building large numbers of ships armed with rockets. Make sure your lethal beam fighter defends well against missiles!

Upon conquering Orion, you acquire the Death Ray—a beam weapon capable of inflicting up to a stunning 1,000 points of damage in one blow. However, it is also very big, and if you've captured Orion relatively early on in the game, you may find the Death Ray can only fit into huge ships. You should immediately pour extra money into researching weapons, construction, and propulsion, as these are the technology areas that yield the biggest improvements in hull space. Once you can build a decent large ship (good computer and all) equipped with a Death Ray, you're on your way. Just don't trade that technology away to computer players!

Final note on beam weapons: Although heavy beam weapons can hit a target from far away, the damage done decreases with the distance. However, the combination of Repulsor Beams with heavy beam weapons is still a winning one, even though you always fire at long range.

Advanced Ship Design

As the game goes on, ship design becomes extremely complex. In addition to all the variations on beam weapons and rockets, a host of special devices becomes available. At the same time, big fleets armed solely with weapons and battle scanners don't cut the mustard any more. That fleet of 50 large and 300 medium ships, with whose help you ruled your part of galaxy, may be wiped out in a confrontation with a handful of big ships bristling with specials.

Some of the specials may be mixed into devastating combos. My own favorite is this trio: Black Hole Generator, Stasis Field, Teleporter. The Teleporter means my ship gets to move first, and that it will appear right next to the enemy, freezing one group of ships with the Stasis field and decimating another group with the Black Hole Generator. When the enemy fleet features a group of 32,000 ships—which happens quite often at high difficulty levels—the Black Hole is the only effective weapon.

Taking the special combo concept one step further, you should design ships with special devices so that they will complement each other in combat. There are a great many combinations possible. My own taste runs towards the aforementioned Black Holes and Stasis Fields. I work towards a situation where I can freeze at least the two most dangerous groups of enemy ships and work on the others.

This is where you can have an incredible amount of fun, and spend many hours coming up with all sorts of variations. Just remember that you have to build a number of ships of any given type for them to be effective.

Around this time, you'll also be building huge ships increasingly often. Don't skimp on shields and protective devices; a huge ship is too expensive to be easily lost.

Because of cost considerations, the composition of your space fleet will change as the game goes on. For instance, small ships make sense at the beginning of the game, when anything bigger is simply too expensive, and also in the endgame, when technological advances have made it possible to fit an impressive array of weapons and devices into a small hull. My favorite choices are as follows:

 Opening game: One small fighter, one medium fighter with a heavy beam weapon and good shield, one fighter-bomber with a good beam weapon and a five-shot missile pack, one large ship with a battle scanner plus the latest in all technologies (best computer, shield, missile protection) as well as heavy beam weapons and missiles (also bombs, if space allows).

 Middle game: Two medium ships—one with at least two beam weapons (one heavy) and strong shield, one with a heavy beam weapon and rockets; two large ships with battle scanners, specials, heavy beam weapons and missiles; one huge ship with all three special slots filled without a battle scanner. I never send the huge ships anywhere without groups of large ships for protection, and during the middle game, huge hulls are the only ones that can take the latest in all technologies, three bulky specials, and still have space for plenty of weaponry.

 Endgame: One medium-sized ship with battleworthy specials (such as high-energy focus, lightning shield, inertial stabilizer, teleporter), armed with a heavy beam weapon and missiles; two or three large-hulled ships with selected special combos as well as beam weaponry, some with missiles/torpedoes; one or two huge ships with plenty of everything, and a big premium on protection.

My fleet lineup usually features a 'custom' design created with a specific opponent in mind. I often have six types of combat ships in action, and scrap a ship type when I have to build a colony ship in a hurry. In the endgame, when even a radiated colony base has become quite tiny, I sometimes build large ships with colony bases as well as assorted weaponry. The endgame features plenty of opportunities to colonize planets, as the computer players mercilessly wipe each others planets out. The player who gets there first has a chance to easily acquire another planet. However, at high game difficulty levels, this opportunistic policy must be backed by plenty of guns.

SPACE BATTLES

Basically, there are two types of battles—the ones you want and the ones you don't. The first kind is usually fought over one of the enemy planets,and the second kind, over yours. Sometimes, however, you'll get lucky and destroy a computer player's fleet with the help of your missile bases. This happy outcome is more frequent at easier game difficulty levels, naturally.

The first requirement of any space battle in *MOO* is that you are stronger than your opponent—in quality, if not in numbers. Three medium ships equipped with good computers, shields, and repeater weapons can easily destroy 20 small ships, and so on. The computer players field huge fleets, and this basic requirement is quite difficult to fulfil.

This is where high warp speeds and the Improved Space Scanner really help. The scanner pinpoints alien fleets' destinations, and if your fleet is fast, you'll manage to assemble your ships for battle before your opponent does. High warp speeds are a savior at high difficulty levels, where you can count on being outnumbered. However, it's possible to destroy a huge enemy fleets piecemeal, taking on each group of enemy ships with your entire fleet.

High warp speeds are also invaluable in planetary defense, allowing you to throw most of your forces into each defensive battle.

Winning Battles

The first prerequisite to winning battles, as mentioned, is assembling as much of your space fleet as you can to face the enemy.

The second prerequisite is having battle scanners along. If the battle is taking place over your planet, and your planet has missile bases, everything's fine. If it isn't, and you don't have a single ship equipped with a battle scanner in your group, you may be in trouble. By providing you with information on the opposing space fleet, battle scanners allow you to lay out a well-informed plan of battle.

There are as many strategies for winning battles as there are battles. Tactics successful against one opponent usually aren't successful against the other. The right plan has to take into account the threat posed by individual groups of enemy ships, and estimate chances of their swift destruction. Spend some time with the scan of the enemy fleet, and note not only the attack levels and armament, but also the defense factor. For example, it's a waste of time to fire salvos of rockets at a group of ships with sophisticated jammers, while another group, just as dangerous, has weak missile defense. Use the same method to select targets for beam weapons, but don't get carried away and ignore dangerous ships just because there are easier targets.

Things are a little different when fighting a defensive battle with ships that can effectively knock out your planetary defenses or even your planet— including biological and conventional bombers as well as hordes of ships equipped with powerful missiles/torpedoes or beam weapons. The rule is to knock out the ships that can hurt the planet first. Repulsor Beam technology is very useful for keeping enemy bombers away, as long as the ships carrying the Repulsors survive long enough.

When attacking an enemy planet, plan around destroying the missile bases. Often, they are the strongest card up your opponent's sleeve. You shouldn't execute any planetary assaults with your ground troops before the enemy bases are destroyed, either, because your transports can be shot down while landing.

Do not use biological weapons, especially at high game difficulty levels! They aren't worth the potential aggravation they may cause. Of course, computer players, while easily angered by your use of lethal microbes, will often use them against you.

If you are confronting an invincible enemy fleet that features colony ships, consider destroying them first. In my experience, this brings about a withdrawal three times out of ten—and even when it doesn't, it often buys you some time. You may be able to assemble another space fleet and send it into action. Provided your first (defeated) fleet did enough damage, your second fleet can often win. Time those brilliant comebacks with the construction of a missile base, if possible.

Beating the Guardian

No matter how big the alien space fleets you'll encounter, the most deadly encounter of them all is with the Guardian of Orion.

The Guardian is armed with an impressive array of weapons that features Plasma torpedoes, Scatter Pack VII rockets, and Stellar Converters. The Scatter Packs are the worst. At the Impossible level, a single salvo from the Guardian can destroy a hundred or more fairly good medium-sized ships. At easier levels, the Guardian may have a smaller number of Scatter Pack launchers, but they are still the most lethal.

The Stellar Converter is the Guardian's second most dangerous weapon. Finally, the Guardian's attack and defense levels, and shield strength, increase with game difficulty level. At the Impossible level, the Guardian has a whopping 10,000 points!

It's much easier to tackle the Guardian once you've acquired the Teleporter. The ability to move anywhere on the screen makes the Guardian's Scatter Pack effort more of an entertainment than a threat; and the inclusion of one very large group of small ships is sure to keep the Stellar Converters busy without much result for some time. Since the Plasma torpedoes lose power with distance travelled and finally peter out, the Teleporter is very handy there, too.

Before you get to the Teleporter, things are much harder. You have to assume the Guardian will destroy at least one group of ships completely during every turn of the battle, and damage others. Therefore, your Orion-bound fleet must meet certain requirements if it is to be successful.

First of all, your ships must be very fast and equipped with good computers (install inertial stabilizers—chances are, you haven't got nullifiers yet—if your warp speed's low). High levels of missile and beam defense are a must. The Guardian should be forced to spend all his weaponry on a single target each turn before he manages to destroy it. Otherwise, you may be losing not one group of ships per turn, but one and a half or two.

Your ships must be fast enough to engage the Guardian with heavy beam weapons during the first turn, and numerous enough to inflict approximately a thousand points of damage in a single turn (at Hard and Impossible difficulty levels). I recommend including a big group of ships designed specifically for the occasion.

POLITICS, OR MANIPULATING OTHERS

The races represented in *Master of Orion* correspond roughly to what we have on our dear old Earth—bears, cats, lizards, ants, and of course humans. There are also the mysterious Silicoids, resembling furry, round-snouted seals more than anything (or anyone) else, and Darloks, always hidden inside a hood.

The races all have their likes and dislikes, which, once again, roughly correspond to our Terran reality. For instance Alkaris(or the birds) are born enemies of Mrrshans (cats). In a touch of whimsy, the game designers have decided that everyone likes Humans, and Humans like everyone. No one, however, is too fond of the Darloks. How can you like someone who doesn't show his face?

You can gauge this inbred attitude when you first meet another race. If the Relations Bar pointer identifies the other party as Uneasy, they aren't fond of you. If they're Neutral, they don't care one way or another. If it's at Relaxed, they like your face. Note that over time, without any external pressures, the Race Relations pointer tends to gravitate towards its starting position—more often than not, to Neutral. If you kick off the new relationship with a new technology, however, this will constantly influence the relationship in a positive way. Believe me, it's much better to go to war with someone that likes you, because it's easier to make peace.

The computer players in *MOO* have long memories, and they remember broken promises as well as technological gifts. (Cash tribute is to be avoided; it only brings about a one-time improvement, if any.) Therefore, the wise player treads lightly, and makes computer players break treaties when desiring war, rather than doing it himself. To do that, actively conduct sabotage and espionage, and maybe provoke a couple of fistfights over planets with no missile bases.

However, before things get to that point, you're wise to start out by keeping everyone happy. If you can get a computer player to like you, chances are you'll succeed in talking him into a war with another computer player. If <u>all</u> the computer players like you, and find your suggestions to go out and fight irresistible, the game is as good as won. All you need to do is build up your forces and include some fast colony ships. Sooner or later, a devastated planet will be ripe for a new landlord.

Be wary of signing non-aggression pacts, especially at the beginning of the game. Although they magically improve relations over time, a non-aggression pact allows your new friend to colonize empty planets even though they are guarded by your ships. Avoid joining alliances! Sooner or later, your ally will ask you to fight someone, and will be offended if you refuse—perhaps so much as to declare war on you in due sequence.

All in all, strive to keep everyone well-disposed towards you, unless you are really ready to go to war. Then start your backstabbing with sabotage, espionage, and getting other computer players to gang up on your intended victim. Do not let any war go on for too long, unless it's basically just you and the other contender for Orion's throne. *MOO's* political sands tend to shift quickly, and you may suddenly find yourself fighting three wars instead of one. Establish specific short-range objectives, gain them, and sign a peace treaty. It's not that difficult to bring the other party to the peace table if you've been successful both at war and in your diplomatic efforts to get other computer players on your side.

Try to hunt down Orion before the others do. Defeating the Guardian is very difficult, but the prize is great, and everyone likes you more if Orion is yours.

Publisher:	Microprose Software
Platform:	PC MS-DOS, Mac.
Release Date:	Summer, 1994
Multiplayer:	No
Rating:	

A game that combines strategy, adventure, and arcade action into one great package. Somewhat tricky controls can be an annoyance, particularly in the MS-DOS version.

General Overview

I read about *Pirates!* before I played the game, and it wasn't in a computer gaming magazine either—it was in *Newsweek* or *Time*. The magazine writer gushed about the game, then made the obligatory complaints about violence (the violence in *Pirates!* is strictly the 'Peter Pan' variety—nice drama, and that's all).

Pirates! was the game that turned me into a computer gaming maniac. I can think of no better game as an introduction to computer gaming, because *Pirates!* mixes elements from many game genres, and does so with charm and grace. Your goal is to gain fame and fortune, of course, and you only have so much time. After ten years of sailing and fighting, your health may not permit another journey.

In the course of your adventures, you will also have the opportunity to reunite your long-lost family, whose members are scattered through the Caribbean. It's worth finding them even if you don't like your family, because every member has a piece of map pinpointing a fabulous treasure. Finding a nice wife is also a consideration, since it affects your disposition. If you do not surround yourself with your nearest and dearest at the conclusion of your pirating career, you may retire a rich man, but also a man that is lonely and bitter.

Pirates! calls for some arcade-action skills as well as strategic planning. If you are bright, but slow with the sword, you'll lose. After all, this is an age in which intellect often means nothing compared with a strong sword arm.

Golden Rules

 The one commodity you can't buy or steal in *Pirates!* is time. Sooner or later, your health will force a permanent retirement— usually, after around ten years of pirating. Remember this throughout your career, and don't waste precious time on sleeping around with barmaids, or doing nickel-and-dime deals.

 Keep a vigilant eye on your crew's morale. I check it several times a month. Morale determines how well your men fight. The most striking difference is in the rate of fire during sea battles. A happy crew gets three or four salvos off in the same time an unhappy crew fires one.

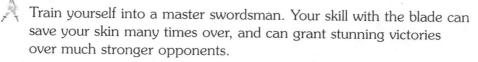 Train yourself into a master swordsman. Your skill with the blade can save your skin many times over, and can grant stunning victories over much stronger opponents.

Do not include any square-rigged ships in your fleet, unless you're selling them off at the earliest opportunity. Square-riggers take forever to sail the Caribbean west to east, against prevailing winds, and time is important.

Time your promotions well. Except at the very start, don't rush to get promoted the moment you think you've scored enough victories. The longer you put it off, the more land you'll get, along with your new title. Don't put it off too much, however, because rank and nobility count heavily towards your retirement.

Make sure you find all four members of your family. Given good knowledge of the Caribbean, this means the opportunity to collect 400,000 additional gold pieces during your career. Also, the more members of your family you rescue, the happier your retirement.

Don't marry anyone but the governor's daughter, and don't propose until you've slept with the daughters of half the governors in the Caribbean. Intimate relationships are an invaluable source of information on the movements of the Treasure Train/Fleet. Learning where both are is as simple as dropping in on the governor and his friendly daughter.

Remain aware of political changes. Nations that were fighting each other at the start of your career may be allied a few years later. France might promote you for attacking Spain one year, and send pirate-hunters after you another. Don't be afraid to change your colors if necessary—if you play as a Spanish renegade, you have no other choice.

PIRATES! GOLD

Gather as much intelligence as you can. Buy information from travellers whenever it's offered. However, releasing captured pirates in exchange for info on the whereabouts of the Treasure Fleet/Train isn't recommended, unless you're pirating off the Spanish Main, and are in a good position to intercept it.

 Make sure you have a place called home. Don't antagonize governors serving friendly nations, unless you have a very good reason. Shoot for a base in every part of the Caribbean by your mid-career. There'll be several less cities to loot, but you'll be able to unload robbed commodities easily. In The Silver Empire, kick off your career by capturing a couple of Spanish towns and installing new governors.

Winning Strategies

The game manual does an excellent job of explaining the game, and also contains some useful strategy hints. My aim here is to point out the not-so-obvious, and to gather all the strands into a coherent whole.

PREGAME OPTIONS

Pirates! can be played in the career or mission mode, the latter consisting of 'leading an expedition'. I recommend you lead an expedition or two to get the feel of things; however, only a full-time pirating career offers real depth of gameplay. Issues such as timing the division of plunder assume great importance. Furthermore, there is your family—well worth looking for. Finding the assorted evil noblemen who know of your family's thereabouts is time-consuming. So is locating the dear relatives.

Choosing Your Era

The pregame options begin with a choice of several historical eras. Following a short description, you are advised of the era's 'difficulty level'. This evaluation is misleading to a large degree. Also, you must realize that The Silver Empire, classified as the game's most difficult era, also offers the biggest profits.

The game's difficulty rating of an era is largely dependent on the degree of French, English, and Dutch presence. Since it is only too easy to capture Spanish towns and install the governor of your choice, the whole issue is null and void.

My difficulty rating for the eras in *Pirates!* is somewhat different. The brief summaries below consider one thing only: that your aim is to end your career, as famous, wealthy, and respected as possible.

Note that the capture of the Treasure Train and/or Fleet yields biggest spoils in the earliest era, The Silver Empire, and steadily decline thereafter. As a rule, the earlier the era, the more gold you can rob. With time, the focus shifts to pillaged commodities. By 1660, most of your take will consist of proceeds from the sale of robbed trade items.

 The Silver Empire: Without any question, this is my favorite era. Almost every Spanish ship carries a handsome sum in gold, and capturing the Treasure Fleet/Train can mean over 50,000 gold pieces. Once you've gathered a large crew and installed a governor or two, you can't go wrong. You can confidently expect to receive French and English titles of nobility. Turn a couple of towns over to the Dutch to make Dutch Captain.

 Merchants and Smugglers: This is a tough era, because no one's fighting anyone except for a couple of brief skirmishes. If you capture a few towns, you'll be rewarded by the new governors, but you need to capture more than one town to make the jump from Captain to Major, for example. My favorite strategy is to lie low the first few years, trade, and get promoted by the Spanish for delivering captured pirates. When the Spanish towns I trade with get rich (partly thanks to my efforts) and doors start slamming in my face, I start pirating. While it's easy to retire in a respectable manner, it's very hard to exit gracefully as King's Advisor.

 The New Colonists: You'll be fighting for the Dutch no matter what nationality you choose. Spain is still fairly rich, so it's fairly easy to retire with a packet. Things may be a bit difficult in the beginning;

after that, it's plain sailing. Although this is a fairly easy era, making King's Advisor means pursuing both the Spaniards and your lost family with beady-eyed zeal.

 War for Profit: The name says it all. One of the easiest eras, a profusion of non-Spanish ports makes things smoother. Expect to be showered with both titles of nobility and land titles.

 The Buccaneer Heroes: This era is almost a walkover. You'll spend quite a bit of time in the Merchant's office, selling hundreds of tons of plundered sugar. This tends to become tedious after a while; however, the spicy mix of nationalities and historical events (the Dutch war with the English initially, and France eventually allies with Spain) helps keep gameplay lively. My most successful game ever was played out in that era while playing under French colors. I started by trading. By a stroke of luck, I made Spanish Major before turning to pirating for the French, then the English. This particular career ended with me as a Spanish Major, English and French Duke, and Dutch Baron (for countless Dutch pirates delivered to Curacao). Yep, it's easy to be a hero at a time like this.

 Pirates' Sunset: This is probably the most challenging era of them all. Although you can make a respectable buck trading, it can never equal the profits made from pirating, yet pirating is a very dangerous business. Apart from one brief skirmish, there are no wars. War galleons and, more importantly, frigates lurk around every corner. You have to be good to get a noble title from *any* of the governors.

Choosing Nationality

The second choice you have to make is that of nationality. This is not as important as it may seem, because you can rise to the rank of the French King's Advisor even though you're a Spanish renegade. However, it is helpful to choose a nation that is at war with Spain throughout your career. An Englishman fighting for the English can expect better rewards than a foreigner in the English service.

Special Abilities

There are only two special abilities you should consider: skill at fencing and skill at medicine. If you're good at fencing, choose medicine—you'll be able to sail the seas longer, or retire healthier. The state of your health is an important consideration when you retire!

Skill at gunnery and skill at navigation are basically helpers for players who haven't mastered the controls. Wit and charm may seem helpful if you're committed to trading for most of your career, but even then, fencing or medicine will serve you better. To win as a Merchant, you must subdue various dangerous pirates, and your merchant operations can work well only if you keep the crew numbers down. Your skill with a blade can save you your pale Merchant's skin.

Difficulty Level

You shouldn't play *Pirates!* below the Adventurer level, except for an introductory game or two. This is because your share of the plunder is minuscule at the easier levels, and you stand about as much chance of becoming a rich King's Advisor as a brothel sweeper.

The biggest difference at higher difficulty levels is not the weather or the nastiness of your enemies (once you've learned how to fight and sail, you've learned how to fight and sail), but the morale of your crew. Your crew is an impatient lot, and you have to keep pouring gold into your holds to keep them pleased, let alone happy.

Also, at the Swashbuckler level, you will be forced into combat whenever you so much as take a look at an enemy. But once you know how to fight, every encounter is just another opportunity to score a victory.

THE FINE ART OF FIGHTING

Whether you choose to become a trader or a pirate, you'll have to fight, or you'll lose. By fighting, I mean fencing, sea battles, land battles, and amphibious assaults.

The morale of your men is crucial to winning battles. Basically, you win when their morale is sky-high, and the enemy's morale hits the bottom. Your men gain morale each time they shoot a couple of enemy soldiers, or each time you hit the enemy leader with your blade.

Fencing

Getting the fencing bit right is one of the most important and difficult aspects of *Pirates!* Once you're good with the blade, you can take on superior enemy numbers with confidence.

The big thing about fencing is realizing that each thrust, slash, or parry is actually a combination of movements. Practice fencing, and observe how the two figures move, and how your guy responds to your commands. You'll notice there is a certain rhythm. Once you've noticed when each sequence of moves begins and when it ends, you've got it. Now all you have to do is issue instructions to your champion just before he finishes the preceding sequence, and he'll move as fast as he can.

You'll notice that certain sequences work well together, and others don't. The manual contains some useful tips on that. My favorite tactic is to start each combat with a high slash/thrust, then close in with mid-level and low attacks. Mid and low-level slashes followed immediately by a thrust (e.g. low slash, low thrust) work particularly well. If the opponent is armed with a cutlass, I move my guy back after each attack. A cutlass has short range, but it's lethal when it connects.

Once you're good, it's possible to win *every* fight with a rapier without even getting nicked. However, I recommend that you choose the cutlass, or at least the longsword, until you know what you're doing. If your crew morale is very low upon entering the fight (something that happens quite often at the Swashbuckler level), I choose the longsword. The extra damage it inflicts raises my guys' spirits faster.

If you aren't sure what you're doing. or your back is up against the wall (same thing), grab a cutlass and attack, attack, attack. Keep in mind that if your guys are really demoralized, a single hit can lose you the fight *even* though you're scoring five hits to one.

Ships

Pirates! features quite an array of ships, most of which are very badly suited for the business of pirating.

The main thing to consider here is your theater of operations, the Caribbean, and its weather. The wind almost invariably blows east to west; most Spanish riches lie in the west, and most pirate bases, in the east. Therefore, you'll be sailing against wind a lot of the time. This practically rules out all square-rigged ships—even the frigate and the fast galleon. The sands of time slip by mercilessly, and the days you waste sailing back home aboard a square-rigged ship will never come back. As your career progresses, you'll find that time is the most important single commodity in *Pirates!* It just doesn't do to waste any.

Without question, the sloop is the best all-round pirate ship—particularly because it can slip over reefs without any problem. However, the sloop only appears in the 1620s. The two remaining fore-and-aft-rigged ships suitable for pirating are the pinnace and the barge. The former, however useful, is a little small; the latter cannot sail over reefs, and handles a tad heavily. Overall, the barque is probably the better choice, although I often form eight-ship fleets composed entirely of pinnaces. These are great for operations in the northern half of the Caribbean, where reefs abound.

You should include square-rigged ships in your armada only for one of the following purposes:

 You can sell the ship without having to do a lot of sailing upwind beforehand.

 You have robbed plenty of valuable commodities that you cannot fit on board of your remaining ships, and you're not in a great hurry.

 You are about to make an amphibious assault on a heavily defended fort. The bigger your ship and the more men you have, the better your chances—as long as you follow the rest of the advice on the subject, later on in this chapter.

Sea Battles

If you're following my advice, you have three ships to choose from: pinnace, sloop, and barge. Barges work best against square-riggers, the others against everything else. A sloop combines the qualities of a barge and a pinnace—it's okay against both big and small ships.

The first thing you should do is raise full sails. Speed and maneuverability are key assets in winning sea battles. You begin each battle with your ship approaching the opponent, who is quite close by. Turn away instantly, and fire a first broadside. While your crew reloads, maneuver your ship so that it can hit the enemy without being hit back—remember that ships fire from their sides; the safest position is slightly in front.

Concentrate on avoiding enemy cannon balls (this is not as hard as it may seem at first) and blast them in the meantime. Watch the crew numbers. The moment you feel you can handle the remaining enemy crew, go in for boarding.

Land Battles

Land battles take place when (a) the enemy town doesn't have a fort, and (b) the size of your force matches the enemy's. If you have a lot of men, the defenders will be too scared to venture out of the fort, and you'll be taken directly to the fencing screen.

You should never attack a town without knowing how strong the garrison is, and once you do, fighting land battles is very straightforward. The situation you're after is one where your guys are in the woods, and the enemy is out in the open, with your guys firing at the enemy. Put your men among the trees. If the enemy is bashful, pretend to run with the weaker-armed group in such a way that pursuing enemy troops will walk into the ambush.

In other words, what you should do is use the terrain. Keep your men under cover, don't walk into any swamps, and if there's more than one enemy group, try to concentrate all your forces on one group at a time. Do not enter melee combat with low morale; morale goes up if your men keep inflicting losses on the enemy without suffering any, and they do it best when shooting from cover.

Amphibious Assaults

The amphibious assault is the most difficult type of attack. Don't attack any town this way if there's another choice. Unfortunately, some island towns—Santa Catalina/Providence, for example, or St. Eustatius—can be taken no other way.

There are two ways to mount an amphibious assault. One is to take a small ship—one that sail over shoals (sloop or pinnace)—and land your men as quickly as possible while avoiding cannon fire from the fort(s). The other is to attack in a large square-rigger (it's good to check on the shoal situation beforehand). A square-rigger loaded to the limit with men can take a hit from a fort and still make a successful landing.

Amphibious attacks work best is you time them well. Watch the main screen before you attack, and wait for strong winds. Attack with the wind, of course—if it's blowing from the east, attack the island from the east. This is the only way to succeed with a square-rigger assault. It needs favourable winds.

When it's time to cross swords, don't choose the rapier. Usually, your men will be outnumbered, and you want a quick victory.

THE SUCCESSFUL PIRATE

A brilliant career involves some planning. The most important single consideration is your poor family, scattered across the Caribbean. Since finding them means finding Incan treasures, you should spare no effort to accomplish their rescue.

The difficulty is twofold. First of all, you need to get promoted before you learn where to find a guy who knows where your family is. If your knowledge of the Caribbean is sketchy, you may need to get promoted several times before you get anywhere. The wicked aristocrats who own pieces of maps showing your family's whereabouts often hide out in out-of-the-way places, and trips to recover the missing relatives involve long voyages, too. Your crew will not take kindly to all this family business, because you could be plundering cities instead.

The best overall strategy to follow is to get your first promotion as quickly as possible, and immediately embark on the search for your sister, then for the Incan treasure. I'm assuming you take the trouble to learn the map, and will be able to find everyone and everything based on a quarter of the whole map. Remember that this way, you can recover four Incan treasures—not just one.

While finding your sister and the first treasure, you should, of course, rob whatever Spanish ship you come across. If you find yourself with a lot of eager volunteers on your hands, you may modify your plan slightly and do some major pirating in the interim; but on the whole, you should keep family

PIRATES! GOLD

business first and foremost. Finding the Incan treasure immediately adds 100,000 pieces of gold to your ship's coffers, and makes the crew happy, allowing you to prolong your first journey.

If you keep looking for your family, yet at the same time take advantage of all the possibilities the game throws your way, you'll be barely able to recover your uncle and the last 100,000 pieces of gold before poor health forces your retirement.

Once you're good with the blade and with guns, you'll realize that a small band of happy men is better than a dispirited, big bunch. You can then devote the retire first half of your career to finding your family and the Incan treasures. The successes you'll score along the way will put you midway up the retirement scale. Then, maybe with just your uncle remaining as a stain on your conscience, you can turn to do some serious pirating. You'll be rich, and thus will find it easy to recruit a large crew without trouble.

The priorities are slightly different when playing in one of the early eras, particularly The Silver Empire. Your first goal then is to recruit at least a hundred and fifty men without mutiny, and take over a couple of poor Spanish towns. Yaguana, Port Royale, and Puerto Cabello are all very good choices; Isabella, Trinidad, and Margarita are a bit out of the way. If you install a French governor in one town and an English governor in another, you'll instantly ensure a constant stream of promotions from both sides.

Remember that it is easier to get promoted to Captain than to Baron, that each nation can only promote you to Captain once, and that each title counts. Try to gather as many promotions from as many nations as you can.

Good Hunting Grounds, or Waters

The *Pirates!* world features several areas which make particularly good hunting grounds. A good hunting ground is one that contains both plenty of shipping, and nearby ports to sell captured commodities.

In the northern part of the map, the best areas are the waters between Cuba, Haiti, and Jamaica. Santiago supplies a steady stream of ships to rob, and at least one other nearby town will willingly trade with you. This is a good spot throughout all the eras. In The Silver Empire, the waters between Havana and Florida are also a good secondary area.

The Gulf of Mexico usually contains many tempting targets. However, it is so remote from the rest of the game world that it is hardly practical to visit on a regular basis. Make one big raid on the cities and ships in the Gulf of Mexico midway through your career, but that's it.

The Antilles play an increasingly important role from 1640 onwards. By the time Pirates' Sunset comes around, the the British, French, and Dutch colonies on these islands are more important than the hitherto powerful cities on the Spanish Main.

The best hunting ground of them all are the coastal waters of the Spanish Main. From Cumana to Cartagena, targets abound. Curacao makes a great base from 1620 onwards. This is also the ideal vantage point when waiting for the Treasure Fleet/Train to pass through one of the nearby Spanish towns.

PIRATES! GOLD

CHAPTER 10

RAILROAD TYCOON DELUXE

Publisher: Microprose Software

Platform: PC MS-DOS, The original *Railroad Tycoon Deluxe* is also available for the Mac.

Multiplayer: No

Rating:

A truly great game that (for once) does not involve shooting or killing anyone. Outdated graphics are its single flaw.

General Overview

Railroad Tycoon Deluxe is not one of the most successful games in the history of computer gaming. It's been around for a few years, and the graphics appear dated, but few games have such well-balanced gameplay. *Railroad Tycoon Deluxe* is an original that will delight anyone who loves a good game!

The premise is simple: Armed with a million bucks (or pounds, depending on the locale) raised from an initial stock issue, you must build a railroad that is also a financial powerhouse. You must select the best area for development. You'll plan the routes and lay down tracks, minimizing grades, curves, and expenditure; and finally,you must play the financial market like a virtuoso. This last aspect of the game is frequently overlooked, yet it makes all the difference.

As time goes on, the game world changes, and so do certain game realities. Cargo rates drop, eroding profits—but at the same time, new and more powerful engines become available, which enables you to increase the number of cars in each train. The character of the gameplay can vary considerably depending on the reality and difficulty levels you've chosen—for example, an Investor or Financier with no Cutthroat Competition will concentrate on building new rail connections. The reality levels you select are very important:

 No-Collision/Dispatcher Operations: You understand that two trains running in opposite directions on a single track will crash into each other, don't you? If so, there's no reason for you to choose No-Collision and forfeit ten percent of your retirement bonus. Yes, laying double tracks and building signal towers is costly, but it's railroad money, not *your* money. Besides, choosing No-Collision can mean seriously delayed Priority Shipments.

 Basic/Complex Economy: You may want to play the first few games with Basic Economy, but as soon as you've got the hang of things, switch to Complex. The reason, again, is an extra ten percent added to your retirement bonus.

 Friendly/Cutthroat Competition: You may want to stick with Friendly until you understand the game fairly well. Basically, choosing Cutthroat Competition means you must either own at least half of your railroad's stock, or be in a position to acquire it at short notice. Owning half of your own stock means you can't be thrown out of office (in *RT Deluxe*, this may still happen if you've bought up half the stock when the stockholders were already looking for a new president). My advice: Buy half your own stock in your first ten fiscal years, and choose Cut-Throat Competition.

You should start playing at the Tycoon difficulty level right away. To start with, only Tycoon lets you manage the railroad for a full hundred years. In addition, opting for lower difficulty means you lose twenty-five percent or more of your retirement bonus. You also can't own stock in all of the competing railroads, or take all of them over. Since taking over competing railroads is the most effective single step in increasing your retirement bonus (you get a staggering two hundred percent bonus if you manage to take over all three competitors!), limiting your choices in that area is simply counter-productive.

The minus to choosing the Tycoon difficulty level is that the game world contains more mountains/hills/uneven ground. You'll encounter more grades, and often will have to think hard when laying tracks. However, the rewards far outweigh these disadvantages.

The strategies discussed below have been developed while playing *Railroad Tycoon* at a hundred percent difficulty level.

Golden Rules

 Don't plan your railroad using the resource map. In fact, don't use that map at all. It doesn't show you the terrain, and in *Railroad Tycoon*, terrain is all-important. It determines how much the tracks will cost, and how fast the trains will run. Take the time to learn to read the map well; it won't take long.

 When laying tracks, remember that speed is all important. The faster your trains go, the more often you get paid—and with cargoes such as mail, passengers, and fast freight, speed of delivery makes a lot of difference to the money you get. Your trains only make money when they're running, and they make most money when they're running fast. Minimize grades and curves, even if this means spending more money on right of way.

Make money by playing the stock market. You may even be able to take over a newly-formed railroad right at the start. If you do, rob it of as much money as you can, and dump its stock. Do not try to hold on to railroads acquired very early in the game. Rob 'em and sell 'em, and you'll fare much better.

Take advantage of all priority shipments. Early in the game, they can easily be the most important single source of profits. Quick delivery of a priority shipment is often worth the price of an engine shop, an upgraded bridge, or a double-tracked line.

Plan any geography wars carefully, for a railroad that's hemmed into a small area is not an attractive takeover proposition. What's more, it is likely to fight its way out by starting rate wars at your stations. Do not let that scare you off from blocking a competitor—just be aware of what's involved.

Remember to play with your own stock—sell a block of shares when you've had a bad year, buy it back the next. You can manipulate the price of your own stock in many ways; one is to build an expensive line in one fiscal period, but only build stations and start running trains in the next. In the end stages of the game, when stock market profits are many times bigger than your railroad revenues, selling and buying back your own stock can make you lots of money.

Replace engines early. I do it when the operating costs of an engine are between thirty-three and forty percent of the purchase price. You can save many thousands of maintenance dollars through quick replacement of outworn engines. Replacing ten engines with a savings of $10,000 maintenance on each means an increase of $100,000 in your operating profit. Adopting that policy also means that your railroads run using the best equipment available.

Know your engines. Broadly speaking, *Railroad Tycoon's* engines fall into three classes: fast engines that can only pull a couple of cars, slow engines that can pull plenty of cars, and engines that can pull a lot of cars at a respectable speed. Use the fast engines for mail/passenger runs, the slow and powerful ones for freight runs, and the third 'in between' kind for freight and passenger/mail routes in mountainous terrain.

 Remember the importance of speed when forming train chains. A short train that can make a round trip twice in a fiscal year is better than a long train that makes the run only once. This is particularly true when you have more than one train using the same line; a slow train can hold up an important passenger express for an agonizingly long time. The Train Income Report gives each train's average speed; of course, you should also monitor train movement. In Dispatcher Operations, it is possible to make trains really move along smoothly by using override signals.

 Aim for a mix of cargoes for your railroad. A railroad dependent on passenger and mail traffic can be greatly hurt by a recession. Try for a balanced mix of fast passenger/mail trains and big freight trains.

Winning Strategies

To win at *Railroad Tycoon,* you must master a specific set of skills and abilities. These are:

 The ability to tell where a good place is to start a railroad, or to connect to your railroad. Do not restrict yourself to well-defined cities. A terminal embraces a great area—seven squares each side, or forty-nine squares in total. Remember this when locating station sites.

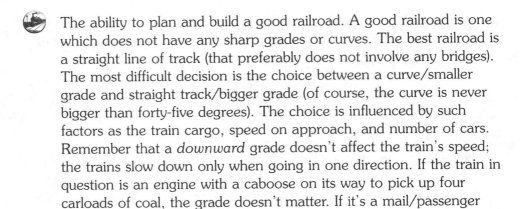

The ability to plan and build a good railroad. A good railroad is one which does not have any sharp grades or curves. The best railroad is a straight line of track (that preferably does not involve any bridges). The most difficult decision is the choice between a curve/smaller grade and straight track/bigger grade (of course, the curve is never bigger than forty-five degrees). The choice is influenced by such factors as the train cargo, speed on approach, and number of cars. Remember that a *downward* grade doesn't affect the train's speed; the trains slow down only when going in one direction. If the train in question is an engine with a caboose on its way to pick up four carloads of coal, the grade doesn't matter. If it's a mail/passenger express with a full load, it matters a lot.

The ability to play the stock market. The stock market can make you more money than your railroad operation *ever* will. In addition, the stock market is where you really can beat the stuffing out of your opponents.

The ability to manage takeovers. A bungled takeover of another railroad can lose you the game. Takeovers are discussed in detail later on in this chapter.

STARTING YOUR FIRST RAILROAD

Your initial network has only one purpose: to furnish you with enough cash to maintain big interest payments, and hopefully also earn a little extra—although that isn't strictly necessary. You can easily estimate, with some accuracy, the number of carloads you can count on per fiscal year. You should have at least twenty carloads available if you want to be successful right from the start—possibly less if your planned routes involve long passenger/mail runs.

Do not start with very long runs. It's better to have more shorter routes, especially when starting in the 1830s, since the engines are slow.

Consider future expansion when starting your railroad. Three big cities in the middle of nowhere will generate a lot of cash, but expanding beyond may be prohibitively expensive/difficult. Sometimes, you may bypass this problem

Note: In *Railroad Tycoon Deluxe*, the engine lineup is a little different from the original version. In the Americas, the Grasshopper has been replaced by the John Bull, a much better engine. Europe, however, has retained the pathetic Planet as the only choice in 1830.

by building a railroad whose only purpose is to make the physical link with a cargo-rich area. Once you've built a connection within the new area, you can dismantle the original connecting track (remember that track maintenance costs are a significant item in your budget). However, you may lose a couple of priority shipments that way simply because there'll be no way to deliver the cargo.

Remember that you can easily spend up to two million on your initial network. Make all the connections first; you only need to have a positive cash balance when laying track involves purchasing right of way or real estate. You can build all the trains, stations, and station improvements you want while in the red, and *Railroad Tycoon Deluxe* also lets you double-track (other versions of the game don't). You should spend at least half a million just on single-track connections—and don't be afraid to spend the whole million if there are more good sources of cargo within easy reach. One of my best games ever involved a railroad that plunged me two and a half million into debt at the very start; however, this money was spent on a network stretching all the way from Portland to Bridgeport, with all the cities in between connected by double track. Revenues for the very first fiscal period totalled nearly a million, and jumped to a million and a half upon building post offices and the introduction of the Norris engine. The moral is: Do not be afraid to take a big jump in the very beginning if you feel it's justified.

Occasionally, you'll come across a natural resource bonanza—a terminal can yield over twenty cars a year. If you can convert the resources into a cargo that can be delivered yet somewhere else , you'll be rolling in dough.

Quite often, it's worthwhile to build the needed industry, as long as its price does not exceed six hundred thousand pounds or dollars, depending on the world.

Link all the station sites with track, then place signal stations and lay double-track where necessary (neither are necessary if there will be just one train running between the two stations). Double-track only if there will be more than two trains using the track in question; otherwise, just build signal stations. The distance between signal stations differs with the era. In earlier eras (1830, 1850), distances between signal stations should never be bigger than *fifteen percent of the length of the line, or three squares*, whichever comes first. In 1870, the minimum distance is four squares; in any later era, it's five. Of course, you may always build more signal stations to help with particularly heavy traffic.

You should double-track any route which features more than two trains. Speed of delivery is crucial in *Railroad Tycoon*—and that applies to all the cargoes, not just the time-sensitive ones. The number of deliveries your trains make each year increases your revenue, but that's only a small part your earnings. The rise in revenue causes a rise of your stock price, and this is where you can make a real killing.

Next, you should build the 'real' stations, the ones where trains stop to deliver cargo or pick it up. Of course, you should have the sites picked well beforehand, bearing in mind that if an increase in station size will yield an couple of extra carloads, it's worth it. You should build post offices right away at every station that generates more than one carload of mail per fiscal year. Build all switching yards, storage facilities, and so on as needed (sometimes, an extra engine shop is worth considering instead of a maintenance shop. Putting an engine to work on a route six months earlier may be worth a hundred thousand in profits in your first fiscal year).

You spend the first six months in office building new trains and issuing bonds to cover your earlier spending, and then some. Your goal is to have a lot of cash on hand when the first competitor appears. You may consider quickly repaying bonds midway through the fiscal period, at the end of the calendar year, and then re-issuing them in January. But if the economic climate changes for the worse, you may find that door closed. It all depends on how well your railroad can carry the interest payments. Broker fees for repaying and re-issuing a single bond total ten thousand—much less than interest payments on higher-priced bonds.

Strike the moment anyone shows their face. Start buying their stock even if the new railroad baron has bought a block right away. If it's evident you won't be able to take them over, bail out when the price is highest—usually, when your opponent buys the last block of his stock still on the market, thus owning fifty thousand shares. Sell all the shares you've just bought; you'll make a modest monetary profit, but more importantly, you've just put your opponent in the worst starting position imaginable. He hasn't built a single piece of track yet, but his railroad has already lost a lot of paper money; he's been forced to take out a bond, paying broker fees and interest. Hit every new tycoon on the scene with this tactic. If your railroad has been making a modest profit on top of the interest payments, in no time at all you'll have enough cash to attempt your first takeover.

Types of Takeovers

Takeovers can be looked at in two ways—in terms of what they're supposed to accomplish, and in how they are done.

First, there are nice-guy takeovers, where you take over a railroad in order to manage it and build it up. Since good-guy takeovers involve injecting a million or more in cash into your new acquisition, they are not an option very early in the game. The only option is the robber-baron takeover—you gain control of a railroad in order to rob it of all the cash you can.

If you plan your moves well, you should always be able to take over a competing railroad in the first ten fiscal periods of the game, and you should

Note: My Mac version of the original *Railroad Tycoon* allowed me to take as much money as I wanted from any acquired company. If that's the *RT* you have, be warned. It makes the game rather boring.

be able to do so by winning a race to buy the majority (most commonly sixty thousand) of the company's stock. The other way of gaining control—through a tender offer—is much more expensive. However, it's also a viable option, as discussed below.

The moment you take over a railroad by buying sixty thousand shares of its stock, all the shares it owns (usually forty thousand) revert to the public, and all the bonds that can be paid off, are paid off (the early Macintosh version of *Railroad Tycoon* does not have this feature). Thus, if the railroad you've bought had nine hundred thousand in cash and one and a half million in bonds, it will have four hundred thousand in cash and one million in bonds when you gain control. This is important, for it lets you estimate exactly how much cash you can rob. Remember, the cash rounds down to the nearest hundred thousand. You can't transfer a hundred thousand over to yourself if there are only seventy thousand dollars or pounds left in the company coffers.

However, once you've taken over a railroad, you can take it over repeatedly, and each time you do, it has fresh cash in the till. It works like this: Upon robbing the lasthundred thousand, you sell the controlling block of stock. The newly independent railroad company immediately takes out a bond to buy up its own stock, and has less than five hundred thousand following its stock purchase. You buy a block of its stock, thus gaining control once again, robbing the till, and so on. This can go on until your victim cannot issue any more bonds, and can net you a million or more. In addition to the robbed cash, all this buying and selling means that when you finally dump all the stock, it fetches a handsome price. Just remember to capitalize on the rise of your own stock, and buy some before it gets expensive!

Given this, a robber-baron takeover may be profitable even if you're forced to make a tender offer. In particular, tender offers are a viable proposition if the target railroad is near collapse, and its stock costs no more than a million to acquire. Since you'll end up with all of the target railroad's shares, you should instantly sell forty thousand, or the minority block back to the public. Then proceed to rob it the usual way.

Try to time your moves with the end of the fiscal year. The ideal situation is when you take over a railroad right at the beginning of a fiscal period, rob it several times, and still manage to dump all its stock before the fiscal period ends.

Engines and Trains

Railroad Tycoon basically features two types of engines: slower engines that pull a respectable number of cars at a respectable speed, and faster engines that pull a couple of cars at high speed. Use the slower engines to pull cargo trains of three cars or more, and the faster engines to pull mail/passenger trains.

I personally found the mail/passenger combination to work much better than forming separate passenger and mail trains. In very late stages of the game, when cities generate six or more cars of mail per year, dedicated mail and passenger trains become more feasible.

As a rule, form passenger/mail trains by putting a car of each type onto the fastest engine you have. Starting with the Ten Wheeler/Stirling, it becomes feasible to form trains of one mail and two passenger cars. They pay off well enough at stations with restaurants and hotels to justify the loss of revenue through lower speed.

Forming a mail and/or a passenger train of more than three cars is something I never do, except for one special circumstance: a run between two very busy stations equipped with restaurants and hotels. In this case, I use a fast freight engine for the job.

Cargo trains should be formed with almost as much attention paid to speed as with passengers and mail. This is particularly true if the cargo is coal, which involves two conversions. You want the train to complete a whole cycle, coal to steel to goods, within one fiscal period. Speed becomes even more important in later stages of the game, with long and busy tracks. A slow freight train can cause horrific traffic jams on a railroad that's being used by several other trains, and if some of these other trains carry time-sensitive cargo, you'll lose more still.

THE SECOND STAGE: BUILDING AN EMPIRE

Your robber-baron tactics should provide you with enough cash to embark on the second stage of your tycoon career. First of all, repay what bonds you can, but keep a million in hand. Wait for the next recession—you may have an opportunity to recycle your bonds if a boom comes along, or to pay more off. When recession arrives or panic strikes, build tracks to at least two new locations, preferably more. Don't build the actual station if you're already in the second half of a fiscal period; you want to maximize double rate revenue. If your construction work cuts sharply into your profits and you're postponing the new stations till the next fiscal period, I suggest you sell some of your own stock before it drops in price. You'll buy it back next year, when profits are up, and so make money twice on every block you speculate with.

Your second-stage expansion always furnishes me with the ability to pay off any remaining bonds that I have. Given this, I then embark on my first real 'good guy' takeover.

Managing Other Railroads

Managing other railroads is simple—it's taking them over that isn't. You have to give your new company enough cash to pay off all its bonds, and possibly some more so that it can instantly build a new connection. This is obligatory if your new acquisition is a brand new puppy, and has been previously ravaged by you on the stock market. It will fold at year-end, and you'll own one railroad less.

Remember to speculate with your new acquisition's stocks. One year, you may want to take some cash and sell some of its stock; next year, when you aren't robbing it, buy the stock again before it rises. There are many variations on this theme once you've got the concept. I'll leave them up to you.

THE MAKING OF A PRESIDENT OR A PRIME MINISTER

You can become President or Prime Minister even without acquiring other railroads if you play the game at the hundred percent difficulty level (which means there's no penalty applied to your retirement bonus). However, the quickest way to reach the top spot is by playing at the Tycoon level and acquiring other railroads. In the middle game especially, the acquisition of a second railroad can catapult you upwards. The acquisition of all three competing railroads with the attendant two hundred percent bonus in your retirement money means you've won hands down. There's nothing more to be said.

RAILROAD TYCOON DELUXE

> **Important Note:** The railroads you took over should always be surveying a new route. Since the computer-controlled railroads cannot build station improvements and otherwise improve the cash flow from an existing route the way you can, the only way they can make more money is through new connections.

However, acquiring the third competing railroad is the hardest acquisition of them all. Quite often, the railroad in question manages somehow to heal after your stock-market attacks and build a decent network. If you run into difficulties during your first or second acquisitions, you may very well be dealing with a powerful opponent with lots of cash and no bonds.

The only way to take over another railroading behemoth is through a steady war of attrition on both the stock market and the railroad tracks. The latter is made possible through rate wars.

Rate Wars

In general, the manual provides a good explanation of what rate wars are about. However, I suggest you remember one item in particular: the second fiscal period following the start of the rate war is the time of the first meaningful vote. Time all your deliveries/pickups for the second fiscal period!

The best way to ensure that you win a rate war quickly is by building a new industry in the contested station's service area. The computer opponent is completely baffled by the concept of changing demand, and you will be able to score double points. You'll be the only one to deliver the newly demanded type of cargo, and also the only one to pick up the cargo produced by your new industry.

Whether you can afford to build a new industry or not, all your trains picking up cargo at the rate-war station should operate under wait-till-full-orders, and feature an impossible number of cars. Detach the cars that are still empty and remove the wait orders just before the end of the fiscal period to qualify for pickup votes on the city council. Also, concentrate on delivering at least one carload of every type of cargo demanded by the contested station.

Making Paper Money

In the end stages of the game, I suggest you try making money by creating false trading activity around your own stock. I found this especially useful since the later part of the game is when railroad revenues tend to get smaller instead of bigger—old routes that pay less and less every fiscal period constitute the vast majority of your railroad network. Shrinking profits for the delivery of the same cargo to the same station are an important feature of *Railroad Tycoon,* one that can easily halt the price of your stock in its tracks, so to speak.

To make paper money, simply sell a couple of blocks of stock, then buy them back, then repeat. You'll notice that the price of your stock rises following this maneuver. Do it as many times as you desire, bearing in mind that at the end of the fiscal year, the price of your stock will be adjusted to a realistic level. I usually end a series of sales and buybacks by selling a couple of blocks for good. Since this tactic is usually employed in the later stages of the game, after your stock has split a few times, you usually own so many shares that you can afford to get rid of a few.

Expect to lose a bit of cash on these transactions. However, you'll make lots of money on the rise in price of all your stock. Check the income statement following a set of transactions to view results.

THE OPPOSITION

Some of the characters you encounter in *Railroad Tycoon* are more dangerous than others. Each of them is assigned abilities in four areas—building a railroad, operating it, his financial acumen, and aggressiveness.

It goes without saying you have taken steps to protect yourself from a hostile takeover (I make a point of acquiring half of my company's stock within the first ten fiscal periods). Therefore, your competition worries are limited to losing good station locations and being hemmed in by the competition's lines.

If you make use of the stock market war strategy presented earlier and combine it with a rate war, you can break any competitor's back. Keeping this in mind, remember the following:

In the Americas, keep a sharp eye out for these characters: Corning, Hill, Forbes, and J. Edgar Thomson. Vanderbilt occasionally makes a strong effort, and Cooke can build a very big network financed by bonds. Railroads owned by Hill, Forbes, and Corning are the most desirable takeover targets. They'll bring you nice profits. The least desirable takeover targets are Fisk and Drew.

In Europe/Africa (or England/Europe in the earlier version of *RT*), the guys to watch are both Stephensons, Rothschild, and Brunel. Brunel and the Stephensons are the most desirable takeover targets.

Avoid Tsar Nicholas II! It's no wonder the Russians grew ripe for revolt under his administration. Von Moltke, Mussolini, de Gaulle, and Lenin make occasional strong showings. Napoleon tends to start well, then flounders.

In general, American tycoons tend move more smartly than their European counterparts.

THE WORLDS OF *RAILROAD TYCOON*

Each of *Railroad Tycoon's* worlds present a different challenge. Understanding the different cargoes which are present in each world is absolutely necessary. It is covered exhaustively in the game manual, which also features a separate conversion chart for each world.

In my personal experience, here's how it all works in practice:

North America

Given the option of choosing the era, North America presents the opportunity for a pleasant career. Cargoes are plentiful in the eastern half of the game world, which is where I recommend you start your first route.

Ports and cities are favored locations for your first stations. Ports supply a steady stream of goods, and also convert coal into steel—which is useful given coal's two-step conversion chain. Try to set up an initial network of three to four routes that include at least two healthy cities and a port, then go on from there.

Eastern and Western North America

Eastern America is, essentially, a smaller version of North America. There's more emphasis on ports and local industries.

The best spots to start a railroad tend to be in New England and south of New England—in the Patterson/Allentown/Philadelphia triangle. Occasionally, Virginia and Pennsylvania provide good starting points. Look for big cities, as usual, but also for groups of coal mines/lumber mills. Remember that coal and grain can be sold at landings.

Western America

The landscape is similar to North America, but the rules are different. Trains running from east to west earn twice as much as trains running north to south, until someone builds a transcontinental railroad. If it's you, you get one million bucks.

To qualify for the title of Transcontinental, your railroad has to start on the east bank of the Mississippi and end on the Pacific. My favorite place to start is somewhere in the Des Moines/Green Bay/St Louis triangle. If you start in the southeast, be aware that a computer-controlled tycoon may cut you off quite easily!

Europe

Europe is all about people and sheep. Coal slips from importance, since the end product—armaments—often needs a separate railroad going to a fort, and forts often disappear in the course of the game. However, sheep farms offer a bountiful supply of wool and nitrates, and are often found in large groups.

I tend to ignore grapes and wine. Grapes tend to perish even if you build cold storage facilities, and since vineyards usually appear singly, it's not worth your while to set up a train for a car-and-a-half of grapes per year.

What are the best cargoes in Europe? Mail and passengers, of course. Long, fast passenger/mail runs—that's where the money is.

Good spots to start your first railroad include the Benelux—the area where Belgium, Germany, and France meet, with Holland nearby. However, I tend to start my railroad in Poland/Germany, and generally do well.

England

This is a world present in an earlier version of *RT*; in *RT Deluxe,* England is merely a part of Europe. The main stress, like in Europe, is on finding an area that can generate a substantial amount of mail/passenger traffic. Occasionally, a well-placed terminal will yield several carloads of hops. Ports are a good source of cotton and a poor of hops. Both ports and landings are at a premium as the only places that demand manufactured goods. Finally, sheep farms act as sources of livestock, which is delivered directly to cities, and, presumably, eaten alive.

If you can't start your first railroad in an area with substantial passenger/mail traffic, look for villages, breweries, and hops. Mixed trains of hops/passengers and passengers/beer are often the only solution in the first few years. Consider building a coal railroad even if there is no demand for manufactured goods at any of your stations. Two payoffs—coal to steel and steel to goods—are good enough even if you hate seeing any cargo waste.

Africa

Ports, ports, and more ports—that's what Africa is about. Ports supply a stupendous total of five cargoes—troops, mail, passengers, food, manufactured goods—and take in practically all freight you'll have to offer in the starting years. Look for cities to connect to ports on the Indian Ocean; you should be able to find at least one spot where starting a railroad is feasible. Run mixed trains—troops/passengers, passengers/sugar, goods/food—remembering that outposts demand food. Cities tend to develop quickly, generating more and more passenger and mail traffic; and making further connections inland isn't a problem as the years go on.

Getting into debt at the start of the game tends to be more risky in Africa than in North America or Europe. Do not borrow over two million pounds for any length of time.

RAILROAD TYCOON DELUXE

South America

This is the toughest game world of them all. Big distances and difficult terrain combine with small cities and a shortage of industry to provide a real challenge both to the human and the computer player. Often, the computer players drop like flies throughout the first twenty years of the game, and that's without any stock attacks on your part.

The best place to start a railroad tends to be in Argentina. Like in Africa, ports are important—try connecting a couple of cities to the seaboard. This is a game world where getting into a lot of debt right at the start of the game is very risky because revenues are on the lean side. Do not borrow over a million and a half pounds for any length of time, and try to save up and build a refinery—there's a shortage of those, but usually quite a few oil wells.

CHAPTER

11

SIMCITY 2000

Publisher:	Maxis Software
Platform:	PC MS-DOS, Windows, Mac
Release Date:	Fall, 1993
Multiplayer:	No
Rating:	

General Overview

In the late eighties, a new game from a new software company swept computer gamers off their feet. The name of the game was *SimCity,* and thousands of people spent many sleepless nights creating the cities of their dreams—and fighting for their survival and preservation in the face of fires, earthquakes, floods, plane crashes, and many other disasters.

In 1993, the long-awaited sequel to *SimCity* finally arrived. Called *SimCity 2000,* it immediately became a bestseller. The original *SimCity* was greatly improved and expanded upon. Most importantly, the new game now features SVGA graphics and an isometric view (*SimCity 2000* is one of the few games that runs exclusively in SVGA. If you don't have SVGA, don't bother getting it).

The game puts you in the position of the founder and ruler of a city. The term 'mayor' does not quite cover it, as you can act like a dictator with total impunity. The only bad consequences in store are that the inhabitants of your city will start moving out if they don't like how things are being run. However, the Sims are a very materialistic lot, and all it takes to lure them back is lowering the taxes.

Your role as city ruler isn't limited to tax business. You actively participate in all the facets of building and running a new city—but the buildings you can erect are limited to public utilities in a broad sense. Industry, commerce, and Sims in general are responsible for the building. Your work consists of zoning land for one of the three kinds of developments possible (each with a low-density and high-density subclass), and then doing everything you can to raise land values so that you can collect more taxes without having to raise the taxation rate. Raising land values is far from a simple process, and cannot progress far unless you've also taken care of basic city issues such as water and power supply, transportation, health and welfare, education . . . The list is long, and is already provided in the game and the manual.

In addition to offering pristine land, *SimCity 2000* also contains scenarios in which you are given the task of achieving a specific goal—be it raising the city's population and filling the treasury coffers, or dealing with a disastrous fire. The goals set by each scenario are achieved by using the same means as you would while creating and managing a new city. If you achieve these goals, you are asked to continue as mayor, which is a tad unimaginative.

SimCity 2000 is an open-ended game. There is no pre-written ending, not even in the form of a time limit; your city can continue for thousands of game years. The game does not have any victory conditions as such, except the scenarios, and there's no Hall of Fame of the best cities you've built (in fact, *SimCity 2000* does away with the point rating system employed by its predecessor). Your success is measured in terms of the size of your city, and its wealth and aesthetics (which may be a trifle watery for gamers who like to see concrete results at the end of a game; in this case, there is no ending, anyway). There's a lot of action going on at all times, and you'll be very hard pressed to satisfy the demands of the rather whiny Sims. Your reward is a big and beautiful city that functions flawlessly. However, personally, I'd have liked to see something—if only a Hall of Fame of the best cities I've built.

One of the biggest plusses of *SimCity* is its originality. Although there are copies of the concept (Maxis proceeded to release *Sim*-Everything: *SimFarm, SimEarth, SimIsland, SimTower*—you name it), there's no other game quite like it. A lot of what goes into the game is an indirect result of your action, which means there's quite a lot of computer magic going on, and this greatly appeals to some gamers. Many people also find the lack of the usual computer-game bloodshed and mayhem very refreshing.

Golden Rules

- Site your city well. The optimum starting location is a flat expanse that has water and hills nearby, but enough space to build a city of at least 5,000 people. Once you've got this many, it's easier to raise the cash necessary for any terrain-altering work. If you're playing at Easy or Medium, you may want to make a connection to a neighboring city right away. It helps early growth.

- Remember the three-tile rule: A Sim citizen can only walk three tiles, and cannot walk between zones. Roads, rails, subways, and highways are the ways in which your citizens can cross from one zone to another. They have to encounter one of the above within those three tiles they can walk.

Subways and other rail transport can only be accessed through stations/depots. The same goes for buses.

Keep commercial and industrial zoning equal to residential (the sum of residential tiles should equal the sum of commercial and industrial tiles). The proportions between industry and commerce are weighed in favor of industry when the city is small, in favor of commerce when it's big.

Make sure every zone has power and water. It has a great effect on land values and speed of development, even when not strictly necessary. You do not have to connect tiles within zones, but doing so quickens things up considerably.

Give your citizens a tax holiday for the first year or two—they'll be flocking to your city as if it were Paradise. Don't destroy the Paradise City image by jacking up the tax rate too high; the maximum comfortable and sustainable tax rate is 7% on the Hard level, 8% on the Easy. You may set the tax higher, but only for short periods of time.

Don't count on city ordinances to help fill your coffers. Even a seemingly innocent ordinance, such as parking fines, can have an adverse effect strong enough to offset any gains. Passing no money-collecting ordinances at all often means you can jack up the tax rate by a point and get away with it.

City ordinances that cost money don't necessarily help your city grow. Anti-pollution measures may help residential zones, but if your city relies on heavily-polluting industries for its jobs, you'll be in for an unpleasant shock. Think about real life and how city authorities always seem to be making things more difficult. Don't mess with your city unnecessarily, and be quick to repeal measures that are having a negative effect.

Make a point of providing all basic city services from the very start—police, firemen, education, health care. You don't need to build colleges right away, and you can set the initial funding of any institutions to 10–15% to avoid breaking the bank. The presence of these buildings means both extra jobs and a better life, and helps your city grow faster.

Keep your Sims healthy and well-educated. Dead Sims pay no taxes; well-educated Sims pay more in taxes. Hospitals, schools, colleges, and so on are *SimCity's* invisible profit-makers.

Monitor traffic from the moment you see animated cars on your roads. When traffic hits the eighty-cars-per-minute mark, it's time to start thinking about public transportation. Buses work best, and are least troublesome. The roads are already there, and all you have to do is build depots. Carve the needed space out of the less-popular spots, but remember to space them well, too.

A port and an airport are absolutely necessary to develop a thriving city. Plan for the expenditure in advance, and give both room to expand. Airports are particularly site-sensitive.

Think twice about accepting a military base. Although it provides help in emergencies and has a positive effect on commerce, a military base also brings increased pollution and crime. Refusal means that every now and then, the Sim Superman will appear to help combat disasters.

Arcologies mean a huge population boost. Be prepared for the crime and pollution they bring!

Winning Strategies

Since you can't win a game of *SimCity 2000* per se, winning strategies here simply mean solutions that allow your city to grow and thrive.

The first step to identifying these solutions is getting to know the Sims, who are the inhabitants of your city. It's important to note that your city is part of a larger SimNation. Unlike the original that preceded it, your city also has neighbors—four other cities, one on each side of the map. The fortunes of the SimNation and the neighboring cities have an effect on your own metropolis. The SimNation's economic climate determines the demand for goods, which has a direct effect on the fortunes of your industrial zones. Making transport connections (road, highway, rail) with the neighboring cities can boost the development of commerce in industry in both cities—yours and the neighbor's that you connected with.

THE SIMCITIZEN

The Sims inhabiting the SimNation aren't a particularly happy lot. Their life expectancy totals just 59 years, and they have an educational quotient, or EQ, of 85 (the current EQ for the United States is estimated at 100).

This is the portrait of the Sim immigrants that arrive in your city hoping for a better life. You must improve their lot if you want to build a truly nice town. Of course, while improving the Sims' lot means expenses, it brings you nothing but profit in the long run. Longer-living Sims pay taxes longer, and then, of course, there are more of them—which means more taxes. More Sims also means more industry and more commerce to serve their needs (although at first, your budding settlement will rely on outside demand to expand industry).

The Population window in the game shows Sims split into many age groups. In reality, only these distinctions count:

- Sims younger than five and older than 55 don't count much. They aren't part of the work force and they don't go to school of any sort.

- Sims between five and fifteen years of age go to school—if there is one. (You have to build public buildings yourself, and fund their operations.) If your city contains colleges, Sims continue to educate themselves until they are 20 years old.

- Sims between 20 and 55 are the work force, and thus, the most important group of Sims you deal with. Unemployment can kill a city; you must make sure your citizens are employed by providing enough industrial/commercial zones, and placing them so that they are within reach of a commuting Sim. Interestingly, many of the public buildings can be placed anywhere without having their benefits affected—more about this later.

Health

Healthy Sims live longer and dead Sims pay no taxes, so build hospitals. That's the long and short of it, perhaps with the comment that low life expectancy makes raising the Sims' educational quotient more difficult.

The education of your Sims isn't an abstract. A high education quotient, or EQ, encourages the development of high-tech industries that pay fat taxes.

Educating Sims

As mentioned, the average immigrant to your newly-founded city is a bit of a moron. Their EQ of 85 is the equivalent of a high school education. It's your responsibility to work on this, and you should welcome it with open arms because providing decent schooling helps increase immigration (this is particularly noticeable at the Hard level). Schools and colleges aren't enough, either. After Sims stop schooling themselves, they tend to forget what they've learned, and their EQ slides year by year. You can help prevent this by building libraries and museums.

The five-year-old Sim enters school with some inborn intelligence—20% of what his or her parents have. Thus, your average immigrant produces offspring that have a natural EQ of 17.

School can improve the EQ of the young Sim by up to 70 points, for a total of 87. However, there has to be enough schools, and they must be well-funded to provide full benefits. Clicking on any public building that provides services to the city's inhabitants will provide you with a rating of the service. Make sure your schools are A+!

A college further increases a Sim's EQ by up to 50%. So, if you send the 87-point Sim to a college that has a good rating, you can see the EQ increase to about 130. Bear in mind that the offspring of this well-educated Sim will enter school with a higher EQ than their parents—in this case, about 26—and will complete college with a higher EQ than the old folks. The same goes for the next generation and the next, until the EQ of your Sims hits the upper limit, set at 150.

Keep in mind that if you don't build libraries and museums, your Sims will turn stupid. One library serves about 20,000 Sims, one museum about 40,000.

The consequences of having a well-educated force are highly beneficial. The high-tech industries your well-educated citizens attract pay more in taxes, and most of them pollute less. Each school you build serves 15,000 citizens, each college 50,000.

STARTING YOUR CITY

It may be argued that cities can only be as good as the ground they're built on, and natural landscape features play a large role. Every game you start generates a random world according to certain parameters. There are ratios for hills, wooded areas, water, etc., and you can adjust each of these more to your liking. I would suggest you make sure there's enough water. City sites that include a river reaching the edge of the map or a seashore are best; otherwise, they can't build a port, which severely handicaps industry. In addition, placing water pumps right next to water squares greatly improves their productivity (although they'll always pump some water). The more water squares around a pump, the bigger the water volume pumped.

Many game-generated maps contain quite a lot of mountains and hills. While these features have a slight beneficial effect on land values, and are indispensable as such (hydro and wind power need them), they make laying your city out more difficult; fooling around with a bulldozer once you've started the city can get very costly.

It's good to keep in mind that hills, trees, and shoreline all boost land values. It makes sense to situate your city accordingly.

PLANNING A HABITABLE CITY

You should start your planning by thinking about power and water. You may see some Sims move into zones that have neither. This is undoubtedly caused by the 85-strong EQ—but most likely, they won't stay.

Choose a flat site which has both water and hills nearby, and make sure it's big enough to accommodate a respectable number of buildings. While it's possible (and sometimes advisable) to build a city that consists of several distinct boroughs, each of these has to be fully independent—that is, each should contain a mixture of all three zone types. The location of hospitals, schools, libraries, marinas, airports (and so on) does not matter, but each type of zoning must have the two other zone types within easy reach.

The Traveling Sim

The workings of an actual city are simulated by making each zone—industrial, commercial, residential—generate trips to the two remaining types of zones. This simulates real-life citizens attempting to get to work, doing their shopping, and so on. If you know about flowers and bees, you can imagine the whole thing: Each zone pollinates the others, allowing them to flower and bloom. The pollination is done by the Sims, who cannot cross from one zone to another on foot. They can only do so if traveling by car, bus, train, or subway.

The Sim that sets out to get to work or to go shopping can only travel a limited distance, which is expressed in "steps." Every Sim has a hundred steps he or she takes before frustration sets in. The maximum distance that it can cover before coming across some means of inter-zonal transport is three map squares, or tiles. That effectively means every square in every zone cannot be farther than three tiles from a road, a bus depot, subway station, or rail depot.

Once a Sim reaches a means of inter-zonal transport, it continues its travels while using up the allotment of steps. Different transport has different movement costs:

- Upon reaching a road, Sims take the car. A car uses up three Sim steps for every road tile traveled, and just a single step for every highway tile. Theoretically, this gives our Sim a range of 33 tiles by road and 50 by highway. Note that highways are only available after 1930.

- If our Sim comes across a bus depot, he/she takes the bus. Amazingly, road-traveling buses can get Sims to places cars can't, because they use up only two steps per road tile traveled. (Like cars, buses use up one step per one highway tile.) Theoretically, our traveling Sim has a range of 50 tiles.

- If the Sim we're watching comes across a subway station or railway depot, he/she takes the train. The train costs just one step per tile traveled; however, the act of finding entrances and exits from stations must be exhausting since it costs four steps. That means a Sim with a full allotment of a hundred steps can only travel a maximum of 92 tiles (four steps are used for getting into one station and getting out of the other).

 If our hypothetical Sim is already traveling by car when he or she comes across alternate means of inter-zonal transport (bus, subway, train), there's a 50–50 chance he or she will park the auto and proceed by bus or train.

Note that the traveling range of a Sim is much shorter in practice than it is in theory. Factors such as heavy traffic decrease the range to 20 to 25 tiles when traveling by road; and since getting onto a highway involves some road and ramp travel, you can't count on the maximum theoretical range there, either. However, highways can handle double the traffic of roads without any jams, so the loss in range, once the Sim gets onto the highway, is less severe.

Remember that unlike in the original *SimCity,* Sims have to make use of a station/depot to use subways and trains.

Dealing With Traffic

Since inter-zonal connections are so important, it's also important to ensure good traffic flow. Heavy traffic robs Sims of steps, and they cannot get as far. As a result, some Sims do not get to complete their trips to the other zones, and when that happens, they get angry and eventually move out of your city.

Heavy traffic also increases pollution, and in *SimCity 2000,* pollution is an evil whose effects are far-reaching and insidious. To check how things are, hold down the Shift key and click on a road tile. You'll get a window informing you of the current number of cars per minute. Anything below 44 cars a minute is considered light traffic, between 44 and 88 is medium, and over 88 cars a minute, heavy traffic—and that's where the trouble starts.

You can attempt to improve the traffic situation in two ways: The first is obvious—build more and better roads and highways. The second is to put the traveling Sims on some sort of public transport, which means they won't be driving their cars, which means . . . you got it. As mentioned, there's a 50-50 chance a driving Sim will park and get onto public transport if given the chance. However, a Sim that hasn't started driving yet is sure to choose public transportation over the car. In other words, you have to create a situation where your Sim comes across public transportation before or as soon as he/she reaches a road. Because of that, subways and trains do not improve traffic flow as much as buses—a funny paradox.

To sum up: Monitor traffic, and when it gets too heavy, consider the bus first, and the train second. Improving your road network is, of course, always a concurrent option, but it has to tie in to a larger plan. Otherwise, it almost always turns out to be a bad move necessitating some form of extra future expense.

THE CHANGING FACE OF YOUR CITY

The first step is to site your city. The second is to lay out roads (it doesn't make sense to build rails right away). Make sure that every zoned tile is not more than three tiles from a road (the only means of inter-zonal travel if you don't build rails). The third is to lay down the water pipes and power grid; it's easiest if you take a cue from real life here, and simply run them along or under the roads. Remember that you only have to make zone connections— the water and power connections inside a zone are made by the Sims themselves. However, if you decide to spend a lot of money and do that for them, you'll be rewarded with faster growth.

When zoning land, you have three basic types of zones—residential, industrial, commercial—and two subtypes for each basic type of zoning: high and low density. The different densities lead to different results—low density zones mean higher land values, but less population to tax. High density zoning means the reverse—more people, lower land value. High density can also result in higher pollution and crime rate. However (yes, there's always a flip side) the lower land values/property tax means quicker immigration, at least in my experience.

Zone low density or high density, whichever you prefer—just make sure you have all three basic zone types. Remember to make sure every tile within every zone is no more than three tiles from a road or rail connection leading to other types of zoning.

Your city needs good balance between the three types of zoning in order to grow smoothly and quickly. This balance changes with city size, being a reflection of the changing needs of your citizens.

SIMCITY 2000

The ironclad rule is that you have to have as much residential zoning as you have industrial and commercial. In other words, the sum of your commercial and industrial zones should equal residential zoning. This is a constant, no matter what size your city is. What changes are the proportions between the industrial and commercial zones. A small city needs more industry than commerce, and a big city, quite the reverse. The optimum ratios start at 3:1 for a city under 20,000 inhabitants, changing to 2:1 at 60,000 people, 1:1 at 100,000 people, 1:2 at 150,000, and finally 1:3 in favor of commerce when your population tops 200,000 inhabitants.

Power

No, we aren't talking political clout. This section is about your choice of power plant.

There is no question that hydro plants are the best type of power plant. First of all, they are relatively inexpensive—"relatively" because the cost per megawatt isn't great, but a single power plant is just $500 ($400 for the plant, $100 for the waterfall needed beforehand. You may cheat a little by putting waterfalls all over the place before you start your city). Coal and oil plants create tons of pollution, plus they consume a major part of your starting funds.

Other forms of power become available later on, but they all have drawbacks. A nuclear plant can melt down, a microwave beam may miss the receiving dish and start a fire, instead, a solar plant won't work when it's cloudy, a wind plant when there's no wind—the list goes on. Hydro plants don't have any of these drawbacks. Their only drawback is low power output, but you can always build one more when needed—it's affordable. What's more, they occupy slopes; there's nothing else you can use those slopes for, really. If you consider that usually you have to leave an anti-pollution band of trees or park around a fossil fuel-burning power station, hydro is the way to go.

SIM MONEY

The finances of your city are, of course, a major element in the gameplay—in fact, the most important single element in the game. Looking at things from a distance, your city is basically a money engine. Every positive event or action, ranging from the city carnival to building a school or a hospital, brings a result in the form of clinking cash. It's those land values, of course, and property taxes. In a way, *SimCity 2000* reflects a sad truth we all know: Living somewhere nice tends to be expensive.

The main thing about your budget is straightforward: make your city make money. Greed is followed by disaster. Your Sims will start moving out if you raise taxes too high, or balk at spending needed to correct a situation, such as improving your transportation network.

The Budget window is pretty straightforward. First of all, you set the overall tax rate. Any tax below six percent means quick growth—the lower the tax, the quicker the growth. Six-to-seven percent allows your city to grow at a reasonable rate (whether it's six or seven depends on how well you designed your city—the better the city, the higher the tax you can set). Eight-to-nine percent means crawling growth, and no growth at all if your city isn't very habitable. Anything over nine percent starts an exodus of your population. If you want to see how fast Sims can move out, set the tax to maximum.

Your budget can be tweaked further through a series of smaller steps. As mayor, you are able to pass various ordinances. Some cost money, others bring in money, and all have some sort of an effect:

- One percent sales tax is a good option once the commerce in your city is strongly on its feet. Earlier on, it has a bad effect on commercial growth.

- One percent income tax can bring in lots of lucre once your city is prospering, but it always has a negative effect on residential zones (it's only applied there). If you're playing at the Hard level, and your city's shaky or in the budding stage, income tax can kill it!

- Legalized Gambling—means increased tourism, extra tax revenues, and a boost to both commerce and crime. Good policing is a must, and that costs, too.

- Parking Fines—this has negative effect on commerce and immigration, but encourages the use of public transportation. Thus, it cuts down on pollution in addition to bringing in a few extra dollars.

- Pro-Reading Campaign—this helps the EQ, though not much.

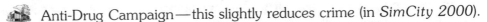

Anti-Drug Campaign—this slightly reduces crime (in *SimCity 2000*).

CPR Training—this slightly increases the life expectancy of your Sim citizens.

Neighborhood Watch—reduces crime, albeit marginally, and only in residential areas.

Energy Conservation—takes a few years to show benefits, which amount to an extra fifteen percent power, or more megawatts, from your power stations.

Nuclear Free Zone—you may get a few nuke-haters moving into your city, and you can't build or replace nuclear plants. That's all.

Homeless Shelters—this can get very expensive. A marginal increase in the work force and an even smaller one in land values is what you get in exchange.

Pollution Controls—can kill your incipient city at the Hard level. Discourages industry, and may keep an airport from growing. The benefits are lower pollution and, consequently, slightly better life expectancy.

Volunteer Fire Department—good for a budding city that can't afford a proper fire station. Not a substitute for the real thing.

Public Smoking Ban—increases the life expectancy of your Sims. In *SimCity 2000,* it has no effect on tourism or commerce.

Free Clinics—expensive, but provide a significant boost to the life expectancy of your Sims.

Junior Sports—increase life expectancy, but the cost is not insignificant.

Tourist Advertising—expensive, but worth every penny if you have lots of tourist attractions. Otherwise, no.

Business Advertising—helps bring in industry. Especially good in the starting stages, when your little town relies heavily on industrial investments.

City Beautification—quite expensive and quite useful. Has a good effect on residential land values.

 Annual Carnival—a little shot in the arm for the tourist industry. Moderately good value.

In addition to passing various ordinances, you may also tinker with the budget by setting individual tax rates for the various industries. You should think less of making extra money there and more about achieving a reasonable, low-polluting mix of industries, with emphasis on the high tech ones in the later stages. In many ways, tourism is the ideal industry because it's practically non-polluting. What's more, encouraging tourism means building such objects as stadiums, marinas, and zoos, which raise land values and immigration rates, thus providing a double benefit.

The Industries

Sim industries should be considered in terms of tech level and pollution. The best industries to have are high tech with low pollution levels: Aerospace, Electronics, Finance, Media, and Tourism, with Tourism being practically non-polluting (personally, in reality I don't think that's the case). Petrochemical and Automotive are also high tech industries, but they are heavy polluters. Everything else belongs in the low-tech, heavy-pollution class, and isn't as desirable.

Unfortunately, the best industries demand high EQ from your citizens. Although they will be present in practically every city you build, they'll grow very slowly. If the EQ of your Sims drops below 80 (five points below that of a standard Sim arriving in your city), development of high tech industries is heavily penalized. They receive a boost, however, if the EQ climbs above 100, and another at 130. Aerospace and Electronics are the most demanding; you'll have to work hard on the Education front before their presence amounts to anything.

In addition to the EQ, industries can be affected by other factors, all of which are just common sense. For instance, don't expect the Steel and Mining industries to whoop with joy when you pass an anti-pollution ordinance. Tourism is affected by a series of factors which include land values and the attractions you've built, as well as some of the city ordinances.

City Services

To grow securely, your city needs hospitals, proper policing, and an efficient fire department. All this in addition to the considerable expense of education may put a strain on your budget. The construction costs of the buildings involved are high, and the maintenance costs very painful.

You cannot avoid building hospitals, police stations, and fire departments. Hospitals can be located anywhere, but police and fire stations have to be carefully situated—they only work within a certain radius.

The effectiveness of all those services, as well as that of your city's educational system, is determined by the level of funding. However, a small city cannot afford full funding for all those goodies without going broke.

The answer is—cut funding. A little town that can't get by with Neighborhood Watch and volunteer firemen can be adequately serviced by schools, hospitals, and police/fire stations that receive just a fraction of what they should. Initially, I often set the rate to as little as ten percent. While the arrest rate leaves something to be desired, schools and hospitals particularly function very well on minimal funding. However, remember to keep an eye on the population stats. As your city grows, you have to increase spending on services!

In large cities, it's a good idea to build a prison. It reduces crime, as long as it's not filled to capacity!

PORTS AND AIRPORTS

Ports and airports are essential to develop your city beyond a certain stage. You do not build them, you just zone the land, and wait. If you've zoned it wrong, you'll be waiting forever:

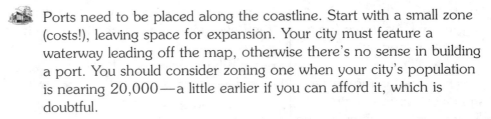

- Ports need to be placed along the coastline. Start with a small zone (costs!), leaving space for expansion. Your city must feature a waterway leading off the map, otherwise there's no sense in building a port. You should consider zoning one when your city's population is nearing 20,000—a little earlier if you can afford it, which is doubtful.

- Airports boost commerce, but they don't make sense until you've got around 50,000 people. However, they become an absolute necessity soon afterwards. Otherwise, the commerce in your city will suffer greatly. The same goes for calls for airport expansion—you'd better heed them, and fast.

Airports are tricky to locate. They need a minimum of five tiles in one direction and three in the other—but allow more space than that. Do not develop the airport area with anything other than parks and such. High pollution levels and plane crashes make airports a hazard. When expansion time comes, it's easiest to add to the existing airport instead of zoning another one. Remember to leave extra space!

Apart from airplanes, your city features a traffic helicopter. Watch out for its propensity to hover near the airport—it may cause a crash. You can cause the chopper to crash if you click on it.

If you cannot afford a port or an airport, or your population hasn't reached the required level, you may try to help your city's commerce and industry by other (somewhat less effective) means. Building off-map connections to your neighbors is what it takes. This tends to cost a bit of cash, too. Road connections help commerce; rail and highway connections help industry.

DEALING WITH DISASTERS

SimCity 2000 features a series of disasters meant to enliven your term as mayor. You can turn them off from the menu, but isn't that cheating?

 Fires are the most common disasters. They often appear following another disaster, just when you really don't want them. Try demolishing everything around a fire that's out of control. It'll stop the fire from spreading. An efficient fire brigade is a must in every city! If you have a military base in your city, you may enlist the assistance of its soldiers through the emergency button.

 Floods are also fairly common. You can prevent them by building tile-high dikes along the coast—but sometimes that's impossible. You can deploy police, firemen, and military in sensitive areas, but mostly, all you can do is wait till the waters fall.

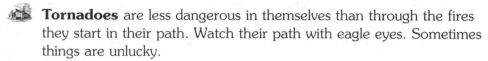

Tornadoes are less dangerous in themselves than through the fires they start in their path. Watch their path with eagle eyes. Sometimes things are unlucky.

Plane crashes cause limited damage if you have a good fire department. Usually, by the time you can build an airport, you already have one. This is of no real concern.

Earthquakes can ruin you in an instant. The resulting conflagration can destroy whatever's left standing! Control the fires first—that's the overriding priority.

Hurricanes can cause widespread damage because they often deliver a secondary punch in the form of a flood. If your city doesn't have a coastline, you won't get a hurricane, unless you ask for it from the menu.

Pollution disasters can be caused by a lot of heavy industry, a chemical spill, or a nuclear meltdown. In each case, there's not much you can do—prevention is the best cure. Try to contain the poisonous clouds with police and the military. Note that fusion power plants aren't at risk of meltdown. If you have to have a nuclear power plant, place it in the corner of the map to avoid most of the meltdown consequences.

Microwave beam disaster occurs when the beam misses the dish of the power station and hits other buildings, instead. The fires that result are usually minor.

Riots and mass riots are caused, first and foremost, by high unemployment and high crime rate, but heat also plays a role. Surround the rioters with cops, or they'll set everything on fire. Keep the firemen handy.

The military mentioned above becomes a possibility once your city passes 60,000 inhabitants. At this point, you may be asked by SimNation's government if you'd like a military base. Say yes, and you get a population boost, a shot in the arm for commerce, help in emergencies, increased pollution, and increased crime. Say no, and every time a disaster takes place, there's a chance you'll see *SimCity's* equivalent of Superman arrive to give a helping hand!

The Mayor's Rewards

As your city increases in importance, so will you. Your newly elevated status will be confirmed by various pleasant occurrences, which start by moving you into a nice mansion when your city's population crosses 2,000 inhabitants. At 10,000 inhabitants you get a city hall which provides you with some extra (but rather useless) statistics about the city; 30,000 sees a statue in your honor; 60,000 the offer of a military base (if you refuse, you'll have the *Sim-City* Superman assisting you in combating disasters from time to time); 80,000 sees the Braun llama dome (an inside Maxis joke). Finally, after the year 2000, you're offered the chance to place arcologies. These self-contained cities cost plenty of money (the previous rewards are free), but increase your city population by immense leaps and bounds. The Plymouth arco, available in the year 2000, accommodates 55,000 people in exchange for a cool $100,000; the Forest arco appears in 2050, and houses 30,000 at the cost of $120,000; the so-called Darco arco appears in 2100, with space for 45,000 inhabitants for a mere $150,000; and finally, the Launch arco becomes available in 2150, houses 65,000 people, and costs a whopping $200,000.

Arcologies are perhaps the greatest reward a mayor could dream of—but they are also a headache. Crime rates and pollution are very big concerns; be prepared for hefty extra expenditures in these areas. Naturally, the jump in your city's population means you must provide a lot of extra services in all other areas, too. The pollution problem can cause chemical spills—don't mass arcologies together! Build parks nearby to appease the criminals and lower pollution.

Unfortunately, the total number of arcologies is limited in most versions of *SimCity 2000* (Windows and Macintosh updates have had this ceiling removed). That effectively limits the maximum population of your city to 9,755,000 inhabitants. However, creating a city this big is practically impossible unless you turn the Disasters off.

SIMCITY 2000

CHAPTER

12

THEME PARK

Publisher:	Bullfrog
Platform:	PC MS-DOS
Multiplayer:	No
Rating:	

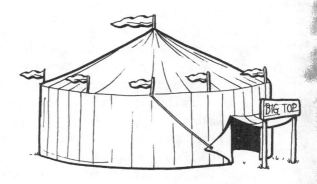

General Overview

Bullfrog is a British company noted for off-the-wall games, so it's not surprising that *Theme Park* is highly original. The game tests your prowess as the owner and administrator of an amusement park. In the process, you'll be captivated by its quirky charm and lively, interesting gameplay.

Theme Park can be played at three "main" difficulty levels, only the hardest of which shows it in its full glory. The necessity of remembering about 20 things at once, familiar to most administrators, is counterbalanced by opportunities such as the one to make a killing on the stock market. Since the game's difficulty can also be tweaked through adjusting the fussiness of the park's customers, it makes sense to opt for Hard elsewhere, and give yourself extra opportunities to make money.

The game isn't strictly about money, however. Facing up to 40 competitors, you must gather top honors as the most successful park owner in the world. You must be the wealthiest, naturally, and your park has to occupy top spots in several categories. It must provide the most satisfaction, be the most pleasant, have best amenities, offer the most excitement, and so on. Money is a necessity to meet all those goals, which means spending very freely in some areas. Tightwads are unlikely to achieve top ratings in more than a couple of categories.

In a sense, getting rich is at odds with building the ideal theme park. First of all, you don't make the big bucks (or top quid) on perfecting one park for years and years. Big bananas can only be made through judicious investments in the stock market (which features the stock of your own enterprise along with all the competitors), and through selling your business at an appropriate moment. Money thus gained can be used to start over in another place, with much more cash and without the burden of a bank loan (it is automatically paid off from the money raised at your park's auction).

The snag is that each time you start afresh, you start only with a gate and a green field. You have to research all the improvements, new rides, upgrades of existing ones, amenities, etc.—right from the beginning. Upgrading existing rides increases their capacity, as well as the quality of the experience.

In addition to all of the above, you must also hire and monitor the park's staff, which can be troublesome. Since *Theme Park* is a real-time game (time is always running, and you cannot do anything if the game's

THEME PARK

paused), performing all the various tasks often involves desperate juggling of priorities.

During the course of your career as the theme park creator and administrator, you'll have the opportunity to start parks all over the world, in varying geographical and economical climates. The ultimate aim, of course, is a park in sunny California. The trouble is, you can't even think about it until you're worth over fourteen million; fourteen million is how much you have to pay for the necessary piece of land in amusement paradise. Along the way lie such contrasting locales as Greenland and Nigeria, each with its own set of characteristics. It takes a brainy entertainer and skilled administrator to succeed!

Golden Rules

 Invest in yourself. It's worth your while to take out a loan for the express purpose of buying your own stock. Given competent performance on your part, your stock will double in value over three to four years, resulting in bigger profits than any number of rides can give you.

 Selling your park at an auction marks a big jump forward. Even your very first park will bring in a tidy sum of money. This will happen only if your park's successful enough to be auctioned, but the beginnings of the game are forgiving—you may even run a profitable, moderately successful park without a single toilet.

 In your initial research, concentrate on giving the masses something to eat and drink first. The catering side of your business easily brings in twice as much cash as the take at the gate does. Although food creates more puke, and possibly toilet problems, grit your teeth and get handymen to clean up as fast as they can.

 Lay out your park thoughtfully. Think of the customers in terms of traffic that needs to be directed along a specific route. Make sure that route takes in all of your rides and other attractions. You can greatly influence things by cunningly placing ride exits and one-way arrows.

THEME PARK

Build paths of sufficient length to accommodate lineups—at least three squares or tiles, and preferably more. My standard (though somewhat unimaginative) solution is to place them along the sidewalk.

 Keep everything in great technical shape. The monetary bonus awarded for ride safety can pay very many engineers' salaries!

 Tweak ratios in skill shops such as the Duck Shoot, Tin Can Alley, and GunShoot. You can be ruined by customers who formerly served in the commandos! My favorite tactic is to lower the probability of winning to 2–3%, while increasing the value of the prize and lowering the price of the ticket. Remember, they have to win sometimes!

 Almost everything in your park induces or can induce vomit. Food induces vomit. Rides induce vomit. Toilets induce vomit. Vomit induces vomit. Hire enough handymen to deal with the vomit. They can't really handle it all, but they can come close if you zone them (assign them to specific areas) properly.

 Pay attention to the relationships between certain structures. An obvious example is the inherent hostility between the food stands and the outhouses. Same goes for airplane rides and similar stomach-turning experiences. However, stomach-turning experiences greatly increase sales of balloons and novelties—place them nearby.

 Check your food supplies regularly. Basically, you have to order them as soon as you're down to 50%, or it's too late. Make increasing warehouse size a not-too-distant goal; a park of any size will regularly experience shortages otherwise. Given the importance of food revenues, shortages are disastrous.

Assign at least a couple of thousand to research on your very first day. To speed up research in a particular area, concentrate all funding there instead of increasing it across the board. It gets frightfully expensive!

Winning Strategies

You start each game of *Theme Park* in the United Kingdom, whose Queen has wisely given you free land for your enterprise. You have 100,000 quid, or dollars, or whatever, and a limited knowledge of amusement rides and other simple establishments. Since the game runs in real time, the very first thing you should do is jump to research and get hired brains working on various ways to make you more money. The five research categories are a little misty in the game:

 Ride upgrades mean capacity and performance enhancements of rides you already operate.

 New ride design simply results in new rides that greatly enhance your park's attractiveness, make you some more money, and greatly enhance your money-making *capability*.

 New shop design embraces all other buildings (with the exception of toilets)—burger stands, full-blown restaurants, and shooting alleys—all of which greatly enhance your park's attractiveness, and make you a lot of money.

 New features embrace toilets and ornamental items such as orange trees, ponds, and fences—all of which enhance your park's attractiveness.

 Improving your staff's effectiveness enhances your park's attractiveness, and saves you some money.

 New facilities work in several ways: better buses increase your gate take by bringing extra customers, better warehouses increase warehousing capacity (what else?), and so on. This category greatly enhances your park's effectiveness, makes you money, and greatly increases your money-making *capability*.

In the beginning, you should concentrate on just two areas: new ride designs and new shop designs. The objects that become available at the start of each game don't provide enough variety, and simply aren't sufficient to

THEME PARK

turn a decent profit. Within these two categories, new shops are more important. They include all catering establishments, and as you'll discover, they pay much better than rides. Rides are just the attraction. They are expensive, they have to be maintained, repaired, and replaced, and overall, they're a lot of hassle. However, every cola and fry stand makes a 100% profit on whatever it sells.

After getting research under way, you should go to the bank and get more money. You are going to run a successful park. In order to fully capitalize on this fact, you need to buy a lot of your own shares right at the start, before they rise in price. You can also expect the computer-controlled competition to start aggressively buying your stock. It's good practice to take an extra 50,000 from the bank and use it to buy up half your shares, especially since the patriots at Bullfrog made Britain a low-inflation country.

Having attended to business matters, it's time to roll up your sleeves and start construction.

LAYING OUT YOUR PARK

Since *Theme Park* runs in real-time, you can't ponder things at your leisure. It helps to have an idea or even a sketched plan of your park before you start. The key to success lies in good traffic flow; basically, you're designing a system of sidewalks that will make your park's visitors go wherever you want them.

In planning your park, you have to consider the delicate relationship between food, head-spinning rides, and public toilets. All three are necessary (though it's possible to make a packet on your first park without building a single outhouse, even with customers set to Fussy), and none works well with any of the others. In *Theme Park,* this inherent conflict is illustrated by vomit. Your customers tend to barf freely and frequently, particularly when fed fat burgers and sweet ice cream, taken on a ride, and subsequently deposited in an overflowing outhouse. Unfortunately, you can't cut food, (the main culprit) out of the picture. Your customers tend to be a crowd of greedy hogs. As their thought balloons will inform you, the only thing they think about upon entering your gates is food and drink. It's up to you to meet that need promptly and rake in a lot of cash in the process.

Michael Rymaszewski

I found that laying out my park in five rectangles joined in a cross proved to be an easy and effective solution. The double sidewalk from the gate constitutes the base of the cross. I extend it enough to fit in a ride complete with path for lineups, and surround it with sidewalk. The center of the cross is occupied by the food-and-drink merchants, while the remaining three arms are filled with rides. The toilets lie at the outer reaches—distant from food, yet relatively easily accessible. The empty spaces between the arms of the cross are great for adding later rides with a minimum of fuss.

I find that the one-way arrows are worth every penny at $250 a pop, since regulating the traffic by the entrance (with two-way lanes) is a must. By placing arrows elsewhere as you see fit, you can steer a potential customer past every single ride, food stand, etc., and deposit him/her on the toilet at a strategic moment.

Make sure that the blocks between the sidewalks aren't too small. You'll need enough space for a reasonably long path (usually, it's easiest to put it parallel to the sidewalk), so that lineups will form outside the main traffic. Consider carefully where you put the exit from a ride. Ideally, you want the customer to be sucked right into your next attraction.

Finally, you may want to consider other relationships between your park's various structures, independent of the puke factor. Balloons and novelties are impulse buys that follow exciting rides, so put the appropriate buildings close, and steer your customers to them in the right sequence. However, putting a Bouncing Castle next to your burger stand is asking for trouble; use common sense, and think what you would like to find in a similar situation.

Toilets hide a trap. The boggy crapper that follows the outhouse is supposedly the better sanitary solution. Personally, I think it's worse. It's worth your while to forego introducing the crapper entirely, and make a clean jump to the super-toilets of the third generation. Whatever toilets you build, put in some sweet-smelling space between them and the rest of the park. A screen of fruit trees works nicely.

Allow everything enough space (crowding can lead to terrible jams) but don't splash space about too freely. The land tax you'll pay after your initial tax holiday is based on the area you occupy. Building longer sidewalks costs more money in construction and maintenance, since they serve as trash cans and vomitoriums—and keeping a long trash can clean is harder than a short one.

THEME PARK

Hiring and Managing Staff

Although rides come with invisible, voluntary help, you still need other staff to run your show. To start with, you don't need many—three entertainers, a couple of handymen, and two engineers (a bit of an overkill, but it guarantees a great safety record, which means benefits in clinking coin) are about all. You'll quickly have to add extra handymen as you add buildings, particularly since most of them will have to do with food. As mentioned, food creates both big profits and big problems.

Your staff is fairly cooperative, provided you take the time to master the tricky interface. Entertainers are uncomplicated. It's enough to remember that the cheaper the entertainer, the less he/she entertains. Engineers are solid, slow-working types; the number needed depends not only on the number of your rides and how reliable they are, but on other variables such as the speed to which the rides are set and their usage. One engineer for every three rides is a pretty high ratio that virtually ensures trouble-free operation. Since you definitely don't want a ride to blow up (you get sued to hell), it's better to play it safe (especially since *Theme Park* gets very busy at times). You should judge your requirement for handymen yourself; a lot depends on how you zone things. I usually zone a handyman in each particularly troublesome area—the exit from a plane ride, or washroom complex, which I usually discreetly locate behind a grove of orange trees. In addition to that, I have a separate handyman patrolling the entrance/exit area, and several freelancing cleanup artists wandering the sidewalks. A relatively clean and tidy park lets you avoid all sorts of consequences, which may even culminate with a visit from a biker gang, as advertised in the manual. I say 'relatively' clean because it's impossible to avoid puke in *Theme Park*—and the bigger your park gets, the more puke there is, irrespective of the number of handymen you have rushing around.

From time to time, you'll have to negotiate pay increases (negotiating pay decreases is theoretically possible, but in my experience, highly unlikely). The key to successful negotiations, with shark-like suppliers of your stocks as well as employees, lies in watching those biscuits like a hawk. You should time things so that your hands meet with a happy handshake just as the last biscuit disappears. Show goodwill during negotiations. Severity breeds hostility and bigger demands from the union. If you fail to reach an agreement, you'll be forced to re-negotiate following a strike, and will be doomed to a 10% increase over and above what was demanded the previous time.

Growing Beyond the Basics

Your research effort can be adjusted downwards as soon as you have the all-important Big Time Fries and Pokey Cola. Generally, it's better to keep researching new shops with gusto until you get Big Time Burgers, too. Burgers carry a very nice profit, and anyway, you are forced to research a couple of non-food attractions on the way to the burger.

However, sooner or later, you'll have to spend more on researching other areas. Warehouses are important, and around that time, you'll start experiencing problems with continuous supply of food and drinks. The time lag between order and delivery means you'll run short of something more often than not, and running short of food means losing big amounts of revenue. Typically, your food business brings in two-to-three times more money than the park's amusements. Just follow the advice of the on-screen advisor. For guaranteed customer satisfaction, make your price increases slightly smaller than recommended. Also, don't forget to adjust prices following an increase in costs.

Keep your park in tip-top technical shape! The end of the year sees awards in various categories. You get a pound or a dollar for every point received, and that often decides your profit in the early stages.

Watching the Stocks

You should be constantly watching your stocks throughout the game—stocks other than food and drink, that is. If you've followed the advice earlier in this chapter, you will have bought a sizable package of your own stock at the outset of the game. Provided you don't make very bad mistakes, your stock should double in value within three to four years.

At this point, you'll probably be asked if you're interested in putting your park up for auction. Grab this opportunity with both hands. It's your chance to pay off that bank loan, and start afresh with a bulging wallet. You can simply choose Britain again—the land's still yours for nothing—and make a real killing this time around, after which you'll be ready to move out abroad.

THEME PARK

When your park is sold, the current price of any shares you own is added onto the selling price, and the bank loan is subtracted from the total. If you sell your park for 300,000 (highly possible) while owning ten shares at 8,300 each, you'll end up with a big chunk of cash, all yours to spend and invest.

If you manage your park reasonably well, you can confidently expect a doubling of your stock holdings every three-to-four years. Making money on other people's stock is also possible, but on the whole, I'd advise you to concentrate on acquiring your own stock, and maximizing the profitability and attractiveness of your park. Positive developments in your park can bring you double profit in the form of bigger immediate returns and an increase in the value of your stock.

Making Renovations

From time to time, you'll be informed that a ride needs replacing. Usually, this is a great opportunity to improve your park layout and traffic flow. Recognize it as such, and see whether it makes sense to replace the ride in another location. You may want to move that Bouncy Castle (a synonym for vomit-inducing rides), and put a serene Treehouse in its place; most probably your food sector will have grown considerably since the opening days, and more and more clients start Bouncing after a substantial meal.

Do not put in more than one food establishment of a kind until you've improved warehousing. An extra retail outlet will drain your supplies very quickly—much quicker than a new order can ever arrive. The first increase in warehouse size, to 110 units, comes free of charge. Subsequent ones cost 3,000 each, but they're worth every cent once your park reaches a certain size.

The first series of theme parks you create and own will serve as a stepping stone to creating the park which can win you the game. However, you should remember that amusement parks are widely renowned for the quality of their rides. Always try to provide at least a couple of really exciting, high-speed choices so that the public likes you.

Michael Rymaszewski

Excitement and Its Consequences

There's puke, of course. Also, since generating true excitement has a lot to do with speed, your rides will need much more maintenance. A ride that's set to slow motion will last long without trouble, but it'll hardly make a name for you.

You can cut down on the wear and tear a little by not filling the rides to their capacity, and shortening their time (this last step especially won't hurt, since good rides always have a long lineup). It's better to provide the public with a brief, hair-raising experience rather than a long, boring one.

You may be tempted to avoid all rides whose reliability is described as poor or worse. Don't. Every ride brings a new element into your park, and increases its overall attractiveness. Remember that the complement of rides you have is an important category; people need variety. Although it's a headache, keep as many different rides going as long as possible.

After you've achieved a good selection of rides, spend a little more on upgrades. Try to capture some of "the World's Longest, Biggest," trophies, not just the one for highest share price. These trophies greatly help in solidifying your park's standing with the paying public. You shouldn't skimp on any investments needed to be the Best, Biggest, or Longest in any category. If it hurts you to spend money for reasons other than generating more profit, spend some time speculating on the stock market. You can make money there any time you walk in. Just pay attention to which stock's going up, which down, and Bob's your uncle.

Do not try to take over another park, unless you've been following its progress closely for quite some time, and know for sure it's the thing to do. It's much safer to paddle one's own canoe. You don't have anything to fear from a vendetta, since the start of *every* game should see you buying at least 50% of your own stock, thus rendering any takeover attempts null and void. You'll notice the computer players—the ones who count like Professor Moneybags and Bingo Highway—always buy 50% of their own stock as fast as they can.

THEME PARK

CHAPTER
13
WARCRAFT II:
TIDES OF DARKNESS

Publisher:	Blizzard Entertainment
Platform:	PC MS-DOS, Windows 3.1, Windows95
Release Date:	Fall, 1995
Multiplayer:	Yes
Rating:	

General Overview

In 1994, *WarCraft: Orcs & Humans* changed the face of strategy gaming forever. Gone were the grids of squares and hexagons. With eye-catching graphics, the relentless action of real-time simulation and a good multiplayer system, this game brought many converts into strategy gaming. The sequel, *WarCraft II: Tides of Darkness,* begins where the first game left off. With a format similar to its predecessor's, *WarCraft II* is no hurriedly released clone. Blizzard made massive improvements to the graphics, as well as developed the storyline even further by the addition of several new types of units. The game is also full of great sound effects. The units respond verbally to your commands and you can always tell when a battle is in progress somewhere on the map. Just listen for the clash of swords, the whoosh of arrows and axes, and the cries of slain warriors. It is no wonder several computer gaming magazines named *WarCraft II* the Strategy Game of 1995.

The player is given the choice of commanding either the Human forces or those of the Orcs. After choosing which side to control, the player is immersed into a campaign of fourteen missions. Animated cut-scenes tell the story of the conflict as the player progresses through the campaigns. While combat is a major part of this game, the construction of towns and base camps, as well as the management of resources, is also important for success. At the beginning of the campaigns, you are limited in the types of structures that you can construct and the types of units you can recruit and train. As the campaigns progress, you can get stronger and more powerful units which are necessary to defeat the enemy's increasingly deadlier units

Having enjoyed the first game, I eagerly awaited the release of *WarCraft II.* I was not disappointed. The units which you can command are no longer limited to only land. You can now control aerial as well as naval units, which are necessary since many of the missions require crossing large bodies of water. This allows the player to create some new and interesting strategies. While most of the missions call for the building up of towns or bases where new units can be trained, a few missions are raids where you are given a set number of units and must complete the mission without reinforcements.

Even after you complete each of the campaigns, the game is not yet ready for the shelf. There are several maps for use in multiplayer games where you

WARCRAFT II

can pit yourself against another human in modem play, or against up to seven other humans with an IPX network connection. There is nothing better than destroying your friend's massive army and town and then sending a taunting message regarding your victory. Also, Blizzard Entertainment has also released an expansion CD for the game. *WarCraft II: Beyond the Dark Portal* takes the player further into the conflict between the Humans and Orcs with two new campaigns, each with ten scenarios. These new campaigns are much more challenging than the originals and require new strategies.

Golden Rules

 Build up your infrastructure first. Train lots of Peasants/Peons and build several Farms early on. The more Peasants/Peons that you have, the quicker your gold and lumber supply will increase

 Send out units to explore the map early in the game. Footmen or Grunts work well since they are relatively cheap and can defend themselves. Once you have flying units, send them over the enemy's bases to see what they are building. It is also a good idea to position units on towers along the routes the enemy would take in attacks on your town. While they stop to attack your observation posts, you can put together a defensive force to ambush the enemy and send them packing.

 Use the special attack values of units to your benefit. Submarines and Giant Turtles are only visible to towers, aerial units, and other submersibles. Therefore, they can ravage a surface force unaccompanied by one of the above units without taking any damage. Aerial units have a similar ability in that they can only be attacked by other aerial units, Guard Towers, Archers/Axethrowers, and magic.

 Upgrade, upgrade, upgrade!!! As soon as you can, upgrade all of your units. Though this can be expensive at first, all of your units will be upgraded, both present and future. You can upgrade armor and

weapons values, weapon ranges, and sighting values. Also, research as many spells as you can to give your Magic Users a larger and more powerful arsenal.

 WarCraft II allows you to build multiple Town Halls/Great Halls. While your first town or base will be built near a gold mine, these mines have a limited amount of gold which you can extract. As your scouts find new mines, send a Peasant/Peon to build a new hall nearby. You may also want to build a Barracks to protect this new mine. You can then train new laborers at this hall. With a nearby hall, they will not waste time in transporting the gold to your old hall. With several mines operating at once, you can mine as much of the gold on the map as possible, thereby depriving your enemy of it. The computer will not send units to other mines until those mines closest to their settlements are used up.

 Plan out your general strategy early in the game. Remember what your objectives are, and stick to them. The best thing to do is create multiple forces. Keep one force back to protect your town. Archers/Axethrowers, Ballistas/Catapults, and towers all make a good defensive force, especially when positioned behind walls for protection. A few Magic Users can also come in handy with a powerful spell at the right moment. Your attacking force should include all types of units, with an emphasis on the most powerful units as you can afford. You may want to create two or more attacking forces. While one is engaging the enemy from one direction, the other force can attack the enemy on their flanks. A third force may even be held as a reserve to throw wherever it may be needed.

 Attacking an enemy town can be very bloody, especially if it is protected by Guard or Cannon Towers. If you have Gryphon Riders or Dragons, you can use these to attack Cannon Towers to open up a way for your ground troops. However, these aerial units are vulnerable to Guard Towers and Archers/Axethrowers. The best tactic is to draw the enemy away from their defenses. Set up a line of your units just outside of the enemy's firing range. Position

Footmen/Grunts in the first line, Archers/Axethrowers in the next, and Ballistas/Catapults and Magic Users in the rear. I refer to this as a line of battle. Give all of these units orders to stand fast. Then send one of your fastest land units into the town. As the enemy's units begin to engage your unit, withdraw him behind your line of battle. As the enemy approaches, your units with ranged fire capability will begin to slaughter those following your withdrawing unit. You may have to repeat the above steps several times in order to pull most of the defenders away from the town. This tactic works very well, but does require some practice and patience.

 Magic can be your friend. The more powerful the spell, the better it is to use. The Human Magi have two very powerful spells: "Blizzard" and "Polymorph". The first spell causes an ice storm to fall upon the target and surrounding area. This is great as a defensive spell against hordes of Orcish attackers. It is also a good offensive spell for attacking towers and Orcish legions huddled together in towns. "Polymorph" is an even more awesome spell. It changes the target into a harmless beast. I keep several Magi in my defensive line for use against Dragons or other powerful enemies.

The Orcs also have some powerful magic. Ogre-Magi can cast Runes on an area, where they'll act as land mines to any unit entering the area. The Death Knights can cast the spells of "Decay" and "Whirlwind." Both act in a similar way to the "Blizzard" spell in that they attack a large area and cause damage to all units within that area.

 Naval units are not just for use against other ships. They can also do much damage to land units as well. Many of the missions will require you to cross a body of water in order to destroy the enemy's base on the other side. Undoubtedly, the enemy will be waiting for you on the shores with towers and other defensive units. Use your ships to attack these defenders and drive them away from the shore. Submersibles are also useful in attacking the enemy's Shipyards, Foundries, and Oil Refineries, as long as there is not a tower nearby that can spot your raider.

WARCRAFT II

As stated above, many missions will require amphibious assaults onto enemy shores. Accomplishing this task is an art form in itself. First, find a landing spot out of range of the enemy where you can unload your troops without being attacked immediately. Position large warships next to the shore to help provide naval bombardment against enemies attacking your troops. Usually three transports full of troops are enough to secure a beachhead. I always take along a few laborers with my troops to construct some towers for defense. I will also build a Barracks on this side of the water so that I can train units here instead of having to transport them all across the water. After I have created my forward base camp and have built up my strength, I then advance on the enemy and destroy them without mercy.

Winning Strategies

In the Golden Rules, I have supplied you with some general strategies to help you win in any battle. However, since each mission you face will be different and provide new and increasingly more dangerous challenges, I have included strategies for each mission as well. Many will refer back to the Golden Rules.

THE HUMAN CAMPAIGN

See page 287 for the Orc campaign.

Mission One: Hillsbrad

Objectives: Build four Farms and a Barracks.

The Plan for Success: First off, build two Farms. Then send your Peasant to mine gold. When you have enough gold, train a few more Peasants. Use them to cut timber, and when you have enough wood and gold, then build your Barracks. After this, build two more Farms, and your mission will be completed. Keep your Footmen to the south and the east of your town to guard against Orcish raiders.

Mission Two: Ambush at Tarren Mill

Objectives: Find and rescue at least one Elven Archer and return him to the Circle of Power inside your base.

The Plan for Success: You have enough forces initially to complete the mission. However, you will have to play very carefully. To be on the safe side, you may want to build a few Farms, mine some gold, train some Peasants, build a Barracks, and train a few more Footmen. Either way, when you are ready to attack the enemy base, set-up a battle line just out of range of the enemy tower. Then send in one of your Footmen to lead some of the enemy units away from their defenses. After a few times, the tower will have no support and you can attack and destroy it. Once the coast is clear, break through the prison walls and release the Elven Archers held captive. Your mission is now almost completed. All you have to do is lead them back to your base camp and onto the Circle of Power.

Mission Three: Southshore

Objectives: Construct at least four Oil Platforms.

The Plan for Success: This mission requires a lot of preparation before you confront the enemy. Keep your Elven Destroyer close to shore for protection against enemy naval attacks. Your first job is to build some more Farms and then train several Peasants. As soon as you have enough lumber, build a Lumber Mill. Continue to mine gold and harvest lumber. You may need to build a few more Farms as well. Forget about building a Barracks—this will be a naval engagement. Your next project is to construct a Shipyard. This should be built on the southern shore, just below your town. Your first vessel should be an Oil Tanker. Once it is built, send it to the closest Oil Patch and begin to build an Oil Platform. While this is going on, you can begin to build your armada. Five Destroyers should do the trick. You may want to build a couple more Oil Tankers to increase the oil supply for building your Destroyers. Once your five warships are completed, begin to patrol the waterways for enemy vessels. Sink any enemy Tankers or Oil Platforms as well. Once the sea-lanes are clear of the Orcish Navy, then use your

Destroyers to attack the enemy structures on the island to the southeast. Your tankers can now be sent to three other Oil Patches in order to construct Platforms. Once this is completed, you can move on to your next mission.

Mission Four: Attack Zul'dare

Objectives: Seek out and demolish the Orc base.

The Plan for Success: The first three missions have just been training for this mission. You will have to make an amphibious assault on the Orc base camp and utterly destroy it. Your first assignment is to train a force of Peasants. Once they are mining and harvesting, build a Lumber Mill and then a Shipyard on the northern shore. Remember to build enough Farms to feed all the workers and troops that you will need. You will also need to construct a Barracks and train some Archers and Footmen for the assault. Once the Shipyard is completed, build some Tankers to construct an Oil Platform; then build an Oil Refinery and a Foundry. You may also want to construct some towers along your coastline to protect yourself against Orcish invaders. This is also a good time to upgrade all your weapons.

Once you have a sizable force of Destroyers launched, send them on patrol and sink any enemy vessels and Oil Platforms they come across. Once the sea-lanes are clear, then move them just offshore of the enemy camp and use them for naval bombardment to clear a landing zone. While this is going on, load up three transports with troops, including a few Peasants, and set sail for the invasion beach. Unload your troops and keep them around to protect the Peasants while they build a couple of Towers and a Barracks. The rest of the mission is just pure destruction.

Mission Five: Tol Barad

Objectives: Reclaim Tol Barad and destroy the Orc Base at Dun Modr.

The Plan for Success: Quickly load up your units on the Transports and sail for the nearest island. Disembark your men and attack the Orc garrison. If you hurry, you can save the Barracks from destruction. Once Tol Barad is secure, build a few Cannon Towers for defense, train several Peasants, and then build a Shipyard. With your Tanker, build an Oil Platform. Have your Barracks train several Archers and make six Ballistas for your assault on the Orc base. Don't forget to build a few Destroyers to protect your invasion fleet.

Once your troops, including at least one Peasant, are ready and loaded into the transports, set sail for the western coast of the Orc base so as to avoid their powerful navy. Once landed, build two Cannon Towers and a Barracks. While you train more troops, lure enemy units within range of your Ballistas and Cannon towers. Once their defenses have been weakened, begin your assault on the base. After that, you can line your Ballistas along the eastern shore and sink the enemy fleet. Also bring up some Destroyers to assist in the carnage. Once the last Orc unit is vanquished, you will be proclaimed the victor.

Mission Six: Dun Algaz

Objectives: Destroy Dun Algaz.

The Plan for Success: First off, train more Peasants and mine gold. You will need to build a Blacksmith and a Keep. Construct Cannon Towers at the eastern and western openings to your base. Train several Knights and build several Ballistas. Upgrade all your weapons. There are three narrow land bridges leading to the enemy. Take your attacking force across the middle bridge. You will come across some enemy units and a Barracks. Quickly destroy everything, and then build your own Barracks in its spot. Lure enemy units away from the defenses of their camp and into the range of your Ballistas and newly constructed Cannon Towers. Once you have killed many of the enemy's warriors, move your Ballistas forward to attack the enemy's towers and then raze the camp. Make sure that you have plenty of troops before beginning your attack. The fighting in this mission will be bloody.

Mission Seven: Grim Batol

Objectives: Destroy five Oil Refineries.

The Plan for Success: Leave your Transports and your Peasants behind for now, and move your combat units south. Defeat the Orc guards and capture two Catapults. Use these to move further south and capture one more Catapult. Now that it's safe, bring down the non-combatants and load up your troops to sail across the river to the other side. As you begin your advance northward, use your Catapults to take out the enemy towers. Once the Orc settlement in the north is leveled, raise your own Town Hall and begin to collect resources.

Since this mission calls for a naval attack, you do not need ground troops except to protect your base against enemy raids. Construct a Lumber Mill and a Shipyard as soon as possible. Then build a Refinery and Foundry, and send a few Oil Tankers to build an Oil Platform at the nearest Oil Patch. You will want to build only Battleships for your attack. At the Foundry, upgrade your guns and armor. As your mine begin to run out of gold, load up a few Peasants on a Transport and sail east to the island with a Gold Mine. There, build another Town Hall, and mine away. Once you have launched at least six Battleships, sail them due south and sink anything they come in contact with. As you get closer to their base, ignore the Refineries and Oil Platforms for a bit while you attack the towers and Catapults guarding them. Once these are destroyed, pummel their Refineries into powder and wait for the Orcs to surrender to your might.

Mission Eight: Tyr's Hand

Objectives: Quell the peasant uprising in Tyr's Hand, construct a secondary Castle in the northwest to maintain order in the region, and destroy all enemy forces.

The Plan for Success: First you will have to kill the rebelling Peasants. Then quickly train new Peasants and put them to work in the mines and forests. You will need to construct a Barracks and a Lumber Mill. Use your combat forces to patrol your base against enemy raids. Upgrade your Town Hall into a Keep. Build farms in the openings of your walls to keep out intruders. Behind these, raise Cannon Towers and position Archers. You should also build some Stables for Knights. Upgrade your Keep into a Castle as soon as you can, and then build a Church to train your Knights in the ways of the Paladin. Once you have upgraded your weapons and constructed several Ballistas, send them out with several Paladins and other troops to the

WARCRAFT II

north, and form a line of battle just out of enemy range. Then send forward one Paladin to draw the Orcs away from their defenses and into your waiting Ballistas. Once they are eliminated, roll the Ballistas into the camp and level it. Follow the same course of action against the town in the southwest, and then against the stronghold in the northwest. After it is razed, construct a second Castle in this area and your mission will be completed.

Mission Nine: The Battle at Darrowmere

Objectives: Escort Lightbringer to the Circle of Power at Caer Darrow.

The Plan for Success: First, assemble your warships into a line of battle. Send one of the Destroyers south to draw the Orcish Destroyers into your trap. Then draw the enemy ships in the western passage into your trap as well. Your next action will be to pick up Lightbringer. Send all four of your Transports, empty of troops, through the gauntlet of Cannon Towers lining the western passage to the shore in the northwest corner. There, load Lightbringer aboard the Transport with the least damage and return him to your temporary base. With the remaining Transports escorted by your warships, rush Lightbringer to the southeastern shore, quickly unload, and rush him to the Circle of Power. You will not even need any of your other land units to win this mission. Speed is your ally.

Mission Ten: The Prisoners

Objectives: Guard the enemy prisoners, construct Transports, and escort at least four Alterac traitors to the Circle of Power at Stratholme.

The Plan for Success: Your first priority is to build up your base camp by constructing a Lumber Mill, a Blacksmith, a Barracks, and a Shipyard. You will also need to build up your land forces to defend against invasions by the Orcs. Build a few Cannon Towers along your southern shore to help deal with them. Once you are fairly secure, build a Foundry so that you can produce Battleships. Prepare your forces for an amphibious assault. You will need at least two Transports full of troops, including several Ballistas and a few Peasants. Secure the enemy camp in the center of the map since it is the only way to get to the river leading to the prisoners. After this camp is razed, you will need to build another Shipyard along the river. Launch three Battle-ships from here to deal with the Cannon Towers lining the river banks. Then send in one Transport to quickly pick up a load of prisoners, take them to the to the forward camp, and then on to the Circle of Power at Stratholme.

Mission Eleven: Betrayal and the Destruction of Alterac

Objectives: Rescue the imprisoned Peasants and Magi from the camp in the northwest, and return them to your base to launch a full-scale assault against the traitorous Alterac.

The Plan for Success: You must first rescue the Peasants and Magi. Take an attacking force north and set them free. Send the former captives south to build up your base while your combatants level the enemy camp. Fortify your southern town and build up a strong attacking force. Remember to upgrade all of your weapons. Advance as you have learned in past missions.

Mission Twelve: The Battle at Crestfall

Objectives: Destroy all Orc Transports, Oil Platforms, and Orc Shipyards.

The Plan for Success: Build up your base camp, train Peasants and get those resources flowing in. Bring your ships close in to shore, and position a flying machine over them to watch for Giant Turtles. You will need to build an Oil Platform and a couple of Shipyards. Build several Submarines, and use them with a Flying machine as a spotter to go after the Orcish Navy. Once they are defeated, build several Battleships and begin to pound the enemy coastline until their Shipyards are leveled.

Mission Thirteen: Assault on Black Rock Spire

Objectives: Destroy Black Rock Spire and eradicate any and all enemy forces.

The Plan for Success: You face several enemy camps in this mission. Take all your warships and your Gryphon Rider westward to sink the Orcish fleet. Then proceed to destroy nearby Oil Platforms and any Transports you may come across. Once the sea-lanes are clear and you have destroyed the Orc's Shipyards, your next target is the Dragon Roost on the central island. While your navy is hard at work, build a few Guard Towers for defense, and then train several Gryphon Riders. You will have to set up new Town Halls next to other mines when your first Gold Mine runs out. After you have built up a large force of warriors, lead them on to Black Rock Spire and to victory. Remember the lessons learned earlier about amphibious assaults.

Mission Fourteen: The Great Portal

Objectives: Destroy the Great Portal.

The Plan for Success: You first need some solid ground on which to build your base. Move west and take out the Ogre village first. On their ashes, build your new base camp. Make sure to defend it against the enemy's powerful Dragons. Your next target is the Orc town to the east. With the use of Gryphon Riders and Dwarven Demolition Teams, you should capture it in short order. To take out the Dark Portal to the north, assemble a large flight of Gryphon Riders, and victory will soon be yours.

THE ORC CAMPAIGN

Many of the missions in this campaign are similar to those found in the Human Campaign. Therefore, I will often refer to those missions if the strategies are similar.

Mission One: Zul'dare

Objectives: Build four Farms and a Barracks.

The Plan for Success: Use the same strategy as in the first Human Mission.

Mission Two: Raid at Hillsbrad

Objectives: Rescue Zuljin and at least one other Troll, then return them to the Circle of Power.

The Plan for Success: Once again, look at the Human Campaign—this time, Mission Two.

Mission Three: Southshore

Objectives: Construct four Oil Platforms.

The Plan for Success: See Human Mission Three.

Mission Four: Assault on Hillsbrad

Objectives: Destroy Hillsbrad and all its defenders.

The Plan for Success: This is just an amphibious assault on an enemy base. See Human Mission Four.

Mission Five: Tol Barad

Objectives: Retake Dun Modr and assault the citadel of Tol Barad.

The Plan for Success: This is just the opposite of the Human Mission Five, but the strategy is the same.

Mission Six: The Badlands

Objectives: Escort Cho'gall to the borders of Grim Batol.

The Plan for Success: This is a tough mission in that you will not get any reinforcements. Use Cho'gall's "Floating Eye" spell to search ahead of your group. Catapults are very effective when massed against Ballistas. Follow the shoreline to the south, and you will avoid much of the enemy's defenses. Once Cho'gall reaches the Circle of Power, you have won.

Mission Seven: The Fall of Stromgarde

Objectives: Recapture the Orc Transports and destroy Stromgarde.

The Plan for Success: Bring your destroyers in near the transports to provide covering fire while all your land-based warriors fight their way to the Transports. With everyone aboard, sail to the island in the center and capture it from the Humans. This is where you will build your base camp. Build up your navy and destroy anything Human afloat. Once you have a good landing force trained, send them across the water to Stromgarde. Build a Barracks along the shore to speed up reinforcements.

Mission Eight: The Runestone at Caer Darrow

Objectives: Destroy the Human Castle and secure the Runestone.

The Plan for Success: Both of your objectives are located on the island in the center of the map. Build up a large fleet of Battleships with some Goblin Zeppelins to watch out for Submarines. After destroying the Human navy, begin to bombard the Human structures near the shore. Lure Ballistas to the shoreline where they become easy targets for your fleet. Once resistance has been reduced substantially, send a couple of Transports full of troops to finish the job. You can neglect the Human village to the southeast. Stick to your objectives and victory will be yours.

Mission Nine: The Razing of Tyr's Hand

Objectives: Construct a Fortress and a Shipyard on the island at the mouth of Tyr's Bay.

The Plan for Success: Build up your base and launch at least six Juggernauts to first wipe out the Human fleet, and then to attack their Shipyards. Once the waters are in Orcish hands, bombard the structures on the island. Assemble an invasion force and land on the island. Ogre-Magi fight well, especially when they cast "Bloodlust" on themselves. Once the island is secured, build your Fortress and Shipyard.

Mission Ten: The Destruction of Stratholme

Objectives: Destroy all Oil Platforms and Refineries; destroy Stratholme.

The Plan for Success: After your Sappers blow passes into the mountains, move your forces inland and build up a base. Timber is limited in this mission, so you will have to get it from the forests close to Stratholme. You will want to build another Great Hall near the mine, in between your first camp and Stratholme. Sappers work wonders on the enemy towers, and even on the Ballistas. Take the enemy base first, and then concentrate on securing the sea-lanes.

Mission Eleven: The Dead Rise as Quel'thalas Falls

Objectives: Destroy the last of the Elven Strongholds.

The Plan for Success: First secure your base and begin to build up a large attacking force. You will be constantly under attack by the Humans, so prepare some good defenses. You will need to control the Gold Mines to your south and to your west. Build Great Halls and Barracks nearby. Begin your attack against the enemy stronghold from the southeast. With a huge army of Ogre-Magi and Catapults, begin your attack. Cast Runes in front of the Catapults to blow up any would-be attackers. Methodically advance until you have destroyed the enemy. Don't forget to use lots of Sappers, as well.

Mission Twelve: The Tomb of Sargeras

Objectives: Destroy the Stormreaver and Twilight's Hammer Clans, and slay the Warlock Gul'dan.

The Plan for Success: First load up your troops and set sail for the largest island to your northeast. With your warships, destroy the defending Destroyers and Giant Turtle, as well as the Tower and Catapult. Then land your troops, raze the old village, and build a new one. Move all of your units inland for protection against enemy warships. Once you have assembled a

WARCRAFT II

large force, cross over to the main island and begin your work of destruction. You will need some Sappers to blast through the rock to get to Gul'dan.

Mission Thirteen: The Siege of Dalaran

Objectives: Destroy Dalaran and all its defenders.

The Plan for Success: Move your forces south, and build your base near the Gold Mine. Build up your forces, making sure to upgrade their weapons and spells. Dragons and Catapults will be your main weapons with other units to support them. You will need to destroy the southern outpost of the enemy in order to get some Peons to the Gold Mine in the east. Build another Great Hall, and train as many troops as possible. Then begin your slow advance on Darlon. Take on one tower at a time. Use Dragons against Cannon Towers, and Catapults against Guard Towers. Before long, the city will be yours.

Mission Fourteen: The Fall of Lordaeron

Objectives: Destroy all that you behold in the name of the Horde!

The Plan for Success: Dragons and Catapults will win this battle for you. Use the tactics and strategies that you have learned so well on prior missions. This mission has no new tricks, just more of the enemy to slay.

Cheat Codes

To enable the *WarCraft II* cheat codes, press [Enter] while playing and type the appropriate message.

CHEAT	CODE
Victory	Unite the Clans
Loss	You pitiful worm
God	It is a good day to die
Cash	Glittering prizes
Oil	Valdez

WARCRAFT II

CHEAT	CODE
Magic	Every little thing she does
Upgrade	Deck me out
Show Map	On screen
Fast Build	Make it so
Finale	There can be only one
No Victory	Never a winner
Lumber	Hatchet
Enable Mission Jump	Orc 10, Human 10, etc.

WARCRAFT II

CHAPTER

14

THE X·COM SERIES
UFO DEFENSE AND TERROR
FROM THE DEEP

Publisher:	Microprose Software
Platform:	PC MS-DOS
Release Date:	Spring, 1994 and Spring, 1995, respectively
Multiplayer:	No
Rating:	1/2

Plot Summary and General Overview

Originally published in the UK as *X-COM: Enemy Unknown*, *X-COM: UFO Defense* proved to everyone that it's the quality of the game that matters, not marketing hype. Practically unadvertised and next to unannounced, *X-COM* proceeded to win a fanatical following. It 's easy to see why. Here, at last, was an original game.

The originality of *X-COM's* concept made it a hit, so naturally, a sequel was published not very long thereafter. Entitled *X-COM: Terror From the Deep*, it basically offers the same game in a different setting (underwater), with a much tougher AI and a wider variety of missions.

The premise of the game could have been used equally well for a hit movie: It is the year 2,000 A.D., and suddenly the skies over Earth are aswarm with alien activity. The activity is far from benign, and that's where *X-COM* comes in as an internationally-funded organization formed especially to combat the alien threat.

You, the player, are in charge of this organization. You are given a starting base featuring essential buildings, UFO interceptors, and a troop transport. The latest Terran technologies are placed in your hands, but, of course, they can't compare to alien know-how. Fortunately, your scientists can research all the alien wonders, thus allowing you to duplicate the technologies and defeat the invaders.

Before your scientists can research alien technologies, however, you must give them something to bite into. This takes the shape of captured alien craft, weapons, ancillary devices, corpses, and finally—live aliens. Of course, in order to get all that stuff, you have to do quite a lot of fighting. The aliens are cooperative in this respect, providing plenty of venues—crash sites, terror sites, even alien bases on Earth.

You can only win the game if you successfully interrogate a series of aliens, culminating in high-ranking officers. The interrogations reveal why the aliens are picking on Earth in the first place, what methods they use and why, and how to end the alien threat. Victory can be yours only if you destroy the main alien base on Mars (Cydonia), along with their Brain. Given the fact that you do not even have the technology to make the trip to Mars, you have quite a lot of work ahead of you, and a lot of heavy expenses.

X . C O M

These expenses are partly (and at the start of the game, wholly) covered by *X-COM*'s funding nations. The amount of money you receive changes in relation to how well you're dealing with the alien threat on any given funding nation's territory. Thus, you may be going great guns in North America, shooting down UFOs left, right, and center, but if you ignore the rest of your rich uncles, they'll cut back your funding—and occasionally, they'll cut it off altogether, signing a secret pact with the aliens and withdrawing from *X-COM*.

Fortunately, *X-COM* is not only a military organization, but also an extremely profitable business. There are legions of eager buyers of such specialties as alien cadavers, weapons, and even food. Alien artifacts fetch phenomenal prices, and within a short time, you can be making money hand over fist. However, it's still essential to spend it wisely.

If you decide that you love this game (it's worth loving) and purchase the sequel, you'll find out that your victory has been in vain. Just as you were trashing Cydonia, the dying aliens activated a process of bringing back to life yet more aliens, but this time of the wet kind. For some reason, the water-loving aliens weren't participants in the first alien invasion; they were sound asleep on the ocean floor—but now they are awake, and an awake alien is an angry alien. If this sounds farcical to you, let me assure you that the game is not. It's one of the best strategy games around. The missions are much more varied than in *UFO Defense*. To start with, part of the missions take place on land, part on ships, and part underwater. In *UFO Defense,* the assault on Cydonia is the only mission consisting of two parts; in *Terror from the Deep,* two-stage missions are common, and the final assault consist of three parts or stages. Furthermore, *Terror From the Deep* introduces hand-to-hand combat. It's the only effective way of dealing with a particularly nasty alien race, the Lobster Men, called so because of . . . you got it.

Both *X-COM* games are independent—you can fully enjoy one without knowing anything about the other. If you aren't familiar with *X-COM* and want to try just one, I would suggest *UFO Defense*. In some respects, *Terror From the Deep* is a better game, especially thanks to the stronger AI. However, things that are too difficult tend to get tedious, and you may feel that way after chasing aliens through several decks of a cluttered freighter—in other words, a tight metal maze. Since researching everything necessary to destroy the main alien base (this time, it's underwater) takes a fair bit of time, you could grow a tad weary when investigating Terror Site #49.

X·COM

It's for this very reason that, unlike with other games, I would recommend playing *X-COM* at the Veteran (the equivalent of Normal) level. Alien activity tends to grow with level of difficulty (while playing a game of *UFO Defense* at the Superhuman level for the purpose of writing this chapter, I led my brave soldiers through over three hundred combat missions). Once you develop a network of 'listening stations' that will immediately detect any alien incursion, it's very easy to find yourself fighting several missions a day (a game day, in this respect, can equal a real day).

Paradoxically, *X-COM* is the perfect game for someone who can't afford to stay up all night. It's very easy to pick up the threads exactly where you left them, and each interception/mission is a mini-game in itself (in fact, *X-COM* is based on a very simple game that mainly consisted of its combat model). What is both original and nice is that here is a game with a real plot, a fascinating mystery, lots of pleasant deal-making, and an excellent combat system.

Golden Rules

- Start ruling *X-COM* with a firm and decisive hand the day you take over. Re-equip interceptors with better missiles, hire more soldiers and scientists, and buy more heavy-damage weapons such as rocket/torpedo launchers and cannon. Build extra facilities for living and storage in addition to alien containment, and base defenses if playing at the Genius or Superhuman levels.

- Vet your soldiers/aquanauts carefully. Fire everyone with Bravery below 40, even when you've just hired them to replace recently fired soldiers with Bravery below 40. In other words, repeat this firing-hiring procedure until you've got a strong team that's also brave.

- Know your own people. Name them yourself, and care for them as if you really knew them. Don't overload them with equipment or push them too hard; the more experienced a soldier/aquanaut, the more protective you should be. This will help you watch losses closely, and eventually groom a killer squad for the Final Assault on Cydonia/T'leth.

Research new technologies as fast as you can. You greatly improve your chances of survival the moment you acquire such basic technologies as laser/Gauss weapons, personal armor, and the Medi-kit. Make capture and interrogation of live aliens a top priority. Remember that every technology you discover contributes to your point total for the month, the other variables being successful interceptions and missions.

Make a point of early acquisition of alien weapons technology. Plasma/sonic weapons are, respectively, the best weapons in the two games. Get ranged-attack stun weapons early; they greatly improve your chances of capturing an alien of rank.

Expand quickly—you should be building a new base every other month at the very least, and preferably every month. Start with a single radar/sonar, stores, and hangar/sub pen; then see what happens to the level of alien activity in the region. Build your reconnaissance post into a full-sized base, or leave it as a listening post, but have most of Earth covered by your detection devices within the first six months. Lay out your new bases so that the access lift/air lock is the only structure connecting hangars/sub pens to the rest of the base buildings.

After researching alien weapons, turn your attention to alien space craft/submarines and to mental warfare. Psionic or molecular control abilities play an increasingly large role as the war with the aliens goes on. Learning how to build alien-type craft is nearly as important. Without the ultimate craft and a team of soldiers/aquanauts skilled at mental warfare, you do not have a chance of winning the game.

Keep a sharp eye on finances. A continuous large deficit can lose you the game. Treat official X-COM funding as pocket money, and make financial self-sufficiency an early goal. This isn't so difficult; by the third month, you should be pulling in much more revenue from sales of mission trophies (all the captured alien stuff) than you receive from X-COM's funding countries.

X·COM

Keep your engineers busy! Items such as personal armor cannot be captured from the aliens—your engineers/technicians will have to make them. Keep a number of personal armor suits in reserve at every base that has soldiers/aquanauts stationed; it's important that you are immediately able to outfit new recruits following heavy mission losses. An alien attack on your base following on the heels of an unsuccessful mission is particularly dangerous.

Show good leadership on the battlefield. Follow all common-sense battle tactics—don't bunch up your guys together (particularly in *Terror*); have them operate in teams, with one covering the other; precede risky advances with grenades; and finally, always, always try to leave your troops kneeling, with cover on at least one side, and with enough time for a snap shot. This policy not only results in more security, it also means that you don't push your guys to the limit—which, in turn, means they don't start dropping from exhaustion midway through the mission. Patience counts!

While battling aliens, remain 'dimensionally' aware—be on the lookout for aliens on higher/lower levels of the battlescape. Aliens firing from upper-level windows, rooftops, and balconies are a big threat, but they can't do much harm if you take proper precautionary steps. Keep your guys close to building walls, and always try to get a lookout/sharpshooter onto a rooftop at the start of the mission. Flying suits prove very helpful!

Do not ever ignore terror sites. You'll lose less points if you make a 'fake' intervention than when you ignore the terror site altogether. Send symbolic troops to the site and abort the mission almost immediately. This tactic does not work as well in *Terror From the Deep*—the number of civilian deaths on a ship is likely to lose you as many points as ignoring the terror strike.

Research the Hyperwave Decoder/Transmission Resolver fairly early. They'll save you tons of troops and money by letting you know in advance when aliens with mental warfare capabilities are present. Sending troops with unchecked/low resistance to mental warfare against aliens that can use it, equals suicide.

X·COM

Be cleverly aggressive. Try to intercept *every* alien craft, but don't tackle crash sites you can't handle—as in the above mental warfare example. Keep a lookout for alien bases/colonies by patrolling sparsely populated/remote areas on a regular basis. Watch for bursts of alien activity that involve numerous supply ships—it's a sure sign a base/colony is under way. Similar intense activity in densely populated areas means a strong possibility of aliens coming to an agreement with the local government, which then often proceeds to withdraw from *X-COM*. Once they're gone, you can't get them back!

Winning Strategies

To win at *X-COM,* you must prove yourself as an administrator and tactician. To put it as succinctly as possible, your success hinges on your soldiers; what you tell them to do, and what you give them to do it with. Of course, ultimately, everything depends on how good your soldiers are—a poor marksman will miss given the best weapon. Perhaps the most important single thing about *X-COM* is that the soldiers under your command improve with experience. With time, they become supermen.

You begin the process of creating an army of supermen the day you take command of *X-COM*.

THE NEW BROOM

On your first day, you take over a base that has been set up by a very conservative and timid commander. There's a short-range detection device (radar in *UFO Defense*, sonar in *Terror*), living quarters, storage space, laboratory (with ten scientists), workshop (with ten engineers/technicians), and three hangars/sub pens containing interception craft and a troop transport. There even are eight soldiers to put into the transport and a fair supply of weapons.

The first thing you should do is order construction of additional buildings. You need alien containment right off the bat. Otherwise, any live aliens you capture will die, and as mentioned, your success depends on interrogating live aliens. In addition, you need more storage space, more living quarters (hiring more people will be your second step), and better radar/sonar (a long-range/wide-array device). If you're playing at the Genius or Superhuman level, I strongly advise you to start building base defenses right away. In the Superhuman games I played, my base was assaulted by aliens right away— on one occasion, defending the base was my soldiers' very first battle! Your base defenses, even if they do not destroy the alien's huge spaceship/sub, should damage it badly enough to inflict casualties on the aliens inside.

Having gotten construction of new facilities under way, you should then turn to reorganizing what's already there.

PUTTING THINGS INTO SHAPE

Although your base is equipped, it's been equipped by the same timid old man that built it. The interceptors are poorly armed, The weapon selection contains yawning holes, and the soldiers on staff haven't even been properly vetted.

Arming Your Boys and Girls

Your first priority is to make your interceptors more battleworthy. The weapons systems available in both *UFO Defense* and *Terror* correspond exactly—even the price of equivalent fighter/submarine weapons is identical. To start with, change the shooters the previous administrator installed on the interceptors. Get rid of the cannon; install missile weapons systems on both interceptors (two long-range systems on one, and one long range, one medium range on the other). In *UFO Defense,* the systems are called Avalanche and Stingray; in *Terror,* DUP Torpedoes and Ajax).

Becoming an Arms Dealer

The next visit you make is to the screens you'll consult following every mission. These are the Sell/Sack and Purchase/Recruit screens.

Sell the peashooters you've taken off the interceptors together with their ammo—storage space is very tight at the start, and you'll have a hard time fitting everything you need in. First of all, buy extra long-range weapons sys-

X.COM

tem launchers for the interceptors, and ammo to match. Then, turn your attention to the weapons for your soldiers.

You'll be hiring new soldiers right away; you should build up their numbers to 20 as quickly as possible. Casualties are a real possibility on every mission, as well as in two missions back-to back. Wounded soldiers are also unavailable for action for long periods of time, and the first thing every general should make sure of is sufficient troops.

The weapons you start the game with are insufficient to equip twenty troops, and the selection isn't the best, either. You need more powerful weapons that will knock the stuffing out of an alien with a single shot. Buy extra rocket launchers (torpedo launchers in *Terror*), heavy cannon (gas cannon), and automatic cannon (Hydro-Jet Cannon). Change all the ammunition for the cannon to HE, particularly in *UFO Defense*—the heavy artillery comes handy for removing walls that are in the way. Stock up on other personal weapons, too. In both *X-COM* games, grenades are a very good weapon choice in early battles, but your base has just a handful—so order plenty. Grenades work surprisingly well in *Terror;* your soldiers have no difficulty in hurling them long distances even underwater.

I tend to buy quite a few pistols for the early days, before my scientists provide me with laser/Gauss technology. A pistol in one hand and a primed grenade in the other is a very effective combination in *UFO Defense*. In *Terror*, the dart guns aren't as good. I stick to the harpoons.

Very importantly, make sure you buy at least a dozen flares, more if you have the space. Flares are essential in missions taking place at night, and you'll have some night missions whether you like it or not. Terror sites only stay on the map for a few hours, and failure to intervene means a huge point loss. Without flares, you'll have a very difficult time!

Round off your revised arsenal whichever way you feel. I tend to buy more arms than is strictly necessary for insurance purposes. However, make sure you re-arm the interceptors, and buy more grenades and heavy weapons. The rifles/jet harpoons your guys are initially issued with are inadequate. Even a weak alien often has to be hit several times to go down. And some aliens feature very tough skin, especially the ones in *Terror*. It's not uncommon to have five soldiers firing at one alien before it will go down. By contrast, it usually takes just a single well-placed shot from a rocket/torpedo launcher or cannon to stop an alien! Battle tactics are discussed in detail later on.

Hiring and Firing

The next step you should take is firing a few soldiers. Invariably, the first eight soldiers (and a lot of the ones you'll hire) have low Bravery ratings. A soldier that's a coward is worse than no soldier at all—a positive menace. This is because the X-COM combat system allows the possibility of a soldier panicking or going berserk. When the former happens, he/she simply drops the weapon in hand and stands there. However, a soldier/aquanaut gone berserk starts firing in all directions, and often succeeds in hitting one of your other guys.

Know Your Men and Women

Every soldier comes with a name and a set of personal statistics. Assembling a squad in which every soldier has respectable stats in all categories is just not possible—it costs too much and takes too long. Also, it helps to know that while some stats may be improved relatively painlessly, others can't.

- Time units indicate how much a given soldier can achieve in his/her turn on the battlefield. This category is very easy to improve; simply participating in a lot of missions quickly adds up to an impressive total. Bear in mind that all actions involving weapons (firing, priming and throwing grenades) always take up a set percentage of a soldier's total time units. Therefore, a soldier that has added time units through experience will use more of them to fire or throw a grenade. However, he/she will still have more time available for other actions—and as you'll find out, the one thing your soldiers have in constant short supply is time units. This is especially true in *Terror*.

- Stamina indicates how much energy a soldier/aquanaut has. If a soldier runs out of stamina, he/she cannot perform any tasks, even though there are plenty of time units left. Pushing a soldier to the limits for many turns may result in their becoming totally useless! Stamina is quite easy to improve.

- Health—this indicates how well a soldier deals with injuries. One fatal wound drains one health point per turn; when there are no health points left, the soldier/aquanaut dies. A soldier's health also determines how quickly he/she will be overcome by smoke inhalation. Health isn't difficult to improve; it tends to show the biggest change for the better after a soldier has been wounded, and spent many days out of action!

Bravery is, as I said, the most important single stat of all. In early missions particularly, you're bound to suffer losses—your weaponry is weak and your guys inexperienced. If the rest of your troops start panicking and going berserk, you've had it. I immediately sack any soldier with a Bravery rating lower than 40, no matter how talented they are in other areas. Bravery can also improve, but only under dire circumstances: When your squad suffers heavy losses, morale drops to below 50, and the soldier doesn't panic during his/her turn.

Reactions determine the chance of whether your guy will fire at an alien during the alien's turn (as long as you've left them with adequate time units!). Reactions are pretty hard to improve. Don't count on it too much.

Firing Accuracy—this is self-explanatory. However, it is different from the actual chance of hitting the target on a battlefield. A soldier's base firing accuracy is then modified by the accuracy of the weapon, size of the target, distance, wounds, and stance (a kneeling soldier always has a much better chance of hitting the target), and of course, the type of shot, with aimed shots being most accurate. Firing accuracy is neither difficult nor easy to improve—it just takes a lot of shooting and hitting.

Throwing Accuracy—this determines how accurately the soldier can throw, not only grenades, but also other items. You may find, for instance, that one guy is running short of ammo, while another has lots. Instead of going through the drop-on-the-ground-walk-over-pick-it-up procedure, the affluent soldier may simply throw his pal a spare magazine (the other guy will still have to pick it up from a neighboring square). Keep this ability in mind . It comes in handy in very dangerous situations, and things that are handy in such situations are good to remember. Like shooting, throwing accuracy improves slowly—not that it matters a lot.

X·COM

Strength—a very important statistic. You'll notice that your soldiers come equipped with a lot of pockets, and backpacks, too. Many players tend to overload their troops mercilessly, trying to put all that space to good use. Don't! A soldier that is overloaded loses time units from the available total, to say nothing of the effect on stamina. Every item you load your guy with weighs something (equipping soldiers for combat is discussed in detail later on). Do not be too concerned with low strength, however—it improves quickly.

Psionic Strength. This statistic does not appear until your soldier has spent a month in a psionic lab, which in turn, is available only later on, after considerable research. Psionic strength is not important when a soldier is fighting aliens that do not use mind control (molecular control in *Terror*). However, the moment the 'mental' aliens appear, watch out! It hurts a lot to find out that the sharpshooter you've cultivated for thirty missions is about as strong as a superstitious peasant, and even more so since it happens when he/she starts shooting at your other guys. In the final stages of the game, psionic strength is even more important than bravery; it's essential that every member of the squad you send out for The Final Mission is great in this department. Psionic strength cannot be increased by any means.

Psionic skill is a measure of a soldier's talent at using mind control/molecular control on aliens. It can be improved by training in the psionic lab, and through actual use in combat. Again, a good proportion of the fire-eaters you send out on The Final Mission should be very skilled psionic fighters. There's nothing better than taking command of a couple of aliens and having them do your dirty work for you—although the aliens defending the main base are exceptionally tough nuts, it's not impossible. Of course, psionic skill can pay big dividends earlier on, too.

You should immediately hire a dozen new soldiers regardless of how good your initial eight troopers are. When they arrive (when any new recruits arrive, any time during the game) immediately go to the Soldiers/Aquanauts screen, examine the stats, and fire the cowards. You'll lose money, true, but this way, you avoid losing even more—and perhaps the game. You can trust me on this.

Once you've decided a soldier/aquanaut is staying on the team, give them a name. Name them after familiar faces—actors, friends, musicians. If a soldier is uncommonly strong, give him/her a name that will help you remember it. Naming your people gives you a kind of bond with those poor guys, most of which won't live very long, and encourages you to spare no effort in bringing as many as possible back alive. This in turn pays dividends in the form of experienced soldiers who shoot straighter and accomplish more within a turn. Also, when the next batch of recruits christened by the computer arrives, you'll have a much easier time sifting through the list to vet the new guys.

You may want to indicate certain features next to the name. Personally, I reserve that option to indicate Psionic Strength or Molecular Control ability. Anyone with a rating of at least 50 gets a star, over 70, two stars, and over 85, three stars. I also indicate which guys are undergoing training in the psionic/M.C. lab. Every soldier/aquanaut that is good at 'mental warfare' is worth a lot as a potential candidate for the Final Assault on the main alien base. However, it's not good practice to store these guys in a cool, dry place; every mission gives them an opportunity to sharpen their experience. A soldier with 90 time units, high shooting accuracy, and a 90+ psionic strength and skill is a terrible killer – but it takes 30 missions or more, plus a score of killed aliens, to reach that level of perfection.

THE IMPORTANCE OF KNOWLEDGE

Research forms a crucial part of your anti-alien effort. The aliens are somewhat timid at first, and this is the only reason why X-COM isn't wiped out in the first month of campaigning. Making even the most basic discoveries in weapons and personal armor technology greatly improves your situation.

The research tree in UFO Defense is far simpler than in Terror From the Deep. While interrogation of live, high-ranking aliens is essential to winning at both games, the overall importance of interrogation is much greater in Terror. In X-COM's 'wet' version, you cannot progress beyond the most basic advances in technology without input from alien prisoners! For these reasons, the research trees of both games are discussed in separate sections. However, read the section on UFO Defense even if you intend to play Terror and nothing else. It describes the overall research logic of the two games.

RESEARCH IN *UFO DEFENSE*

Better weapons are the highest priority in both games. Upon starting a new game of *UFO Defense,* set your scientists to work on Laser Weapons right away. They take only a short time, and the laser pistol/rifle should follow right afterwards.

I usually don't bother to research the Heavy Laser at this stage. It's not really necessary—the heavy laser is a bulky weapon incapable of automatic fire. I usually research the last three Laser technologies towards the end of the game, when my scientists have nothing else to do. Every new technology discovered counts towards the monthly score!

I make Alien Alloys and Personal Armor my next research choice. Even the most rudimentary type of Personal Armor greatly increases your soldiers' life spans, thus resulting in a better, deadlier soldier. This is why I follow Personal Armor with the Medi-kit, an item that can save tons of money in the long run. I tend to continue outfitting new recruits with Personal Armor throughout the game; once they increase their value by improving their stats, I issue them with better protection. Rookies often have short lives, and it's a shame to waste a Power Suit—brutal, but such are things in times of war.

My next effort goes towards securing better weaponry. Alien grenades are great and available for free, so I take those first. I follow it with plasma weaponry. I would suggest you research Heavy Plasma and Heavy Plasma Clip before the rifle and the pistol. Heavy plasma is the ultimate gun in the game.

By that time, I always have more bases, and at least one also has a laboratory. *X-COM* does not accumulate research done in separate labs on one topic, so from that moment onwards, I always research at least two topics concurrently—one technology in one base, another in the other. Therefore, simultaneously with plasma weapons, I acquire such landmark technologies as Elerium 115 (leads to practically everything else that's important), the Power Suit (best value in personal protection, hands down), Motion Scanner (invaluable for big alien ship assaults), and finally, the Small Launcher and Stun Bomb. These two last technologies make capturing live aliens much easier, and so lead to a long chain of interrogations that yield information about the aliens, as well as the Hyperwave Decoder. This last device is extremely useful, as it will allow you to identify the alien race forming any UFO's crew. This lets you successfully employ soldiers with weak psionic capabilities—otherwise, they become next to useless. Sending a squad of soldiers against Ethereals can turn into a suicide mission if many (or even any) squad members have low psionic strength.

The moment I've got decent (plasma) weapons, decent personal armor (Power Suit), and a couple of helpful extras (Medi-kit, Motion Scanner, Small Launcher, Stun Bomb), I make it a priority to capture a live Sectoid leader, whose interrogation allows me to research the Psi Lab and Psi Amp—two crucial mind-control technologies. This information can also be obtained from an Ethereal leader, but I don't advise trying to capture an Ethereal before you've made significant psionic progress with your troops.

Alien Interrogations

The interrogation of live aliens is an option practically from the moment you complete the Alien Containment facility. The first wave of live aliens is caused by the inadequacy of your weaponry; aliens are often stunned instead of killed. I strongly advise against using the hand-held stun rod. If you need to capture a live alien before you obtain the Small Launcher and the Stun Bomb, I suggest you try Terran grenades. A couple of them dropped next to an alien, not on him, often knocks him out without killing.

Of course, alien interrogations bring results that depend on who you're talking to. All alien races have subclasses that correspond to their military function in the ongoing alien invasion. These are: alien soldier, navigator, engineer, medic, leader, and commander. Leaders and commanders are much deadlier than mere soldiers, of course. In fact, each class has its own ability score; given the variations between the alien races themselves, this results in a great many combinations.

Interrogating live aliens will provide you with a wealth of information on your enemy. Every interrogated alien of any race will provide you with data on that race. Alien medics additionally yield information on one other race—autopsy data or race data, depending on your luck. Interrogations of engineers bring information about UFO construction (although they are not essential to obtain UFO technology). Interrogations of navigators will give you data on various types of UFOs, including important combat stats. Interrogation of any alien leader will put you on the path towards the Final Solution, or the assault on Cydonia. To discover the Final Solution, you'll have to cap-

X · C O M

ture an alien commander. These high-ranking guys can most easily be found in alien bases, and there's always one on battleships.

As mentioned earlier, interrogating a Sectoid or Ethereal leader will give you the start you need to learn mind control, and discover the psionic capabilities of your soldiers.

UFO Technology and Heavy Weapons

Even if you've got all the information about Cydonia, you still have to obtain the means to get there. The long road to Cydonia starts with a fork in UFO Navigation and UFO Power Source—two technologies that may be researched as soon as you've captured the items in question.

There are three types of craft you can construct as a result: the Lightning, the Firestorm, and the Avenger. All differ in that they use precious Elerium 115 for fuel. However, given some initiative on your part, Elerium should not be a problem. All you have to do is capture an undamaged alien spaceship from time to time. This is not much more difficult than dealing with a crash site. In fact, I haven't noticed much difference. Also, every alien base contains a small quantity of Elerium.

There are many opinions as to which ship is better. Practice seems to make its own demands: At the Superhuman level, I found I needed two Avengers, three Firestorms, three Lightnings, four Interceptors, and three Skyrangers to keep things firmly under control. As your successes grow, the aliens are likely to launch a counteroffensive that includes a number of big, powerful ships. A lot of your fleet can be undergoing repairs at any given time.

RESEARCH IN *TERROR FROM THE DEEP*

X-COM: Terror From the Deep is more complicated than its predecessor, and especially so in the area of research. Most technologies involve interrogating live aliens, and remain unavailable otherwise.

However, the basic technologies for survival are there. Upon starting the game, get scientists going on Gauss Technology, which leads to Gauss weapons, Get those as quickly as you can, because the weaponry *Terror* starts you with is simply laughable. It's important to note that several weapons work only underwater—as their name indicates (Torpedo Launcher,

X·COM

Hydro-Jet Cannon). The Heavy Gauss is about as useless as the Heavy Laser in *UFO Defense.* All other discoveries in the Gauss area are best left for later.

You won't be able to develop any kind of personal armor until you get hold of a Deep One corpse. This alien race makes its first appearance during a terror attack. If, by some chance, you haven't gotten hold of his precious corpse by the time you've got Gauss pistols, rifles, and the appropriate clips, get going on the Medi-kit (the underwater version) and the Particle Disturbance Sensor (equivalent of the Motion Scanner). You'll also have a live Aquatoid or Gill Man to interrogate. For sure. Almost every other early mission in *Terror* results in capturing live aliens because of your weak weaponry—a nice and unexpected benefit!

A Deep One autopsy allows your scientists to research Aqua Plastics (equivalent of Alien Alloys) and finally Aqua Plastic Armor (Personal Armor). The capture of a live Deep One is necessary for the next generation of personal armor, the Ion Armor, which incidentally (just like the Power Suit in *UFO Defense*) provides the best value. Autopsies of Calcinite and Gill Man corpses provide advances in the field of hand-held weapons (which play an important role in *Terror From the Deep*). Most importantly, construction of the Leviathan—the only sub capable of the Final Assault—is impossible without the interrogation of a Lobster Man commander. This requirement alone makes it very desirable to research the Molecular Control Reader (it's enough to capture this item), which—like the Mind Probe in *UFO Defense*—reveals the data of any given alien. It's a total waste of time and aquanauts to try and capture a Lobster Man without positively identifying him as a commander.

The ultimate intelligence, of course, comes from the interrogation of a Lobster Man Commander—like the Ethereal Commander in *UFO Defense,* the toughest adversary of them all. It is preceded by getting data on Alien Origins from any live alien, and information on alien objectives (The Ultimate Threat) from a Gill Man or Lobster Man Navigator or Commander. You do not need any alien help to research Sonic Weapons, which is good.

As with *UFO Defense,* make it a point to study alien weapons that stun instead of kill (Thermal Shok Launcher, Thermal Shok Bomb). They make things much, much easier—though you shouldn't expect to stun a tough alien with a single bomb. You have to capture a live terrorist (an alien of a species used to terrorize humans) in order to begin work on Molecular Labs—*Terror's* equivalent of Psionic Labs from *UFO Defense.* Finally, a live

X · COM

Tasoth is necessary to research the Molecular Control Disruptor—the Heavy Blaster of *Terror From the Deep*.

Dealing with Terror

The aliens in *Terror from the Deep* are much more dangerous than the ones in *UFO Defense* not only because of their superior intelligence, but also their toughness. Several alien races are difficult to kill—impossible to kill if you try to rely on Gauss weaponry. This is a very different situation than the one in *UFO Defense,* where there is only one relatively tough (and rather stupid) alien race to deal with—the Mutons.

The problem in *Terror* is compounded by the weaponry available. Most of the alien races prove very resistant to Gauss beams—practically the only ones that react the way you want them to (i.e.—die) are the Aquatoids, Gill Men, and Deep Ones. Gauss beams bounce off Lobster Men, Calcinites, Tasoth, and other aliens, and the fact that Gauss is the only weaponry to offer out-of-fire is no compensation. Sonic weapons are much better, even though they use up more time units and don't offer the auto-fire option. Probably the best ranged weapon of all is the Thermal Shok Launcher. (The Disruptor Pulse Launcher, while invaluable under water, does not work on land.) Make sure you research the Thermal Shok Launcher and Thermal Shok Bomb early on, and use them extensively, even if you have to keep manufacturing the expensive ammo. The large number of live aliens you will capture are an added benefit.

You should also make a point of equipping your Aquanauts with large quantities of grenades. Alien Sonic Pulsars are best. Since the grenades in *Terror* can be thrown vast distances, over barriers, and onto different levels of the battlescape, they are very useful weapons.

Finally, there are the blade weapons (Vibro Blades, Thermal Lances), my favorite means to deal with such terrors as Lobster Men and Bio-Dromes. The problem is, your blade-wielding guy has to get to the alien without getting shot before he/she can stick the blade in. Lobster Men are equipped with an ultra-accurate targeting system and Bio-Dromes can fly, so getting your guy next to them is a little difficult.

My imperfect solution is to additionally equip my swordsman with sonic pulsars and sonic pistols. They use grenades when closing in on a Lobster—

dye grenades come in handy too, to provide cover—then switch to a pistol in one hand and a blade in the other.

RUNNING THE X-COM FACTORIES

Your first base comes complete with ten engineers (technicians in *Terror*). They get down to work the moment your scientists research the Laser/Gauss Pistol. You'll quickly want to hire more, and to build additional workshops in your subsequent bases, with at least one base containing at least two workshops. This 'factory' base is subsequently used to build advanced spaceships/submarines based on alien technology. The bigger the project, the more workshop space it takes up, leaving less for the engineers. Multiple workshops are necessary if you want to build any advanced craft, and they're essential to build the ultimate fighter/transporters—the Avenger and the Leviathan.

Your engineers will most likely be hellishly busy just trying to meet your demands. Some periods of slack may happen in the second part of the game, when your production capabilities are quite big. Following a big defeat, the momentarily discouraged aliens may suspend their activities for a time, and suddenly, you have all those highly-paid people with nothing pressing to do.

You won't make any big bucks, but you can at least make your guys earn a living by producing items for sale. Any item from both the *X-COM* and alien arsenals may be traded for a good price. Laser/Gauss Pistols are an obvious example of a good deal; so are Medi-kits, and the lowly Alien Alloys/Aqua Plastics. They don't fetch much per unit, but they are easy to manufacture in quantity. Don't build big-ticket items for profit—it's not any better, and you may be forced to suspend production because of an emergency, without completing anything. Never, ever build anything involving Elerium 115 or Zrbite for sale; these two are simply too precious. They can only be obtained from relatively lightly damaged alien craft or bases. Good management of this precious resource will mean pretty much total freedom in the use of your Elerium and Zrbite-powered advanced craft.

Most of the game, your engineers will be busy churning out personal armor of all kinds, heavy weapons platforms, and miscellaneous items such as Medi-kits. You'll get all the ammunition and weapons you need from the battlefield.

X·COM

ARMING YOUR FORCE

The weaponry in *UFO Defense* is mirrored in *Terror,* where it bears other names and differs in utilization details. Each type of weaponry has an equivalent in the other game. Lasers equal Gauss technology, plasma equals sonic weapons, and so on. However, in *Terror,* some weapons work only underwater—do not make the mistake of taking them along to a terror site! They include the Hydro-Jet Cannon, Torpedo Launcher, and the all-powerful Disruptor Pulse Launcher. The Magnetic Ion Armor, which functions as a Flying Suit underwater, doesn't work on land either (though the actual protection from hits stays the same).

Terror also features three hand-to-hand combat weapons: Vibro Blade, Thermic Lance, and Heavy Thermic Lance. These work great against practically all aliens, and are particularly devastating against the otherwise all-powerful Lobster Men. The drawback is obvious—you still have to get your guy in close for the attack, and he's likely to get shot at in the meantime. Employing *Terror's* brand of surgery demands a lot of cunning and experience, and anyway, the necessity of attempting it adds a lot to the difficulty of the game.

You should always keep a good stock of weapons handy! If you sell every surplus rifle and pistol, chances are you'll be sorry you did. The first year of battles (I found it impossible to win the game inside a year) brings plenty of loot, and you may well sell off some, but it's also a year in which you'll be constantly building new bases and equipping new soldiers. It goes without saying you shouldn't even think about selling any alien ammo, unless it's absolutely coming out of your ears or your stores are bursting, and you need space for something else right away. Even then, it pays to check whether another base of yours couldn't use the surplus items.

Not surprisingly, how you arm your men and women has a decisive effect on the outcome of your battles. This means not only what you issue your soldiers/aquanauts, but also, how much of it.

Preparing For Battle

As mentioned before, every soldier has a Strength rating. This determines how much he or she can comfortably carry. Each item in the game arsenal has a specific weight. Once the sum of the items' weight exceeds the strength of a soldier, they start losing time units from their movement allotment. Do not ever allow this to happen! If it does, immediately order the soldier/aquanaut to leave some of his/her gear behind.

As a rule, Medi-kits, pistols, and pistol/rifle clips weigh no more than 5; grenades (alien and others) weigh 3, rifles weigh 5–8. Heavy weapons of Terran technology tend to get very heavy—up to 20—and the ammunition is progressively heavier as well—between five and eight. It does not make the slightest sense to total all the numbers for each individual guy before each mission. The numbers above are just meant to provide you with some sort of an idea of the numbers involved. Beyond that, all you have to do is follow these common-sense guidelines:

- Soldiers basically fall into three categories: lightweights (below 26 strength), medium weights (27–38 strength), and heavyweights (39+ strength). Each type neatly fits a certain weapon combination:

- Lightweights fare best if you use them as grenadiers (pistol, possibly spare clip, four-to-five grenades and/or flares) or light infantrymen (rifle, spare clip and/or grenade or two, Medi-kit).

- Medium weights perform well with a heavy weapon and nothing else, save for a spare clip (for example, heavy cannon/gas cannon and clip) and a single flare/grenade, or a rifle with heavier extra load (spare clip, three grenades, Medi-kit, flare).

- Heavyweights are obviously used as beasts of burden for anything. They're the best choice for rocket/torpedo launchers because of the heavy weight of the extra ammunition. Also, the limited ammo these weapons have makes it advisable for them to carry a pistol and a grenade or two. Naturally, heavyweights are naturals for Heavy Blasters and M.C. Pulse Disruptors with their bulky ammo (I suggest you also issue them a pistol). I usually spare my heavyweights the necessity of lugging a Medi-kit, too.

The main rule to keep in mind is this: Don't overload your guys. Most of the time, all they get to fire is a couple of rounds (this isn't as true in *Terror* where things tend to get vicious, but it's still no reason to load an aquanaut like a camel). In 95% of *UFO Defense* missions, none of my guys ever needed an extra clip of ammo (in any case, after you discover alien weapon technologies, there's always some ammo lying around, complete with weapons). Things are slightly different in *Terror,* where the early Jet Harpoons carry just ten rounds to a clip, and where you may have to fire a dozen shots to bring one alien down. In *UFO Defense,* things are easier, although a tough alien still requires several hits.

Which Weapon Works on Whom

Various alien races react differently to diverse types of ammunition or weapons. However, in *UFO Defense,* Heavy Plasma rules the battlefield. The small damage bonuses that are available for firing phosphorus at Reapers, for instance, do not outweigh the bother of fooling around with your guys' ammunition on a constant basis.

Things are different in *Terror.* Hallucinoids, which look like giant jellyfish, are quite tough, except when you use phosphorus ammunition. Lobster Men are almost immune to most weapons. Surprisingly, it's easier to stun them with a stun weapon than to kill them with a heavy cannon, and they are very vulnerable to all blade (hand-to-hand combat) weapons. Xarquids, or giant snails, are very tough to everything except blade weapons and traditional armor-piercing ammunition. Overall, sonic weapons are the best for dealing with a large range of *Terror's* aliens—however, Lobster Men are excluded.

Assault Vehicles

A heavy weapons platform or vehicle is a good addition to your fighting team, especially right at the start of the game and in the middle stage. At the beginning, your guys are pitiably weak and can use all the help they can get. In the middle game, mental or telepathic warfare changes the face of the battlefield. Vehicles have this one big advantage over soldiers/aquanauts: They are not susceptible to any kind of mind or molecular control.

There is only one drawback to using vehicles: They take up a lot of space, and so less of your guys can gain experience. In terms of available firepower, trading four guys for a single vehicle is not that great a swap, unless the vehicle in question has one of the late-generation, fusion-ball or pulse-wave torpedo launchers. In the early stages, the best choice is a vehicle

X · C O M

that fires exploding missiles. Although more expensive to operate than a cannon-armed version, it's much more effective. Again, that distinction doesn't apply as strongly to *Terror,* where missile-firing vehicles are limited to underwater operations.

All the same, many extremely dangerous missions are made much easier by vehicles. The final assaults in both games can be said to require them. In both cases, you have to wage a furious battle on the surface before you get to enter the base itself.

TYPES OF BATTLES

The two *X-COM* games both contain a variety of missions, but the ones in *Terror From the Deep* are both far more varied and more difficult. Even terror sites—a feature of both games—come in more shapes and varieties: Island resorts, cruise ships, ports. . . . On the other hand, one bit of sea bed tends to look like another, even if it's got oil pipes here and there. *UFO Defense* offers you the opportunity to do battle in a diverse collection of geographical regions and settings: Desert, arctic wasteland, jungle, village, forest[Ellipse] The one kind of battle that is identical in both games is the one that's most unpleasant—defending your base from alien assault.

Here's a brief rundown on the *X-COM* missions:

Crash Sites

Whenever you down a UFO or a submarine, your next step should be to send along a transport of troops to beat up the surviving aliens, take some in custody, and gather up whatever spoils possible. The difficulty of these missions varies greatly with the size of the ship you downed (the bigger it is, the greater the difficulty) and the alien race or races aboard.

When dealing with small and medium ships, it usually pays to take along a vehicle. Not so with the very large ships—a lot of the fighting goes on indoors, where vehicles can't enter, and four extra soldiers are worth their weight in gold.

Each crash site investigation consists of two phases. In the first phase, you clear the field of any aliens. If you're patient, it's not a bad idea to lay an ambush for the aliens still inside the ship with proximity grenades placed at all exits and carefully arranged fields of fire. However, most often you'll be storming the enemy ships. Watch out for friendly fire casualties. Don't push your troops too hard; try to leave them with time for a snap shot and in a kneeling position, preferably with cover on at least one side. Use motion detectors to estimate the positions of aliens inside the ship, then grenades— your guys can throw them one level up—to clear up your chosen points of entry of unwanted presence. Crash sites usually take a couple of days to disappear, but it's best to storm them quickly, while the aliens are still reeling from shock.

Landed UFO/Stopped Sub

Missions against these are very similar to investigating crash sites, only the operation is conducted against an undamaged craft that has landed as part of its mission. There are more healthy aliens around, and they all have their wits about them, so you have to be a little more careful. On the other hand, the prize always includes Zrbite or Elerium 115.

Terror Sites

From time to time, aliens land in a city (port) and proceed to murder the inhabitants. You'll encounter two types of aliens on these missions—'standard' aliens and terrorists controlled by them. For instance, Floaters habitually terrorize cities with the assistance of Reapers, and Sectoids with the help of Cyberdiscs. Your objective is slightly different—to minimize deaths among civilians (of course, you shouldn't kill any yourself, but sometimes that can't be helped) as well as wipe out all aliens.

Terror sites can be tricky, particularly in the opening stages of the game, when your weaponry and soldiers are weak. Often, you have to fight at night. Terror sites stay on the map only for a few hours, and any delay is inadvisable. If you ignore a terror site, you lose lots of points (and money down the line). At the higher difficulty level, the government on whose territory the ignored act took place, often signs a secret pact with the aliens in consequence.

In *Terror From the Deep,* appropriately, terror sites are rich and varied. Some of the missions, such as those aboard terrorized cruise ships, are split into two stages. Having dealt with aliens on the passenger decks, you proceed to clear them out of the holds. Even more difficult than cruise ship attacks are those on cargo ships. A cargo ship is more or less a labyrinth of narrow corridors, little rooms, and vast chambers with overhead catwalks that are usually festooned with snipers. A very systematic, thorough, and careful search is the only solution.

Port and island resort missions are also a common occurrence. The worst thing about terror site missions in *Terror* is that your potent underwater weaponry is inoperational. While I welcome the absence of M.C. Pulse Disruptors on both sides, in the early stages, the lack of a couple of Hydro-Jet Cannons or a Torpedo Launcher can hurt. Furthermore, island missions feature particularly dangerous, hilly terrain, while port missions can sometimes end in a very disagreeable manner. If you happen to blow the steps off one of the towers every port seems to feature, and there is an alien hiding inside one of the structures they have on top, you may be forced to abort the mission, even though it's as good as won. It has happened to me repeatedly— the single terrorist is terrorized with fear and won't come out, and my guys can't get in.

Alien Base/Colony Assaults

You assault alien bases in *UFO Defense,* and colonies in *Terror.* In *UFO Defense,* things are fairly simple: You must kill every alien in the base, and the mission's over. Your soldiers start in two separate spots, not far apart. Linking them up is the first priority; after that, it's a fairly long search-and-destroy operation, with aliens doing the searching and destroying if you aren't careful. Watch out for snipers in two-level structures, and take flares along—they come in very handy. Assaulting an alien base is not unlike fighting in a maze; you'll want to decide whether you want to blow the walls apart or use them as cover, and follow through on your chosen tactic. If you can't or won't blow up walls, use grenades in groups of three or four to clear out suspect areas.

Alien base, or rather alien colony assaults in *Terror* are much more complex. They consist of two stages—each is effectively a mission in itself. They are rather similar to the Final Assault in *UFO Defense.* The first battle takes place on the dark seabed, very deep down, and the second deeper still, in the colony structures under the sea bed. Gaining entrance is really difficult—your guys have to cross an open area while being fired upon by snipers equipped with Pulse Disruptors.

You end the first part of the mission when you've killed all the aliens, or gain access to the Exit Area that leads to the colony underground. This choice is present in every multipart-part *Terror From the Deep* mission, and is much better than chasing aliens around the landscape and losing men and ammo while an even tougher battle awaits.

Your aim is to get into the cross-shaped structure guarding the entrance to the colony. You can do so the hard way—through one of the existing entrances—or create an entrance yourself with a Pulse Disruptor. Blowing a wall off the two-level central structure usually exposes a bunch of aliens who had been waiting for your aquanauts to pass under them—and boy, are they surprised.

The Exit Area is right under the balcony where the aliens like to congregate. Assemble your troops there, on the specially-marked tiles, and click the button with which you usually abort the mission. This time, you're transported into the alien colony instead of back to your base. Your units are scattered on several levels around one of the Exit Areas. Your job: Link them up, find the colony's Synomium device, and destroy it. The device is highly explosive, so take care! Best tackle it from a distance with the reliable old Pulse Disruptor, after you've blown apart a few interfering walls. Otherwise, you'll have to make your soldiers run like rats in a maze crawling with aliens. If you don't have the Disruptor, use lots of grenades every step of the way.

The colony is a multilevel-level maze of dark rooms and corridors. Concentrate on finding and destroying the device while keeping your aquanauts alive. Don't go looking for extra trouble. After you blow up the device, you must assemble all your guys in an Exit Area and click the Abort button to complete the mission (as at the end of the first half of the assault, it works differently here).

Synomium Activity Sites

These are another *Terror From the Deep* specialty. However, they only exist for a few hours. If you've missed the bus, that's it, like with terror missions. As with colony assaults, you should look for the Exit Area; it's in one of the buildings, sometimes quite close. Don't bother exploring beyond looking for the Exit Area.

You'll have your hands full simply keeping your aquanauts relatively safe.

Having found the Exit Area in one of the pyramid-shaped buildings (watch out for guards!), use the Abort button when your guys are all assembled to begin the second part of this mission. It consists of a multilevel-level maze similar to the alien colony's, but the room you're looking for is on Level 3. However, your soldiers can only access it through an entrance on Level 0. It goes without saying the entrance route is stacked with aliens waiting for your aquanauts. You may want to try storming the building in an unconventional way—by using *Terror's* equivalent of a hovercraft, the Displacer craft. The Displacer can slide onto the elevator leading to the Synomium device by entering the building through an opening above the entrance steps. After taking the elevator up, it can destroy the device without much trouble; by staying in the elevator, it's safe from the ensuing explosion.

If you go after the device in the conventional way, you'll want to use plenty of grenades before you enter. Particle disturbance grenades thrown into dark corners may trip up any remaining aliens moving out to attack your aquanauts.

Don't let your guys shoot at the device—use a timed grenade. If they shoot, the resulting explosion could wipe them all out. After destroying the device, assemble the aquanauts in an Exit Area and use the usual Abort button to end the mission.

Defending Your Base

This may sound like the worst scenario possible, but actually it isn't. First of all, many aliens might have been killed by your base defenses. Secondly, aliens can only enter your base through hangars/sub pens and the access lift/air lock. If you lay your base out well, aliens can only come in through a single entrance—the lift/air lock connecting the block of hangars/sub pens to a block of other buildings.

Your chances of having to conduct a base defense rise with the game's difficulty level. If the aliens have been getting particularly hammered in an area, they may decide it's time for retaliation. There are a few steps you can take to minimize the probability of this taking place: Conduct all interceptions as far away from your base as possible. Install plenty of missile/torpedo defenses (replace them with better defense systems, at least partly, when they become available. I also recommend installing protective and detection devices such as Mind Shield/M.C. Generator, Grav Shield/Bombardment Shield, and Hyperwave Decoder/Transmission Resolver. Inevitably, all of these involve advanced research.

The Final Assault

This is the most difficult battle of them all. It is much harder in *Terror* than in *UFO Defense*. For starters, it consists of three stages, not just two. Just like in some other *Terror* missions, you may complete each stage by killing all aliens present, or find the Exit Area and use the Abort button. This second option is, of course, infinitely more preferable.

The assault on Cydonia in *UFO Defense* begins on the surface of Mars. You must find the one pyramid among others that contains the elevator leading inside the base. There are plenty of aliens everywhere, and the placement of the elevator pyramid is random. Once you've managed to find it and to get everyone inside, you instantly begin the second part of the mission (no Abort buttons here). This resembles a very grueling alien base assault, only here the adversaries consist of hand-picked Ethereals. Also, you don't have to kill all the aliens. In fact, it's better even not to attempt it, but to start looking for the alien Brain right away. It is accessed by a double elevator at the end of a T-shaped corridor. Upon ascending, your guys emerge into the midst of a group of the deadliest aliens there are—Ethereal commanders. If you cannot take them out the easy way with a Blaster Launcher, consider a semi-suicide trip by a soldier or two with a pack of High Explosive and grenades. Following the disposal of the guards, you have to destroy the Brain—each of its four sections. By then, other aliens may come running, so speed is important.

Speed is even more important in the Final Assault in *Terror From the Deep*. The first of its three stages usually consists of traversing the whole battle map to get to the Exit Area, where you assemble all units and employ the trusted Abort button. The Exit Area is right above the only Level 0 room with four elevator pads. The second stage consists of the same, in much more difficult circumstances. Instead of relatively wide corridors, you get threads one square wide, and there are tons of tiny rooms crammed with nasty aliens. Once again, find the Exit Area and assemble your troops. You may have a nasty surprise, because this second Exit Area is smaller than the previous one, forcing you to leave guys behind. Also, this time, you have to access it through Level 1, although it's located on Level 0 (it's right next to a nine-pad elevator). Of course, each stage can also be completed by killing all aliens, although it's questionable whether you'll end up with more troops that way.

The third stage sees you destroying the Ultimate Alien (it resides in a coffin, Dracula-like). You cannot destroy it directly—you just cut its life support by shooting out the eight power nodes supplying it. They don't explode, and just need a couple of hits each. However, before you get to this easy-sounding ending, you have to fight a small horde of select aliens that will make mincemeat of any but the best troops.

In both games, it's essential that your Final Assault team is composed of veterans with high psionic strength and skill. Mind-controlling the aliens makes the whole affair suddenly easy. However, you'll do well enough if none of your guys lose their heads to an alien influence.

Having destroyed the Brain and enjoyed the process, you'll probably want to destroy the Ultimate Alien. The creators of *X-COM* are betting that the Ultimate Alien still isn't enough—*X-COM: The Apocalypse* is scheduled to arrive sometime in the not-too-distant future.

Computer Game Books

1942: The Pacific Air War: The Official Strategy Guide	$19.95
The 11th Hour: The Official Strategy Guide	$19.95
The 7th Guest: The Official Strategy Guide	$19.95
Aces Over Europe: The Official Strategy Guide	$19.95
Across the Rhine: The Official Strategy Guide	$19.95
Alone in the Dark 3: The Official Strategy Guide	$19.95
Armored Fist: The Official Strategy Guide	$19.95
Ascendancy: The Official Strategy Guide	$19.95
Buried in Time: The Journeyman Project 2: The Official Strategy Guide	$19.95
CD-ROM Games Secrets, Volume 1	$19.95
Caesar II: The Official Strategy Guide	$19.95
Celtic Tales: Balor of the Evil Eye: The Official Strategy Guide	$19.95
Cyberia: The Official Strategy Guide	$19.95
Computer Adventure Games Secrets	$19.95
Dark Seed II: The Official Strategy Guide	$19.95
Descent: The Official Strategy Guide	$19.95
DOOM Battlebook	$19.95
DOOM II: The Official Strategy Guide	$19.95
Dracula Unleashed: The Official Strategy Guide & Novel	$19.95
Dragon Lore: The Official Strategy Guide	$19.95
Dungeon Master II: The Legend of Skullkeep: The Official Strategy Guide	$19.95
Fleet Defender: The Official Strategy Guide	$19.95
Frankenstein: Through the Eyes of the Monster: The Official Strategy Guide	$19.95
Front Page Sports Football Pro i95: The Official Playbook	$19.95
Fury3: The Official Strategy Guide	$19.95
Hell: A Cyberpunk Thriller: The Official Strategy Guide	$19.95
Heretic: The Official Strategy Guide	$19.95
I Have No Mouth, and I Must Scream: The Official Strategy Guide	$19.95
In The 1st Degree: The Official Strategy Guide	$19.95
Kingdom: The Far Reaches: The Official Strategy Guide	$14.95
Kingís Quest VII: The Unauthorized Strategy Guide	$19.95
The Legend of Kyrandia: The Official Strategy Guide	$19.95
Lords of Midnight: The Official Strategy Guide	$19.95
Machiavelli the Prince: Official Secrets & Solutions	$12.95
Marathon: The Official Strategy Guide	$19.95
Master of Orion: The Official Strategy Guide	$19.95
Master of Magic: The Official Strategy Guide	$19.95
Microsoft Arcade: The Official Strategy Guide	$12.95

Microsoft Flight Simulator 5.1: The Official Strategy Guide	$19.95
Microsoft Golf: The Official Strategy Guide	$19.95
Microsoft Space Simulator: The Official Strategy Guide	$19.95
Might and Magic Compendium: The Authorized Strategy Guide for Games I, II, III, and IV	$19.95
Myst: The Official Strategy Guide	$19.95
Online Games: In-Depth Strategies and Secrets	$19.95
Oregon Trail II: The Official Strategy Guide	$19.95
The Pagemaster: Official CD-ROM Strategy Guide	$14.95
Panzer General: The Official Strategy Guide	$19.95
Perfect General II: The Official Strategy Guide	$19.95
Prince of Persia: The Official Strategy Guide	$19.95
Prisoner of Ice: The Official Strategy Guide	$19.95
Rebel Assault: The Official Insider's Guide	$19.95
The Residents: Bad Day on the Midway: The Official Strategy Guide	$19.95
Return to Zork Adventurer's Guide	$14.95
Romance of the Three Kingdoms IV: Wall of Fire: The Official Strategy Guide	$19.95
Shadow of the Comet: The Official Strategy Guide	$19.95
Shannara: The Official Strategy Guide	$19.95
Sid Meier's Civilization, or Rome on 640K a Day	$19.95
Sid Meier's Colonization: The Official Strategy Guide	$19.95
SimCity 2000: Power, Politics, and Planning	$19.95
SimEarth: The Official Strategy Guide	$19.95
SimFarm Almanac: The Official Guide to SimFarm	$19.95
SimLife: The Official Strategy Guide	$19.95
SimTower: The Official Strategy Guide	$19.95
Stonekeep: The Official Strategy Guide	$19.95
SubWar 2050: The Official Strategy Guide	$19.95
Terry Pratchett's Discworld: The Official Strategy Guide	$19.95
TIE Fighter: The Official Strategy Guide	$19.95
TIE Fighter: Defender of the Empire: Official Secrets & Solutions	$12.95
Thunderscape: The Official Strategy Guide	$19.95
Ultima: The Avatar Adventures	$19.95
Ultima VII and Underworld: More Avatar Adventures	$19.95
Under a Killing Moon: The Official Strategy Guide	$19.95
WarCraft: Orcs & Humans Official Secrets & Solutions	$9.95
Warlords II Deluxe: The Official Strategy Guide	$19.95
Werewolf Vs. Commanche: The Official Strategy Guide	$19.95
Wing Commander I, II, and III: The Ultimate Strategy Guide	$19.95
X-COM Terror From The Deep: The Official Strategy Guide	$19.95
X-COM UFO Defense: The Official Strategy Guide	$19.95
X-Wing: Collector's CD-ROM: The Official Strategy Guide	$19.95

Video Game Books

3DO Game Guide	$16.95
Battle Arena Toshinden Game Secrets: The Unauthorized Edition	$12.95
Behind the Scenes at Sega: The Making of a Video Game	$14.95
Breath of Fire Authorized Game Secrets	$14.95
Breath of Fire II Authorized Game Secrets	$14.95
Complete Final Fantasy III Forbidden Game Secrets	$14.95
Donkey Kong Country Game Secrets The Unauthorized Edition	$9.95
Donkey Kong Country 2—Diddy's Kong Quest Unauthorized Game Secrets	$12.99
EA SPORTS Official Power Play Guide	$12.95
Earthworm Jim Official Game Secrets	$12.95
Earthworm Jim 2 Official Game Secrets	$14.95
GEX: The Official Power Play Guide	$14.95
Killer Instinct Game Secrets: The Unauthorized Edition	$9.95
Killer Instinct 2 Unauthorized Arcade Secrets	$12.99
The Legend of Zelda: A Link to the Past—Game Secrets	$12.95
Lord of the Rings Official Game Secrets	$12.95
Maximum Carnage Official Game Secrets	$9.95
Mortal Kombat II Official Power Play Guide	$9.95
Mortal Kombat 3 Official Arcade Secrets	$9.95
Mortal Kombat 3 Official Power Play Guide	$9.95
NBA JAM: The Official Power Play Guide	$12.95
Ogre Battle: The March of the Black Queen—The Official Power Play Guide	$14.95
Parent's Guide to Video Games	$12.95
PlayStation Game Secrets: The Unauthorized Edition, Vol. 1	$12.99
Secret of Evermore: Authorized Power Play Guide	$12.95
Secret of Mana Official Game Secrets	$14.95
Street Fighter Alpha—Warriors' Dreams Unauthorized Game Secrets	$12.99
Ultimate Mortal Kombat 3 Official Arcade Secrets	$9.99
Urban Strike Official Power Play Guide, with Desert Strike & Jungle Strike	$12.95

TO ORDER BOOKS

Please send me the following items:

Quantity	Title	Unit Price	Total
_____	_____	$_____	$_____
_____	_____	$_____	$_____
_____	_____	$_____	$_____
_____	_____	$_____	$_____
_____	_____	$_____	$_____

Subtotal	$_____
Deduct 10% when ordering 3–5 books	$_____
7.25% Sales Tax (CA only)	$_____
8.25% Sales Tax (TN only)	$_____
5.0% Sales Tax (MD and IN only)	$_____
Shipping and Handling*	$_____
TOTAL ORDER	$_____

Shipping and Handling depend on Subtotal.

Subtotal	Shipping/Handling
$0.00–$14.99	$3.00
$15.00–29.99	$4.00
$30.00–49.99	$6.00
$50.00–99.99	$10.00
$100.00–199.99	$13.00
$200.00+	call for quote

Foreign and all Priority Request orders:
Call Order Entry department for price quote at
1-916-632-4400

This chart represents the total retail price of books
only (before applicable discounts are taken).

By telephone: With Visa or MC, call 1-800-632-8676. Mon.–Fri. 8:30–4:00 PST.

By Internet E-mail: sales@primapub.com

By mail: Just fill out the information below and send with your remittance to:

PRIMA PUBLISHING
P.O. Box 1260BK
Rocklin, CA 95677-1260

http://www.primapublishing.com

Name_____ Daytime Telephone_____

Address _____

City _____ State _____ Zip _____

Visa /MC# _____Exp. _____

Check/Money Order enclosed for $_____ Payable to Prima Publishing

Signature _____